AF609219

THE RELUCTANT RUNNER

A Steven Popoford Spiritual Thriller

Book Two

Robert Wood Anderson

Tautly Sharp Publishing

Bellevue, Nebraska

Robert Wood Anderson / Tautly Sharp Publishing
c/o PO Box 1566
Bellevue, NE 68005-1566
www.rwanderson-author.com

Publisher's Note: This is a work of fiction. Names, characters, places, and incidents are a product of the author's imagination. Locales and public names are sometimes used for atmospheric purposes. Any resemblance to actual people, living or dead, or businesses, companies, events, institutions, or locales is completely coincidental.

Cover design by Martellia at Fiverr.com

The Reluctant Runner / Robert Wood Anderson. -
- 1st ed.,
ISBN# 978-1-7347698-6-9

J/M/J

The *Reluctant Runner* is dedicated to my dear wife who continues to encourage me with her love, forgiveness, patience, and belief in me. I also honor all those who have supported me and helped bring this story to print especially those who read *The Reluctant Runner* and provided their critical insight.

For a copy of *Resurrection Runner*, Book One
of the Steven Popoford Series,
please visit Amazon with this link:
https://rwanderson-author.com/db15

"Let all the poison that lurks in the mud, hatch out."
Robert Graves, *"I, Claudius."*

CHAPTER ONE

In the Grand Room of a High-Sierra compound fit for the richest person in the world, a man unwelcome anywhere even among the most perverse megalomaniacs sits on a stool up to his chest in a warm-bath mixture of Dead-Sea saltwater and coal tar. He is a bag of wretched flesh, ravaged by erythrodermic psoriasis and advancing psoriatic arthritis, so dry he might spontaneously ignite if exposed to intense sunlight. Ultraviolet light fixtures provide the room's artificial portion of the light. The sun allowed in the room is shaded.

He's known only as Vladdrac, the secret leader of The Supreme Five, in ancient Greek, "to anótato pénte," TAP, commanding his four generals in their sinister international war.

His end game is advancing steadily from its audacious beginnings generations before. His opponents have scoffed at his determination to dominate the world, but he and his predecessors have led TAP with patience and skill through the ages and his is the long game, not an adolescent fancy of speedy conquest. Some of TAP's enemies had relaxed and softened while many more had folded into his vast army: duped, drafted, or conscribed. Some, once seen as his most righteous opponents, mighty and true, are the most precious pawns Vladdrac has purloined for his master's domination of the human race and all the beasts of the world.

Vladdrac's head is long and feral. His arms rest on cushioned, ventilated platforms positioned above the black water. He scans several computer monitors in front of him as the shaded sunlight enters through an expansive window directly ahead. The view is a glorious expanse of rolling hills descending to a lake whose waters reflect the snowcapped mountains beyond. The blue sky offers false hope against the whirlwind he continues to inflict on America and the entire free world.

To his right, and just behind him, Junko Abrams, his attendant and bodyguard, is ready to accede to his every need. Junko is the grandson of a Stasi colonel and a student of *Zersetzung*, the specialized psychological warfare techniques used to destroy so many patriots in Soviet-occupied East Germany. He is also known as John, once the butler of P. Y. Mous, the deceased arms dealer. He rarely leaves Vladdrac's side.

"Where is Lamia?" Vladdrac asks, his phlegm-choked words gurgling in his throat.

Three of the monitors show people calmly waiting for the meeting to begin. A fourth screen is dark. A fifth screen is tuned to a compilation of the world's leading financial markets. A sixth scrolls international headlines. Vladdrac can see his generals but they cannot see him for there are no cameras in Vladdrac's room.

Finally, Lamia's face pops up on the darkened monitor.

"A reminder should be sufficient to all," Vladdrac hisses. "Punctuality is required to remain a member of TAP."

"My apologies, Leader Vladdrac. It won't happen again."

"If it does, Lamia, you will be eliminated. Do you understand my meaning?"

"Clearly," she said.

"Let's get on with it. Lamia, your report."

"I have continued good news from the education segment. Last evening our Brilliance in Basics program passed the Senate without changes to the House bill. It was sent to President Halbertson for his signature. All public schools will institute the BIB program immediately. Our growing influence in universities will insure their BIB participation as well. Schools not following our lead will be subjected to social conformity measures calling their loyalty into question subjecting them to cries of racism, fascism, and perversion of public norms. We will rely on Diomed's propaganda expertise to turn attention away from the actual curriculum by destroying dissidents. Our press will be turned against them and disgrace will drive them from their livelihood and public view. Our pliant constituents will be righteously proud for naming the unsavory among them."

"Well done, Lamia. Diomed, is your team fully prepared for this?"

"Prepared and already active. As you know, they're circulating talking points to all our tied-in outlets who have laid the groundwork in the minds of common men. The promotion of BIB and the claimed results of the program will be supported everywhere. The storyline is written for the next six months with my action team monitoring and reporting any deviation to Blagden."

"And Blagden, are the DCFC shock troops ready"?

"Vladdrac, all Community Organizers are prepared and ready for battle. The Downtrodden Community Fighting Corp is armed and organized. All DCFC wolf packs are mobilized and are on standby waiting for their orders."

"Excellent," Vladdrac said, a tight smile stretching his thin lips. "Tamisra. Your report."

"Our judges are in place and well prepared for any legal pushback on BIB. No lawsuits other than our own will advance in any courts. Law enforcement will stand down in the face of the DCFC protests. Local lawmakers know their future lies with us.

"Furthermore, after a brutal confirmation hearing, Jenkins Stent, the "Constitutionalist," has been confirmed to the Supreme

Court. As one of ours. He'll surprise his faithful supporters with his revisionist decisions.

"Everything is in place and running smoothly" Blagden continued. "Your final effort to transform America's education, history, and the government is about to unfold on the people, the economy, and soon the world. I'm proud to be among the few who will lead the country to a new and glorious Constitution and crush this evil republic. Congratulations, Vladdrac. My Leader."

Vladdrac sat quietly for a minute. He savored the knowledge that it was neither the end nor the beginning, but it was a masterful segment in a never-ending crusade, an unholy and eternal war by his dark master against the weak supplicants of the Other One, the one they call Savior and his mother whom they call the Blessed One. Fools, all fools. No one could match the power of his master, not given the folly and weakness of men: believing fools who had fallen for a chimera, a dream of freedom, a promise that they'd be saved and reborn from the emptiness of death. The world was full of foolish chattel disposed to his domination, offering themselves as a sacrifice upon whom he would feed as he waited for his master's reward.

"Your reports give me many reasons to smile," Vladdrac said. "You have done well. Now, it is time to get back to work. Keep a close eye on your operatives. Take nothing for granted. And remember, there are would-be heroes among the masses, people who know exactly what we are doing. They all must be disgraced, destroyed, eliminated. Wrath must fill their days and nights and they must be driven mad looking for peace they will never find.

"We will meet again soon. Until then, send all your updates to Junko. If it is an emergency, handle it. If you can't, you had better just die because your suffering at my hand will have you begging for death. Too bad for you that I have studied the ways of cruel torment and know how to keep you alive even as your skin is peeled away in one continuous strip of bleeding flesh. Not a pretty sight, but you will see it all when your eyelids are cut away with a dull knife. Go do your job. Do it well and have pleasant dreams. Fail, and suffer my fury."

He pushed a button and all the screens that his leaders watched went dark but the cameras secretly mounted within their screens remained on. Vladdrac studied them as they gathered their things and left their offices.

"What do you think, Junko? Did you catch any weakness in them?'

"No, sir. But they're good actors. I'm sure they'll hold their feelings until they think they're beyond your view."

"Which they can never be."

"Yes, Sir. They can't hide."

"No. Never. If they turn on me, others will take them down and replace them."

"Yes, Sir," Junko said and helped him out of his bath.

Vladdrac smiled as Junko toweled his ravaged body.

"I'm their creator, Junko. It's as if I'm the son of the dark one himself."

"Yes, Sir," Junko said without emotion, for his mind, devoid of sentiment, was equally loyal to Vladdrac's master and his own ambition.

CHAPTER TWO

He had a slack-sided, demented mind, forever drifting off point for that's what nightmares are made of. When conventional wisdom said, "steer left," he turned around. When it said, "turn right," he rolled over. Downhill was up to him. Sideways, the shortest distance between two points. Tell him what to do, and he didn't. Tell him not to, and he did. He wasn't so much a contrarian as he was a straight-up guy. He didn't give a crap what was expected of him since he had no regard for the fools he encountered. That was the way it was until he spotted her across the mowed wheat field that late August day, the sun a haloed veil dimmed by her radiance.

They had a lusty rolling in the hay, drawing each to each other as if willed by the ancient gods to perform a frail chapter of human necessity upon the god of fertility Priapus' stage, consumed with life, assured they had solved its mystery.

Then, a dark mist swirled up from his perverse imagination and embroiled him in a terrible fantasy.

It took three slugs to kill her, two in her back and the third in her throat as she spun towards him whipping an arch of blood about the room. She fell at his feet, staining his khaki pants. It was a messy kill, his first, an embarrassment, but he'd done it.

Her name was Gretchen and they'd been lovers, but she had deceived him. When H.O. read him in on her true identity there was no doubt what he had to do. She was a master spy and the brains behind a sophisticated ring of enemy agents tasked to disrupt, confuse, and cripple the lives of ordinary Americans. He'd done his duty for his country.

His nightmare swirled from the depths of his guilt. Her ever-staring eyes pierced his soul with eternal recrimination.

Steven Popoford's eyelids popped open in the waning light. An empty glass slipped from his hand and crashed to the hardwood floor shattering into ragged chunks. He was slouching in his chair and the whiskey bottle he was staring at was empty. He had a screaming headache, and his crusted eye itched and throbbed. The room's lone curtain was pulled back from the window framing a doe and her fawn grazing in the gloaming. Tears filled his eyes and remorse crumpled him into a seething ball.

Slowly his booze-soaked nightmare of Gretchen faded and he awoke in the real day; one lazy eyelid drooping over its empty socket, his good eye doing the work of two. A wry smile stretched his lips and crinkled his face. Gretchen was an illusion; a woman who never existed yet never ceased haunting him. These figment memories were only remnants of the psychological damage he had sustained under the thumb of Alex Hendricks and Home Office. She was a ghost created to mold him into the pliant assassin he had become, a tool of his enslavement. He rubbed his good eye and gazed out the window.

It was at the aging end of a long summer day when fireflies hovered in the meadows as the sun lowered toward the pines. The scent of warm sap mingled in the breeze with the sweet expectation of an approaching thunderstorm.

His small house, tucked away in the Whimsy woods, was much the same as it had been when he first moved in, a little large for one person and perhaps too small for two, yet comfortable, nonetheless. He sat alone as he had for much of his last six years, his headache hammering his skull, temples, and eyes. But he hadn't hit the bottle that hard for at least three weeks. The drunk wasn't worth the pain but no fool seriously considered action before the damage was done.

Popoford had a plan to go hunting in the morning. Maybe he'd follow through. Probably not. For now, he had to get his head adjusted and walk his nightly perimeter patrol. Cameras and trip lines needed to be inspected, trails checked for animal and human tracks. Above all, he had to perform the daily test of his EID grid. The electronic intrusion detection grid that surrounded his home and the woods to the perimeter of his land was a sophisticated early-warning system that could identify intruders and report on their movements. It was an important part of the complex security system he had developed since returning to Whimsy. Popoford was paranoid. He knew too much about how the world worked to be a fool.

After he slapped water on his face, he chased three Advil tablets with two glasses of water. He checked his bloodshot eye, skipped putting the eyepatch on the other one, and grabbed a half-eaten American cheese sandwich from his refrigerator. Then he stepped onto his porch and took a quick look around the yard.

It was more of a gravel-covered clearing with nothing but a few rose bushes planted near the house. It was just a natural opening in the trees where the road came to an end and the original owner had settled down. Popoford liked it that way. From where he stood, he could watch as twilight deepened the shadows and the woods became active with foraging raccoons, coyotes, endless squirrels, and occasional cougars. Fireflies began to dance on the breeze as it slowly rose to the approaching rain, and he could smell the thunderstorm building above the mountain peaks as night fell.

Popoford was still dressed in a black shirt and black pants. His headache still pounded as he walked across the clearing and entered the woods where he'd spent so much time that he could tell any little thing that had been disturbed. As his head slowly cleared, his awareness rose. He listened and caught an unexpected sound coming from the road. It was a soft and strange whoosh.

He swore he also heard the crunching sound that tires make as a car rolls *down* a hill with a dead engine. But this sound was coming up the road, and he couldn't find any evidence of a motor in the steadily growing whish.

He reached into his pocket and removed a pair of earbuds and slid them into his ears. He pressed a button on the right bud and it connected to his EID grid. As he began his perimeter check, a quiet warning announced intruders.

"Multiple subjects acquired. Advancing in ranks to the clearing."

Popoford immediately moved toward an earthen mound slightly deeper in the woods. Once there, he put his hand out and found the latch he was seeking. He turned the handle and a pneumatically assisted hatch quietly opened. Attached to the hatch's underside were a Sig M18 9mm pistol and two extra mags. He grabbed the gun and the mags and closed the hatch.

"Subjects dispersing. Four units entering woods. Two units staying the course."

Popoford again moved closer to the clearing edge so he could have an unobstructed view. Hidden there, he could look across the clearing and see everything. He stood silently concealed behind an old redwood as the sound grew steadily louder advancing slowly up the hill. Suddenly, the crunching sound began to change. It got softer but it kept coming without changing speeds. The calls of fleeing creatures arose from the woods as something advanced through the trees and up the road toward his house.

"Four subjects spreading at equal intervals across the eastern clearing perimeter."

CHAPTER THREE

A pair of headlights appeared and two riders on silent bicycles braked to a stop just as they entered the clearing.

"All stopped."

Seconds after that, a half-dozen headlights appeared from four other bikes positioned uniformly around the clearing, waiting. Popoford remained undetected among the four bikes. Then, without a noticeable signal, all six bikes silently advanced into the clearing and proceeded to make a semi-circle facing the house's front door.

"All advancing. All stopped."

The riders dismounted and approached the front of the house. Three of them carried short-barreled shotguns while the other three had pistols at the ready. One of them turned back to the woods and put a device to his eyes that looked like binoculars. Popoford suspected they employed heat-seeking technology. He was satisfied his heat signature wouldn't be picked up as long as he remained hidden among the trees.

Finding no signs of defenders, the invaders entered the house as a swat unit would: efficiently, rapidly, with no B.S. Popoford thought it looked oddly like a rugby scrum as he moved quickly back to the hidden hatch. He opened it and climbed down a ladder into a tunnel and closed the hatch behind him. Touching down on the tile floor, he moved rapidly towards his house. The lights ahead of him snapped on as he approached, while those behind him slowly dimmed. The security system continued to stream live updates as he advanced.

"Six-actor assault team clearing location…searching cabinets…in kitchen…bedroom."

Popoford reached a staircase at the end of the tunnel and opened a small door installed on the wall. There was a gas mask hanging inside, and he put it on. Then he turned a valve. The sound of gas whooshed through the pipe as pressure was released. He quietly climbed the stairs and listened carefully. The trap door above him opened into his bedroom closet and was covered with a carpet. There was a latch on the other side.

Two actors exiting building. Four actors immobile in place,"

Popoford listened closely as he turned the latch and lifted the trapdoor.

"We have the files and the serum!" one of the two on the porch called over his shoulder. "Shut it down. Let's go!"

Popoford could hear him through his headset.

There was no response from the others still inside.

"Actor turning back toward the door."

"I said, let's go!" their leader repeated.

By this time, Popoford had scrambled out of the cave. He moved to his bedroom door where he snatched a glimpse of the man at the door, startled, with his mouth hanging open. The man's partner grabbed him by the shoulder.

"Don't go back in there!" She was young, in her twenties he guessed, but he couldn't say what either of them looked like because their faces were covered with lamp black.

"They're all down," the man said. "But how?"

"I don't know. Let's get out of here. Now!"

Without saying another word, the two of them jumped off the porch and grabbed their bikes. They accelerated rapidly as

Popoford jumped to his feet and went back to the tunnel to shut off the gas. He gathered a coil of rope and ran back upstairs. He had to secure the attackers and discover what the others had stolen. Then, he had to hustle out of there before the other two came back.

He stifled his erupting anger at the sight of the rummaged room and hogtied the first invader he reached stuffing a gag in his mouth and locking it in place with two long strips of duct tape wrapped tightly around his head.

After securing the other three intruders, he opened his safe and confirmed his suspicion: they'd stolen the doctored Resurrection Runner files and the phony vials of the Home Office serum he'd made himself. They weren't interested in his guns. And they hadn't had time to discover the tunnel where the real serum and the original files were hidden.

When he'd cinched the other intruders, Popoford backed his truck up to his front porch and immediately jumped out and moved two of the electric cycles aside. Then he opened the tailgate and removed a three-quarter inch sheet of plywood that he inclined off the truck's bed. Next, he deployed a hooked cable and dragged it into his front room where he snagged one intruder after another and hooked them to his winch. He dragged them in one bundle to his tailgate where they slid into the truck bed.

Once in place, he grabbed his rain gear and locked his front door. He was slamming the tailgate shut when he noticed the letters "S. M. C." embroidered in black thread on the captive's black jackets. Wondering what they stood for, Popoford jumped into the driver's seat and sped out of the clearing. He was halfway to the county jail in Whimsy when it came to him that he might know one of the intruders.

CHAPTER FOUR

A thunderclap rattled Popoford's head. He ground his teeth. A lightning bolt struck a tall pine just feet from his truck splitting it in two and setting it ablaze. As if God had sprung open an immense hole, the rain came in wind-driven torrents making driving the last mile into Whimsy treacherous. When he pulled to a stop in front of the county jail, his captives were soaked, but still unconscious. He let them wallow in the rainwater and made a call to George Florter, the county sheriff.

"What's going on, Steven?" Florter answered.

"I've got a load for you, George. A bunch of folks thought raiding my house was a good idea. I think they've changed their minds. They need a place to sleep."

"Where are you?"

"In front of the jail."

"Good. I'm inside. Drive around back so we don't cause a stir."

"On my way," Popoford said, starting the truck up. The street was empty except for a couple of parked cars. He made a cursory check of them as he passed and confirmed they were empty. Florter was waiting at the backdoor when Popoford arrived.

The sheriff was a big man, round-faced and strong. His biceps were larger than Popoford's neck, his shoulders big enough to block half a defensive football team. He stood six foot two and wore a grey Stetson wherever he went, ducking under most door jambs. He was the kind of cop whose countenance was forever pleasant even when he needed to slap a man down. Life worn as the sheriff did was a beautiful thing. He was Popoford's only friend.

Florter and Popoford worked together and dragged the lot of them towards the tailgate where Sheriff Florter handcuffed each of the recovered culprits' hands in front before they were untied. Then they marched them one-by-one into the one-cell jail. They were told to sit on the bench that spanned the back cell wall. The four of them, three men and a woman, were bleary but were recovering when the cell door was locked.

Two of the men were in their forties, one looked to be in his thirties. The woman was also mid-thirties. They all expressed varying degrees of anger on their faces, but the older men displayed a certain calm that caused Popoford to study them closely as he gave his account of the affair to Sheriff Florter.

"Their leader ditched them," Popoford said. "He was with a woman and they just left them for dead."

"Not our notion of brotherhood," Florter said. He was a Marine, and he knew by the things he'd gleaned from quiet conversations over a glass of scotch that Popoford had some combat history. He expected that his service wasn't from regular duty. He was probably CIA or FBI. Maybe he'd been in an unnamed ghost agency. It didn't matter to Florter. He just knew that he and Popoford were of kindred spirits.

"You're right, but I wonder what they were after."

"Steven," Florter said with a scheming glint in his eye, "I think you can tell me something about that."

"I could, but I'd have to kill you," Popoford said with a smile.

"I believe it, but you won't," Florter said. "Why don't you tell me what you can."

Popoford walked over to the bars and studied the faces of the older men. One was craggy, all wrinkles and squints. He had three days of whiskers scrumbling about his face. His hair was short; no barber needed. His eyes were light blue and his pale skin was burned red without a tan. He was an outdoors type who didn't believe in sunscreen.

The other man appeared as though he hadn't been out in the sun for years. His skin was smooth and pink, but his blond hair, while turning white, was the muddy color of too many tints mixed on a pallet. If he possessed a character, it didn't show in his face.

These two men Popoford could put a name to. The woman and the younger third man he didn't know.

"I believe I know the older ones," Popoford said.

"Who are they?"

"George, I'd have to lie to you to answer that."

"Old mates?"

"Something like that."

"I take it you parted over some disagreement," Florter said.

"I wouldn't know. After training, we didn't see each other again until now."

"I see. Then that's all you've got for me?"

"Yes, except that I suggest you dump them off on another agency when the sun comes up. They're trouble you don't need."

Sheriff Florter studied Popoford's face for a moment and then shrugged. "Will you be around tomorrow? I'll need to get some details from you."

"I'll be at the house or in the woods. You can reach me if you need something."

"Okay. Get some sleep and give a call in the morning," the sheriff said.

Before he turned to go, Popoford had a few words for the captives.

"Hey, Jack. Hey, Bill," Popoford said under his breath. "You guys running a Home Office op on me?"

Singleton and Masterson only glared at him.

"Did you say something, Steven?" the Sheriff said.

"Just muttering. You better keep a close eye on these four. These slobs had two other accomplices. They may try to bust them out."

"They won't be going anywhere until they get transferred to Sacramento for arraignment. I'll be hanging around the jail until the deputies come to get them. Nothing's going to happen in my jail. You can count on it."

"If you say so," Popoford replied. "Talk to you in the morning."

"All right, Steven. I'll get your statement then."

"Right," Popoford said and zipped up his coat.

The rain drummed steadily on the jail's tin roof as Popoford stepped out the back door and got into his truck.

One of the older men's names was Jack Singleton and the dirty blond was Bill Masterson. Both had been agents in Home Office's Resurrection Runner program, the source of all his nightmares.

Visibility was terrible but he knew the road well enough and drove slowly. Situational awareness was his habit and he practiced it as he pulled out from behind the county jail and headed home. The two cars were still parked on the other side of the road. They still appeared to be empty, but he slowed as he passed and shined a flashlight in their windows to confirm. Revealing nothing, he continued up the hill. When he turned onto his driveway, he activated his earbuds, but he heard no warning. He drove slowly into the clearing and parked in front of the house. He shut off the ignition and listened to the rain's pounding racket on his cab. Finally, weary from all that had happened, he went inside, locked up, and went to bed. He was engrossed in a masseuse-table dream when he shot bolt upright. He slapped the alarm off. It was six-thirty.

CHAPTER FIVE

Even without a hangover, Popoford was bleary. He made a pot of coffee, took a quick shower, and got dressed. He went to his kitchen and retrieved a cup from his cluttered sink. He rinsed away the dry coffee rings and filled it up. As the coffee cooled, he dug out his only cereal bowl and used his hand to scrape the dried cornflakes away. He didn't bother to rinse it out but filled it with cereal and milk. He ate his breakfast at his kitchen table while looking around at the mess his attackers had made. Slowly his headache dissolved, and as if directly connected to his relief, he saw the rain coming to an end while the sun's rising light filtered through the trees. His day was beginning with an ascending note.

He was anxious to get to town, but he took a minute to call Sheriff Florter to let him know he was on the way. He let the phone ring for a long time but there was no answer. He figured the sheriff was in the head or doing his rounds about town so he slid his pistol into his belt holster and pulled on his jacket. He arrived in Whimsy twenty minutes later.

As Popoford neared the county jail, he noticed the two cars that had been parked there the night before hadn't moved. He drove by them and past the jail spying a man at the wheel of one of the cars. At the end of town, he turned right down an alley and then right again back into town on the access road running along the back of the main-street businesses. He parked behind the post-office-telephone-company-hospital-general store called Dr. Marshall's Emporium which was closed until 9:00. It was directly across from the county jail and the person Popoford was interested in was parked at its curb.

Popoford grabbed a pair of binoculars from his glove box and got out. Then he lowered his tailgate and got into the truck's bed. The Emporium's backdoor had an overhang, and he easily pulled himself up onto it, but he had a tense moment as he reached for the roof. There was a crunching sound underfoot and the shingles he stood on began to split under his weight. He made a frantic leap against his foot's receding foundation and just managed to get a grip on the roof's edge as he scrambled up and over to the top. The tarpaper on the roof was soft but not sticky, yet soon, as the sun rose higher and heated it, it would turn to a viscous ooze. Because of this and the fact that it gave him his only cover, he took a seat in the shade of the chimney. From there, he had a perfect view of the police station and the jail. He could also see the sidewalk and curb across the street, though without exposing himself, he couldn't see anything on his side of the road.

Then he realized that the windows opposite him reflected everything at the curb and sidewalk on his side. He focused his binoculars on a man scrunched down in the front seat of the car parked in front of Dr. Marshall's Emporium. He looked to be asleep, but within the hour he was stirring. At 8:00, the police station would open. Now was the time for Popoford to act.

He scrambled back to the edge of the roof and lowered himself onto the back-stairs awning, placing his feet wide so they rested on top of the joists. He then jumped to the truck's bed and cautiously walked down the alley on the left side of the building. At the sidewalk, he stopped and peered around the corner looking for early morning walkers. Seeing none, he moved with purpose to the parked car and quickly drew his Sig P18 pistol as he slid into the back seat.

To his surprise, the driver displayed extraordinary speed as he spun and pointed his gun at Popoford's chest. Their eyes locked and neither man fired.

Popoford held his gun trained on the driver's head. At first, he thought him a stranger, but then he let a small smile catch the corners of his mouth. The driver held nothing back as he grinned full-on and slowly lowered his pistol. The standoff melted with mutual recognition and Popoford took control of the situation.

CHAPTER SIX

"Hand your gun to me, grip first," Popoford said. "No fancy tricks. I took up my trigger slack. Any quick moves and I'll pull it without a thought."

The driver slowly transferred his pistol to his weak hand with its barrel aimed at his chest his finger off his trigger. He carefully handed the gun to Popoford.

"You're supposed to be dead, Simon. Hendricks told me you died."

"Hendricks was lying, as always. Singleton and Masterson, the other Runners at Home Office, are also alive. We've had our struggles as you must have had, but we didn't die and we didn't go crazy."

"Really?" Popoford said.

"Well, we didn't stay crazy."

"That remains to be seen," Popoford said. "What are you doing making an armed attack on my house?"

"We're in a war, Steven. There's no time for niceties."

"That's bullshit! 'Niceties?' How about just talking to me about whatever crap you're involved with instead of staging a raid. I could have killed you all before you got off your bikes, but I thought I'd employ some 'niceties' and let you live long enough to explain yourselves."

"I'm indebted to you."

"Bullshit, again! What are you doing parked at the county jail? And don't tell me you're planning to turn yourself in."

Simon Contlerust wore a sheepish grin as he answered. "I'm staging another raid: a jailbreak. You know I can't leave anyone behind."

"How admirable. I can't leave anyone behind, either. Toss me the car keys. We're going to add the ringleader to the clown show."

Popoford slid behind Contlerust and got out of the back seat on the driver's side. He opened Contlerust's door and held his gun on the man as he got out and crossed the road to the county jail without a word.

He was a man with mostly elfen features, older than Popoford by ten years, but oddly youthful. His skin was so translucent and his complexion so pale he appeared to be lit from within. His veins showed through and contributed a blue cast to his face. While crows' feet were beginning to mark Popoford with maturity, Contlerust's contrasting dark eyes and transfused lips were unwrinkled and projected a virile air of youthful innocence. His ears were slightly pointed and his long, prematurely white hair added a Valinor lord's detail to one's first impression. He looked sly and regal while Popoford, by contrast, appeared candid and plebian. Though they were nearly as tall as each other, their baring, stride, and posture separated them more than the pistol Popoford held on the once-Home-Office assassin. Had anyone been there to see them entering the County jail, they'd have never remembered the gun or Popoford. Contlerust commanded attention wherever he went while Popoford slipped unobtrusively through life.

"Open it," Popoford ordered when they reached the jail.

Contlerust opened the door and stepped in stopping dead in his tracks.

"Keep moving," Popoford barked at him and nudged the pistol in his back.

Contlerust reluctantly took a couple more steps, allowing Popoford to enter the jail himself and close the door. What he saw made him grab Contlerust by the collar and march him further into the room and shove him into a chair.

"Stay right there," he snapped as he backed to the front door and threw the bolt. It was a horror scene. "What is this?"

Popoford's friend Sheriff George Florter was lying on his back. A bullet hole in his chest oozed blood. His revolver was loosely clutched in his hand, the cylinder open. Six empty shell casings were on the floor between his legs. A pool of blood, already drying at the edges, seeped from under his back.

The jail cell wasn't empty, but it was quiet. The seated bodies of two older men and a younger one were splayed against the back wall where they'd been dropped by two shots each. One to the center of mass. One to the head.

That's Jack Singleton and William Masterson," Contlerust said. "The younger one is Masterson's son, Bill."

They had not struggled in death because they were shackled to bolts in the wall. Chains hung from a fourth spot on the bench. They were empty. The jail door was open.

"One of your tribe is missing," Popoford said.

"You're right," Contlerust said.

"Who is it?"

"It's Sarah, Sarah Tufftang, Jack Singleton's granddaughter."

Popoford kept his gun on Contlerust as he moved to the back door and found it locked. "What do you make of this, Simon? Who would do this?"

Contlerust ran his hand through his white hair and slowly shook his head. "It looks to me like someone killed them all with the sheriff's gun. And seeing that there's a cartridge missing from his belt, that someone killed him first and then killed the others while they were locked up. That same person then pulled a final round from the sheriff's gun belt and put a coup de grâce between the eyes of the third prisoner. On top of that, Sarah is missing. It looks like she turned on them all.

"You think she could do this?" Popoford asked.

"I don't like to think that, but it sure looks like it."

"Really?" Popoford said. "You think one of your own did this?"

"She might have. She was in a lot of trouble for striking a student when she was kicked out of her job."

"So, you think it likely that she'd just go crazy and murder her friends; her father?"

"Not really. I guess that sounds pretty unlikely."

"Yeah. Seems that way to me, too," Popoford said. "Take a close look at the gunshot wounds. Tell me if you see anything strange."

"You going to let me stand up?" Contlerust asked and Popoford gestured with his pistol to get up and take a look.

"It looks to me like whoever did this wants it to look like the sheriff went crazy and shot all the men and then killed himself. But the headshot of the man on the right appears to be from a larger caliber than the others."

"Excellent," Popoford said. "Can you draw any conclusions from that?"

"Looks like Sarah had a friend to help her," Contlerust proclaimed.

"Maybe yes, maybe no. I think it's more likely that someone kidnapped her. I think someone's been following you and they were pleased to take advantage of four of you locked in jail. The question is, why was she kidnapped instead of killed?"

Contlerust didn't have an answer for that.

"George was a friend of mine. About the only friend I have. You need to tell me what you've been up to and who's been after you. You're coming with me back to my house so you can come clean."

Contlerust gave Popoford a peculiarly impish smile which he ignored.

"Get going. If we get caught in here, we'll be locked up for a long time waiting for our trial. Let's strip everyone including the sheriff of any identification. Careful with your fingerprints. I'll wipe down the doorknob in front. We're heading out the back door as soon as we have what we need."

Popoford locked the front door and checked through the window to be sure no one was coming. Then he searched Sheriff Florter's desk and file cabinet and came up with the arrest report on Contlerust's crew. Included with the report was a thumb drive. He palmed the drive and folded the file into his back pocket.

"Okay," Popoford said. "Wipe anything you touched. No one needs to know we were here. Let's move."

After smudging all their fingerprints, they went out the back and Popoford wiped the knob clean, pulling the door closed with one last nod to his dead mate. Anger and sorrow mixed a violent stew in his guts and brains. His mind was already considering horrific retribution for the death of his friend, George Florter.

They walked down the alley past a few buildings. Then they crossed the street to Contlerust's car.

"Pull your car around to the back of this building. We're going to leave it there for now and take my truck up the hill."

Contlerust drove the truck back to the house and as he drove, Popoford remembered his friend the sheriff.

They'd hunted together many times and they shared a deep love of the country, both the grandeur of its encompassing nature and the magnificence of its foundational natural law. Together these qualities were the cornerstone of their friendship and patriotism. Florter's death brought agonizing mourning to Popoford's guts; a sour, slow-burning madness consumed him as they parked and he walked Contlerust to his front door.

Popoford holstered his P18 and took out his key. As he reached for the knob, he stood up straight and froze. Contlerust had his gun stuck in Popoford's back.

"You forgot this, didn't you. You left it in my car. You always had a reputation for screwing things up, but it's your lucky day. Let's go in and have that little talk. Okay?"

Popoford shoved his door open and made a desperate leap inside. He swung the door closed locking it with one hand and grabbing a shotgun he had hanging on a hook with the other. He placed his face close to the door and peered at Contlerust through a peephole.

"If you want to talk, Simon," Popoford said, "you can do it on my terms. Drop your gun and put your hands behind your back."

Contlerust just stood there and smiled.

"Well? Do you want to talk or not?" Popoford said.

Contlerust still said nothing, but suddenly the hair on Popoford's neck bristled.

"You sure are an acrobat, aren't you?" Her voice was lilting, almost purring. "Put the shotgun back on the hooks and open the door. I'm a crack shot so just be easy about it. There's no reason to put a bloody hole through the front door. People would talk."

"How long have you been here?" Popoford asked as he followed her orders.

"I let myself in when you took off this morning. I've been watching the house all night. Turn around."

As Popoford turned, Contlerust brushed by him walking into the kitchen where the girl was sitting at the table, her revolver centered on his heart.

Her eyes were the first thing that threw him. He did a micro double-take that she noticed and cocked her head playfully. Contlerust was pulling a chair up to the table and hadn't seen a thing.

"This is my daughter, Millie. She's on my team. Don't mess with her. She bites."

Millie cracked a smile and almost imperceptibly parted her lips. Popoford saw her teeth tapping together like a ravenous hound. It was meant for him alone as her eyes lingered on his.

Her large flirting eyes flustered him and aroused him.

"Uh, hello," he stammered. "Good to see you."

"Same here. Want some coffee?"

"Yeah, sure," Popoford said nonchalantly, failing to pull it off. He turned his blushing face away, embarrassed at his awkwardness. But as he took his seat, she stood and slowly turned towards the coffee pot. She gave him a good look at her lissome self: front, side, and rear. He closed his eyes at the sight of her comely body just so he could get a grip. His thoughts were inappropriate amid his memory of the vulgar mass murder.

"What are you planning to do, Simon? With your little gang, I mean. Who are you working for?"

"I work for myself, just like you do."

"Bullshit! I don't support myself with armed assault and theft. You're crazy."

"Some say that about you, Steven," Contlerust said.

"Don't try to put me in the same boat as you. Just level with me. What are you planning to do with the serum and my records? Why didn't you talk to me about whatever crap you're involved with before attacking me"

Millie, her long, auburn hair pulled forward over her shoulders framing her Gaelic beauty, a gift from her mother, no doubt, took her seat again and handed them each a cup of coffee.

Contlerust shrugged and placed his gun on the table. "I believe I've fallen into a trap of my own making. What I'm doing is a matter of conscience, a practical matter of moral and social recovery. Our cause is a final attempt to stop the incessant perversion of moral norms: the same moral principles long held dear by Americans and enshrined in the Constitution; the same principles that radicals have threatened since Creation itself, and whose continued erosion is fomented by purposeful tyrants everywhere. We intend to reverse their perversions. We intend to take the country back."

Popoford studied Contlerust's face for a moment. He saw an earnest light in his eyes, the passion of a true believer.

"You sound like a fanatic," he said. "I know what you're talking about, but what in the world makes you think you can do a damned thing about it? The forces against you are insurmountable. You're getting old, Simon, and the days are growing short. You'd be better off to mellow out and let the inevitable cycle of a great nation's rise and fall proceed. What lasting good can you expect to accomplish; you and your diminished tribe against the powers that run the country?"

"What are you talking about?" Millie said. "What do you mean by diminished. We're as strong as ever."

Popoford couldn't look at her but continued to bore a hole in Contlerust with his good eye. "Well? You're the ringleader. Tell her."

Contlerust hung his head and didn't respond.

"You've got to be kidding me?" Popoford said and looked directly at Millie. "The other girl on your team has been kidnapped."

"My God! How? When?"

"She was taken from the jail during the night or early morning."

"She was locked up. How could that happen?"

Popoford then told her that they had found the other three of her team and the sheriff dead in the jail.

She was overcome with grief, but she maintained a stoic countenance and merely stared at Popoford. He saw tears forming in her eyes and turned away to let her grieve. He looked at Contlerust with a disapproving glare. "You should have told her yourself. I asked you what lasting good you expect to achieve now that there are three of you and one is out of service. This is a fool's game!

"Have you no faith?" Contlerust said. "Is nothing worth the attempt and the sacrifice? Look at my daughter here. She alone is worth the attempt. So are the lives of the others. Their memory is reason enough to do what must be done. We believe that God sent us on a mission. We can't turn our backs even though we may be destroyed. I'd think your experience would cause you to jump at the chance to join us."

"It's my experience that tells me to keep still, prepare, and protect my own."

"Then we agree, except I must act and you must sit and ignore the future of coming generations."

Popoford took this in and finally said. "And how do you plan to accomplish your mission? Surely you'll be crushed and it'll be over. You don't have the resources and men to overthrow anything, not even my little house. And now that there's only three of you and one's a hostage, how could you stand a chance against dark powers so strong and established?"

Contlerust slowly looked at Millie and then back into Popoford's eye. When he answered, all he said was "Resurrection Runners."

CHAPTER SEVEN

Months before her kidnapping, Professor Sarah Tufftang answered a summons from the dean of the history department at Claramon College. She entered his office and closed the door taking a seat at the dean's desk. She had come prepared for what she received.

"You've gone too far, this time, professor, I have no option but to censure you. You're the consummate example to our students of an intolerant, fascist, racist thug. Good luck, Professor Tufftang. The students will have their rage and you will quietly slip away. I warned you, but you wouldn't toe the line. Now, leave my office."

The professor, an attractive brunette of thirty-six, stayed seated for a moment. When she rose, her long-held anger was released upon the History Dean.

"How vile you are: the epitome of an unforgiving tyrant unfit for education. You have no business being at a university. The Stasi would have loved you. Your lies are transparent, but your accomplices are so reliant on your views, they have atrophied and can only whine, cry, and accuse. I will not be driven out and you cannot fire me. I'm tenured. Oh, and I did nothing wrong except question the unquestionable. Do your worst, Dean. I won't be making it easy for you."

Dean Wrenbutt smiled. "You can't touch me or the college. You have agreed to our curriculum criteria but have continuously failed to follow those rules."

"I never agreed to that crap you call a curriculum," professor Tufftang responded. "I never agreed to any such thing. Not verbally or in writing."

"You're out of your league here, Sarah."

"Call me professor, you Nazi."

Wrenbutt's eyes squinted perceptibly as he smiled. "Seeing that we are at an impasse because you will not use the required first-term Brilliance in Basics American history book but insist on twisting our student's minds with old, racist accounts of America's misogynist history, you may consider yourself relieved of duty. Return to your classroom. A security guard will meet you there to escort you off campus."

"You'll never get away with this! I'll take you to court."

"Oh, really? You don't have the resources to fight me. Just try and you'll be canceled at once. The rampage against you will fry your brain, in a manner of speaking. You'll be hounded down a rabbit hole, never to work another day in this business."

"What are you, a slimy movie producer? You have no idea what hell I'll bring down on you for this."

"Get out of here. Now! And shut that mouth of yours if you expect to survive."

"That sounds like a death threat!"

"Take it any way you want. You're through: you might as well be dead."

Sarah Tufftang stormed out of Wrenbutt's office slamming the door behind her as she marched past his mousy secretary, Miss Shlenterby, and into the hallway. As the door closed behind her, she took a deep breath. She had anticipated what would happen and had come prepared. She reached into her purse and shut off her recorder. Her quarry was snared and would make a perfect experimental subject for her impending plans.

She returned to her classroom and cleaned out her desk. She took her copy of *American History Volume I, ver.3*, the persistently inventive and responsibly revised *Brilliance in Basics* edition of American history. Her students were no strangers to the ideas it held as these same notions had been instilled in them at home. In kindergarten, even before their first formal introduction to the canted thoughts enshrined between the book's covers, teachers taught that the world would be much better off if America had never existed. Offered no alternative and roundly discouraged from any research of their own, especially research found outside the internet, they didn't know the Dewey Decimal System existed. And why not? Libraries all over America and Europe had closed due to disinterest. Histories and first-person accounts of historic events were just fabrications of corrupt authors dedicated to the rule of the few. Indeed, those caught with the writings of Jefferson, Washington, Adams, Lincoln, and Solzhenitsyn were viewed as un-American. Certainly, they did not enhance the social construct of progress. Without a public recanting of their sins against the people, they'd be diminished, reconditioned, or canceled. These were marked for extermination. Not death necessarily, but isolation so complete that no one would dare to publicly associate with them. No one would give them a hand up. They'd be the new living dead, ostracized, exiled, and untouchable. So pitiful, really. All they had to do was to embrace *Brilliance in Basics*. Where's the harm in purging history?

Sarah lamented the state of the union. She knew that children are always born ignorant of all but their immediate needs. She also knew that they had to be taught to discern good from evil. No one had to teach them to love. But someone needed to teach them to hate and fear. It turned out that this truth was quietly perverted and its message flipped from good into evil. One must hate and fear whoever does not pull the party line: the new, true, and correct history of the world.

As Sarah was finishing collecting all of her personal belongings, a security guard and the president of the student body entered her classroom.

They both approached her and reached out to take the box she was filling from her personal things. Startled, she grabbed the box herself and pulled it back.

"Give us the box," the student snapped.

"No. You have no authority in this matter," she said.

"Give him the damned box," the guard ordered. "We need to see what you're taking out of here."

"These are my things, not the school's."

"Let me see them," the student barked and yanked the box from her arms. "You're through here, so shut up and do as you're told."

"Why you little brat, I'll sue you and your idiot parents for this! And what the hell are you doing just standing there and letting this assault go on? Do your damned job, officer!"

"Professor," the security guard said. "Please calm down. No good can come from you getting all worked up."

"What? You spineless idiot. You're allowing this child to do this? What's the matter with you?"

"I've got a family to think about, professor. If I get involved I could lose my job."

"How pathetic. I hope the little woman never finds out she married a coward."

"Sit your butt down," the boy ordered. and Sarah raised her hand to wallop him like she used to do to her older brother.

"Just do it! Go on. Smack me one. Won't you look good on the ten o'clock news?"

Sarah let her arm drop to her side but she didn't sit down. "Take the damned box," she said. "But you're not keeping any of my things."

"We'll see about that," the boy said as he rummaged through the contents and removed a few personal items and several books.

The boy's pompous smile broadened into a sinister grin. "I'm confiscating these things. They're all symbols of your systemic racism and your ongoing Fascist curriculum to pervert your student's minds. All, that is, except for this school-issued copy of The Brilliance in Basics *History of the Americas*. There is no reason for you to steal the book you intend to undermine. It's not yours. And the lipstick and the compact will be a fine gift to my girlfriend. You might remember her. Mary Lou Tinker? You flunked her last quarter for daring to tell the truth about this corrupt, oppressive society, you repressive bitch."

Sarah's reaction was spontaneous and violent. She swung both arms up and, cupping her hands, she delivered a concussive blow to both of his ears at once. Gasping for breath, he couldn't scream as the pain of his bursting eardrums brought him to his knees.

The guard looked on, baffled, as Sarah, fuming still, put everything back in the box and walked toward the classroom door.

"You two have a pleasant day," she said turning back for a moment to look at them. "I'll be unavailable for a while as my lawyers prepare assault charges against the both of you. That's how it's done, right? Blame the other party for what you have done? Why don't both of you think about growing up before you end up in jail?"

With that, she left the room and the campus with her head held high, and a plan of retribution already forming in her head.

CHAPTER EIGHT

Popoford's jaw went slack and his good eye bulged. "Why don't you all have a seat? You've got something crazy on your mind, and you might as well get to it."

There was a tension within him like none other he'd known since he'd destroyed Home Office, its leaders, and the politicians who embraced the Resurrection Runner operation. The memory of it was always in his head; his mantra as rhythmic as his heartbeat imploring the thought to be gone. It rose again in all its horror with Contlerust's mention of the cursed program and with it an unexpected curiosity. Popoford clenched his jaw.

"Do you believe in God?" Contlerust began. "In other words is there a plan that God has provided for our redemption?"

"What does that have to do with this?" Popoford said.

"Everything, Steven. I believe that His plan is on the verge of collapse. It's man's way from the beginning to ignore God. Right now there is an organization actively dismantling the structure of this country. You've seen it yourself. You've been a tool of it. So have I. And you know as well as I do that all we have will be destroyed if we sit back and watch."

Popoford remained silent while Millie expressed quiet agreement with an earnest expression.

"The organization I'm talking about has worked for many years openly destroying our way of life, past and present as if nothing we stand for is of value. They call themselves The Supreme Five, "*to anótato pénte,*" in Greek, or TAP. One incremental step at a time is their practice, eternal patience and steadfast loyalty are their strength. Many recognize their evil work but don't take it seriously. Some recognize the threat but think we have beaten them when we win a minor victory. More have no time for the fight and are consumed with their jobs and families. Still more wear out or think the threat is past when there's a lull in the enemy's campaign. Even more figure the tar baby du jour is deserving of their contempt and are too ignorant to escape the cunning foes snapping at their heels. Most never pay attention to what their children are taught, their politicians are scheming, and that the freedom in their schools is eroding. And, way too many think that the talking heads on the big networks are unbiased, reasonable, and unimpeachable. They put their faith in political operatives posing as reporters and news analysts. They read *Brave New World* and point their fingers at the other guys never suspecting that their guy's Big Brother."

Popoford nodded at Contlerust but didn't speak up. Millie listened to her father's speech like she'd heard it many times before, with lowered lids and fidgety fingers. Popoford was distracted by a perfume evaporating on Millie's throat. She looked up and caught him sneaking a peek.

"Look at you, Steven. You're obviously prepared to defend your little piece of earth, but are you willing to defend the nation again?"

"I'll defend what's mine. I won't waste my time tilting at windmills."

"You haven't answered my question, Steven. Do you believe in God?"

Popoford nodded.

"Of course you do. Even though the crucifix on your wall is dusty, you haven't taken it down. So tell me, even for a lapsed

Catholic like you, does your God ask you to do what is best for the least of His people?"

"Just what are you selling? I already have a bible and a priest."

"I know."

"Do you, now. What do you know about that?"

"I'll get to that later."

"Really? Well, why can't you get to it now so we can understand how loco you are?"

"I'm not loco. I'm probably the sanest person you know."

"Please get on with it," he said. "What's your plan?"

"I want the real Resurrection Runner Files and any serum you have."

"Hell no!" Popoford snapped. "That'll never happen. I won't help you do anything involving that program."

"Maybe I can convince you otherwise."

"Try me. But better still, why don't you get lost. That way you could get back to your special shelter all snuggled up in your favorite straight jacket."

"I'm serious, Steven."

"An old federal druggy with a gang of dead, ill-trained, special-ops posers wants to save the world? Ridiculous and dangerous."

"No more ridiculous and dangerous than sitting on your butt doing nothing. You're too holed-up to notice the pervasive corruption. It's especially heinous where it's deployed in our school systems and our local governments. Our military is riddled with Marxist crap. From top to bottom TAP's loyalists are leading the way down. With honey-coated lips, they kiss our children's cheeks and poison their hearts. With perverse logic, they accuse their detractors of what they, themselves are. With devil's tongues, they seduce, cajole, and promise heaven on earth while leading their demented subjects to damnation. We need to fight them using their tactics. We have a plan to do just that. We need your help to go to war against our enemies within."

Popoford raised his eyebrows. "You got a codename for this nutty operation?"

"Yes. We are nearly ready to launch."

"Humor me. What is it."

"The Devils Hand-Basket. DHB."

"How cute. Sounds like posies for the damned."

"Spot on. Steven. We'll fill his basket with community organizers, school principals, and politicians infected with robust patriotism. They'll replace the lies with the truth going unnoticed until we've organically revived many more. The desire for freedom and the willingness to fight for it will grow exponentially."

"You're a dreamer Contlerust. There's no hope for success with such an illegal plan."

"I appreciate what you're saying," Contlerust replied in earnest. "But tell me, how can you embrace hopelessness? Have you no faith?"

Contlerust sat quietly for a moment waiting for an answer.

"I see your picture of our Blessed Mother Mary with roses by it on the mantle. Have you no faith?" he asked again.

Popoford sat silently for a full twenty seconds before answering.

"Yes, in God"

"As do I."

"But this is different. I don't see it. It can't work," Popoford replied.

"Faith does not depend on seeing, Thomas," Contlerust paraphrased Christ's admonition of his apostle. "You know there are times you just have to jump right in even when the water's infested with piranha. Especially then. Our founders did that when most thought there was no hope."

"Do you have any idea what you're up against?"

"All I know is that sitting around waiting for the wreckage to be complete is an easy bet. The hard way is to start a small fire that will give people hope. In that hope, courage will be born. This is God's work for me and you. I need your help to light the fire."

"Don't tell me what God wants for me. He has already shown me my path."

"Yes, and it led you to us."

"You lead yourselves to me. Don't blame God."

Contlerust shrugged. "You frustrate me, Steven. Why can't you see reason?"

"Reason?" Popoford said. "Speak for yourself. You want *me* to help you get that depraved program up and running again? You think your arguments will excuse the use of the Resurrection Runner program. You think you can use evil to overcome evil because God is on your side. After what I've been through, you want me to place my life on the line for your naïve dream. The result of your easy bet is plain to see, and I don't like it."

"All war is depraved in its implementation," Contlerust said. "but one must defend what God has given us. And we must fight to win. And don't be fooled. The enemy is working on an improved version of the Resurrection Runner program. Our children are trained in the new-world order every day. It's a tyrant's prime weapon repeated throughout history: get 'em while they're young and they're yours forever. With patience and focus, you too can rule the world in two generations. After that, it's self-sustaining. Duped parents train the young who grow into duped parents. Whether by drugs or brainwashing, the result is the same. The time has come again for you to fight for your country."

"I have my own life to protect. I don't want to lose what I have."

Contlerust sighed heavily while he shook his head in dismay. "We are at war and you know it. By thinking you can save your little piece of freedom by hunkering down and letting the rest of it go to hell, you'll end up in the same grave that's waiting for you no matter what. You just won't die with much to be proud of. And, you'll have a hard time explaining why you wouldn't help your fellow man."

"Guilt trips?" Popoford said. "I can't believe you'd stoop to that."

"It's not a guilt trip as much as it's the truth."

"And why would God want us to have you lead us into this evil? Surely He would never allow that?" Popoford said.

"He allowed it with Adam and Eve, and with Jesus, himself, in the desert and Gethsemane. Aren't you a man of free will? Don't you see that your life and faith have prepared you for this? You were called to serve in this way. It won't be easy, but you can do it. You look like you're in better shape than the last time I saw you. Obviously, you have the skills needed to be effective. And, most importantly, you would hate yourself if you didn't step up when your country needed you. You did it once, and you must do it again."

Millie broke the long silence that lingered after Contlerust's last words. "I don't know about you, but I'm hungry. Can I get us some breakfast while you all are hashing this out?"

"I'm not hungry," Popoford said. "See what you can find for yourself."

"How about you, Dad?"

"I'm good," he said and jumped right back into his monologue.

"TAP is brainwashing students, indoctrinating voters, inventing history, and programming innocent minds. The courts have become tools of politicians. Enforcers keep the people silent while skimming funds from neighborhoods. You're only seeing what directly affects you, so you're missing the depth of corruption that pervades so many American Institutions."

Popoford put his head in his hands. He was about to tell Contlerust to shut up.

"Look," Contlerust continued. "We can only win this war by topping the tenacious stubbornness of the enemy, and by fighting them with the most powerful weapons in our arsenal. The Resurrection Runner program is our most powerful weapon. We must have it and improve it to win. And we must stop defending only our little plots of land. We must also defend the ideas that are crushed by doublespeak and outright lies. It's time to free ourselves and return our constitutional republic to the people. We need the Resurrection Program whether we like it or not. You, Steven, are the only one standing in the way of hope."

"Don't you ever take a breath?" Popoford said as Millie put a bowl of shredded wheat on the table. "I need a break."

For once Contlerust was quiet, but the fire in his eyes stayed hot. Popoford got up and went outside where he paced the length of the clearing until Contlerust followed him out with a bit more to say.

"What can I do to convince you, Steven? You must see that what I'm saying is true."

"Not entirely. You sound like a lunatic looking for the devil in everything you see, or maybe you're a cunning sycophant of the forked-tonged master himself beguiling me into damnation."

"That's a pretty speech and you may be right, yet who would believe you if you said that in public? No one would side with you. It's just too dangerous an idea. I'd advise you to drop that notion now. It's just stupid."

"And yet you're asking me to help start a war against my own country. That sounds like insane treason and the Devil's own work to me. I see threats more deadly to my soul than you see."

"How sad," Contlerust replied. "I guess you've been living off the grid for so long you can't realize that your own paranoia is based on only a whisper of what is really happening. You've been holed up so long, you don't know what's going on outside of Whimsy."

"Really?"

"Yeah. Really."

"I doubt it," Popoford said.

"Are you forgetting the woman who was kidnapped from your quaint county jail?" Contlerust asked.

"What about her?"

"She's Jack Singleton's granddaughter. You remember Jack. Right?"

"Yeah. You already told me that. So what?" Popoford said.

"Help us find her! Let her tell you what's happened to her over the past few months. Wake up and join us."

Popoford ignored Contlerust's order. "I think a better idea is to get on the phone and report the killings in the jail."

"I'll stop you from doing that," Contlerust said emphasizing his threat with a growl. "We'll lose Sarah if we have to spend time with the cops. They'll make us stick around here when we need to get on the road."

"That sounds like a good thing. Let the FBI search for her."

Contlerust let out a big sigh. "Pull your head out, Popoford! The sheriff was killed, too. You're going to be a suspect along with us. You need to understand what's going on here and calling in the police before we all get out of town will only embroil all of us. Sarah's life is in danger, and Millie and I are going to find her."

Popoford looked at Millie as they returned to the kitchen. He hoped she'd disagree with her dad. By what she said, that wasn't going to happen any time soon.

"You need to get with the program," she said. "Sarah's life is in danger. Her life was ruined and now someone has more plans for her. That can't be good. You must hear her story. What can it hurt to listen to her? We can't hang around waiting for you. Anyway, we need your help. It would do us all good."

Popoford gazed at her while he thought about it. He thought about George Florter then about Millie and finally about the eternal consequences for what he was about to do. After a meager attempt to discern the Holy Spirit's path, he silenced all heavenly alternatives and told himself that correcting the evil he had seen was worth the suffering that reintroducing the Resurrection Runner program would bring. And though it is written that "Vengeance is Mine, saith the Lord," he promised himself he would personally rain cruel justice on Sheriff Florter's killer and blurted his response.

"If it'll get you off my back, I'd go almost anywhere. But I keep control of the serum and no one gets my notes."

Contlerust's elfish smile grew wider.

"You drive a hard bargain, Steven," he said sarcastically. "If I had known this was going to be this easy, I wouldn't have bothered to say half of what I did."

"Don't be too smug. You don't own me. I'll be playing this one day at a time. Right now, we have to get your car out of

Whimsy. We'll take my truck into town and you can bring it back here. After that, I'll gather what we need and we'll get started. I'll take both of your guns before we do anything more."

"Millie? Give the man your gun."

"Carefully," Popoford said, turning to face her.

Millie looked at Contlerust with uncertainty but handed her pistol to Popoford.

"Your's too, Simon."

Contlerust slid his gun across the table.

"Now," Popoford said. "When we're driving to town, Millie will be up front with you. I'll be in the back keeping an eye on both of you."

Millie gave a small laugh. "'Both of us?' That's a good one."

"It wasn't meant to be funny," he said.

"But it was, wasn't it?"

She batted her lashes a couple of times and he blushed.

CHAPTER NINE

Sarah Tufftang could smell the sweat of the driver and the scent of the other man's pedestrian aftershave. The one she thought had worn the mask was behind her in the back seat while she sat handcuffed up in front next to the driver. The flour bag over her head had no eye holes. She didn't know what either of them looked like since the driver had never come into the jailhouse and the other guy still wore his mask.

Sarah had an eerie feeling that there was another person in the car as well, but there was no third aroma and no sound of movement or breathing, let alone speaking. Still, her skin crawled as she felt someone unidentified staring at her.

The attack had been a quick and efficient operation. Before she was kidnapped, a person had entered the jailhouse through the back door with a suppressed pistol leading the way. He had a mask covering his face: the fright mask of a deranged woman. Though he had elegant hands that had been spared hard labor, there was no doubt he was a man.

He wasted no time with pleasantries. Before Sarah could fathom what was happening, the sheriff was sprawled dead on the floor. The killer had taken the cop's revolver and had heartlessly shot him in his chest. Then he'd casually killed her grandfather, Jack, and the young man, Bill, with two shots each from the revolver. William Masterson got one of the revolver slugs in the chest and a .45 ACP round in his forehead from the killer's gun.

Her terror burst her heart and petrified her, but she didn't surrender to the terror. Her mind was branded with what she saw, and she would never forget the terrible eyes that peered out from the killer's mask. The pupils were onyx jewels as black as his irises, beautiful and cold, framed only by a hint of white as they filled the mask's eye cutouts.

Still, she cowered on the jail bench awaiting death, managing a quick Hail Mary as she held her breath. Her astonishment sent waves of relief and thankfulness through her soul when her prayer was answered and the assassin turned without a word and left the way he'd come in.

But her troubles had just begun.

She was still chained to the wall when another man wearing a hood entered the jail through the front door. He'd found the jail keys on the sheriff's belt and, instead of shooting her, he entered the cell and slapped handcuffs on her, and pulled a sack over her head. She was alive and had no idea why she was spared, yet she prayed she'd survive what was to come. Then, succumbing to the strain she had undergone, she passed out.

Now, she sat still taking in any information she could gather. The road was winding, of course: the road that passed through Whimsy wound both east and west. But she knew they were traveling eastward now because the sun was warming her face under the flour sack. Their speed was moderate as one might expect given the curving mountain road. Once they slowed to a crawl when they fell in behind a ranch wagon or a semi that lumbered up a grade in front of them. Whatever it was, it must have pulled off the road as it reached the top of the hill, because the kidnapper at the wheel stepped on the gas and blurted an unexpected curse.

His voice was deep with a foreign accent: perhaps Slavic or Germanic. Sarah couldn't decide. But the instant the curse was hurled, the killer behind her growled and she heard a backhand head thwack coming from the driver's direction.

There were no further outbursts and presently they were gliding along the Interstate still heading east.

The sun was behind them by the time the car slowed and took a series of turns eventually pulling off the paved highway and onto a gravel road.

Sarah started counting the seconds as they slowly progressed. When the car finally came to a stop, she had counted to three hundred and eighty-two, about six minutes. That meant they were about three miles from the paved road.

These observations, though small, gave her hope that she might gain enough information to find where they took her. If she could only get out alive.

Sarah was pulled from the car and marched a short way into a building where her handcuffs were removed. She heard a door close and a lock turn. Her arms ached as she pulled the flour sack from her head. Only the dark greeted her as there were no windows. But her eyes were already used to the total darkness and she could easily see the cracks of light which framed the door.

Sarah crept up to the door and listened. She heard voices but they were indistinguishable, just mutterings, yet proof enough that there were three people outside.

Using the meager light from the door, she turned around and was able to see faint traces of two chairs and a desk. She cautiously approached the desk and moving around it she found a drawer which she opened a little way. Putting her hand in the drawer, she felt for any object that might be of aid.

Much to her surprise, she felt a sharply-pointed letter opener. Taking what she believed was an answer to her prayers, she pulled the blade from the drawer and slid it under her shirt at the small of her back. Then she put her hand back in the drawer and was amazed to feel a handgun resting there.

As she started to grasp the gun, she heard the door lock turn, she immediately released her grip, closed the drawer, and slid out from behind the desk.

The glare of the day's final minutes of golden light blinded her and she couldn't make out who had grabbed her, blindfolded her, and tied her down in one of the chairs.

All was silent for several minutes except for the quiet breathing of her captors. Just as her eyes were getting accustomed once again to the dark, the blindfold was removed and the lights in the room snapped on. Sarah was blinded for a second time.

"Good evening," a woman said. "We meet at last."

She was standing directly in front of Sarah and gradually her face became more distinct. There was a haughty beauty about her, an air of confidence and power. Her voice was soothing but with a threat of menace. She was simply dressed in a black skirt and a white blouse. Without shifting her eyes from Sarah, she took the raincoat she had draped over her arm and placed it on the desk. Sarah took her for a business professional. And, as if in acknowledgment that Sarah was sizing her up, the woman continued.

"I like to get the job done, Sarah, and done right the first time. I assume you will not fully understand my commitment right away, but soon you will believe everything I tell you without question. Your time has come."

Sarah, a woman with a spine, looked her in the eye, and calmly asked, "What is your name?"

"I'm Lamia," she said.

"Ah, the serpent goddess. How much baby blood have you sucked today?"

Lamia's right fist snapped hard into Sarah's gut and her left hand delivered a devastating slap to Sarah's face.

"The first rule is to never speak until I tell you to."

Sarah tasted the blood in her mouth and spit it in Lamia's face. "You bitch! You killed my grandfather!"

Lamia punched her again, this time on her left temple. Sarah swooned but the two men held her up.

"Slow learner? I'll see if I can't improve your shortcoming," Lamia said, and without glancing at her backup man, she continued. "Prepare the syringe and get the other equipment ready. A beautiful mind, untamed, is a waste."

CHAPTER TEN

Contlerust drove Popoford's truck to Whimsy with Millie beside him in the passenger seat and Popoford behind them, his attention at first on her.

His head had been full of rage and plans for vengeful murder but when Millie laughed at his unintended one-eyed Jack joke, his mood change startled him. Except for the invented affair he had with Gretchen, Popoford never felt any lustful desire. He'd been a monotone man, singing a one-note tune, perfectly flat pitched, a dullard with no manly awareness of women. He couldn't carry a tune and he couldn't make time. Little did he know that no matter what revenge he had planned for Sheriff Florter's death, God would have the last laugh. He caught himself humming a light tune but silenced himself immediately.

"Don't stop," Millie said. "I like that song, and you put a spark in it."

Popoford was dumbfounded, but he self-consciously picked up the tune where he'd left off. All the rest of the way into town his eye lingered on her shoulders and the nape of her bare neck. With her hair pulled back in a ponytail, his imagination flourished until Contlerust put on the brakes just as Popoford was overwhelmed with a desire to graze her throat with his lips.

He snapped erect, startled that he had been leaning towards Millie, and abruptly covered his foolishness with an order.

"Get out, Simon," he said. "I'll drive the truck back to the house. You drive ahead of me in your car."

"Come on, Millie," Contlerust said.

"She stays with me," Popoford said. "That way you won't ditch me."

"Is that the only reason?" Millie said, turning towards him, her lips parted and her eyelids heavy.

Contlerust was already walking to his car when Millie asked her question, so he didn't see her reach into the backseat and pull Popoford's head close enough to hers that he couldn't stop from accepting her full lips on his, her tongue lightly teasing, her breath and perfume pungent, urging him on.

Then she snapped around and sat straight up in her seat staring straight forward. Her father was just getting into his car.

"You're a wildman, Mister P.," she said. "I'm going to have to tame you real soon. What do you think of that?"

"No one can tame me," he said, his whole body proving him a liar. He was already tamed.

On the drive back to his house they kept silent, but as Popoford turned onto his long driveway to his clearing, Millie reached over and put her hand on his leg gently stroking his thigh. The thrill and the embarrassment were almost too much for his pent-up desire, but Millie had enough experience to go only far enough and not too far. When he got out of the car, Popoford kept her handiwork concealed from Contlerust until it had lost its power.

It took little effort to gather what they needed from Popoford's prep stash and only a minute to load the bugout duffel bags he had stashed in his bedroom closet. Finally, they returned to the house and Popoford gathered a redundant set of his falsified files. He took three vials of Resurrection Runner serum from a small refrigerator nestled in the floor under a trapdoor next to his bed. Then he filled a large cooler with the food he cleared out of his main refrigerator and packed several boxes of canned goods from his pantry. When everything was loaded, they sat down in the kitchen again.

"You're dragging some bad folks behind you," Popoford said.

"No kidding," Contlerust said.

"Who are they?"

"All I know is someone was following us before we got to Whimsy, but we shook them two days before we got to your place."

"Not really," Popoford said.

"No. I guess not."

"You seem pretty nonchalant about it," Popoford said. "Three of your people are dead. My friend, the sheriff, was murdered. And you have what looks like a kidnapped team member to find. That's a pretty shitty score if you ask me."

Contlerust and Millie scowled.

"Tell me again why I should care about your paranoid plans."

No one said a word for a few minutes, then Popoford continued.

"What's done is done," he said. "We need a new plan to find the woman right now. What's her name again?"

"Tufftang. Sarah Tufftang," Contlerust answered.

"Yeah. Let's start with you telling me her story. The one she would have told us herself."

Contlerust's story was brief. He'd read about it online after hearing about it on News at Eleven. Sarah had been fired for refusing to include the federally mandated *Brilliance in Basics* history textbook in her classroom curriculum. She was attacked by a punk Marxist student-body president and she slapped him down. The word went out to cancel her and by the evening news, she had become the latest martyr of the revisionist movement.

The news at eleven led with the accusation that she had beaten a child senseless in the presence of the Dean. The child she had struck was, in fact, twenty-seven years old, a man who had returned to finish his undergraduate work after having flunked out nine years before. She considered fighting it in court but was advised by her lawyer not to bother. He explained that the circumstantial evidence was overwhelming. The lawyer acted like he was an operative of the Supreme Five. Who knows, he may have been.

"We went to her after reading about her problems and convinced her that joining us would be her best opportunity to recover her career and reverse the history rewriting campaign sweeping the country. She's a member of our small force. Joined just under a year ago."

"How much do you trust her?" Popoford asked."

"With my life."

"Really?" Popoford said. "What about you Millie? Would you trust her with your life?

Millie looked at her father, and with her eyes still on him, she said, "Not so much. I don't trust anyone with my life."

"How old are you, Millie?"

"Twenty-one. Why?"

"I just wondered how you got so cynical."

"I was just kind of thrown into it when my uncle killed his sister, my mother, and tried to blame it on me."

Popoford paused for a minute as that sank in. "So, what happened to your uncle? Where is he?"

"In hell, I guess. I killed him," she said matter-of-factly. "Self-defense."

Contlerust frowned at this but said nothing.

"Your brother-in-law?" Popoford asked Contlerust.

"He deserved it," Contlerust said.

Popoford paused again.

"Do you two think that Sarah could be in on the murders? Has she done anything to make you suspicious?"

"No. Nothing," Contlerust replied.

"And you, Millie?"

"No."

"So, what was your plan when you got the files and the serum?"

"We were going to infiltrate their Downtrodden Community Fighting Corp operation."

"How?" Popoford asked.

"We were going to capture Dean Wrenbutt and put him on the Resurrection Runner program," Contlerust said. "We were going to turn him completely around and make him an undercover operative for American values. He would quietly help subvert the Brilliance in Basics program and support teachers like Sarah."

Popoford considered the idea.

"And what keeps you from doing it now?" Popoford asked.

"Nothing, but we need to get Sarah back."

"I agree, but I think we can do both at once.

"How so?" Millie asked.

"With your help, Millie. I think you should go back to college for a while, for the sake of the cause."

Millie looked stunned and gazed at Popoford as if he was crazy.

"Who's going to buy that?"

"Everyone. No questions asked. You're a transfer American History graduate student. You don't have to prove anything to anyone. No one's going to ask for your credentials. All you have to do is look the part and walk into a lecture hall. Then you can sidle up to Dean Wrenbutt on campus and strike up a conversation. You take it from there. The plan will be for you to lure him to our location and we'll see to it that he returns to school with a new perspective on life."

"I think that's a bad idea. Wouldn't people notice his about-face?" Millie asked.

"Hopefully not if we do a proper brain wipe and a fresh memory transplant. He'll become a champion of justice working to weed all out the perversions he's currently fostering," Popoford answered. "For your protection, we'll make him forget you ever existed so he won't keep coming around looking for you."

"I guess it could work," Millie said.

"Then you'll do it?"

Millie looked at her father who shrugged and said, "It's up to you. If you say yes, I'll be keeping an eye on you all the time."

Millie tapped her fingers on the table a few times and then nodding slowly as if she was convincing herself.

"How about you, Steven? Will you keep an eye on me, too?"

"With pleasure," he said suddenly aware of his unexpected familiarity. "Of course."

"I'm in," she answered. The morning wore on as they discussed Millie's cover. Contlerust took charge of planning the details.

When it came to rescuing Sarah, Popoford insisted on handling that part of the mission.

"I don't know just what we're facing, but my gut tells me it's a lot bigger than we imagine. There are only three of us. On the face of it, the best thing to do is just let it be. Do nothing. We don't have what it takes to win."

The others looked at him in disbelief.

"Don't get me wrong. I'm not a quitter, and I'll never leave one of my own behind. That's not what I'm driving at."

"Well, then what is it?" Contlerust said.

"I've decided to use one of the Resurrection Runner doses on myself."

"That's crazy," Millie said. "Why would you need to be reprogrammed?"

"I have a lot of skills, a lot of experience. I don't need reprogramming, but I do need strength. I'm not as strong or as limber as I once was. I know I can still hold my own for a while. But it's the "for a while" that I need to correct."

"And just how do you think brainwashing will help?"

"I want the confidence, determination, and stamina that an operation like this will require. I want the power of my brain to reject all negativity and weakness. The serum and some stimulants can do that for me."

Popoford fell silent as Contlerust and Millie considered his words.

Finally, Millie broke the silence. "You can do that?"

"I'm certain the mind has powers to convince the body to endure hardship. With the serum, my mind can become more resilient to pain and weariness than ever. I'll need that if I'm to do what must be done."

"You sound like you want to be a superhero," Contlerust said.

"Hardly. I have a job to do and I want the best tools to get it done."

Millie was silent.

"I'll do it with you, Steven," Contlerust said.

"I wish you could," Popoford said, preparing to lie. "But there are only two vials: just enough for two doses. We need one for Dean Wrenbutt and one for me."

"Are you certain about this?" Millie asked.

"Yes. Certain."

"Then it's settled," she said, and Contlerust agreed.

"Well then," Popoford said. "We better hit the road. We should get Millie on campus as soon as we can. If we can get Wrenbutt in our trap right away, we could get his mind corrected so he can be at the college Monday morning ready to alter the history curriculum and get Sarah back ."

Popoford set all his alarms, his video and audio recorders, and his notification software. As Contlerust got into his car, Millie waited, then jumped into Popoford's truck as he walked the clearing perimeter watching and listening for intruders. The eight-point buck he'd kept an eye on for the last three years was bedded down twenty yards deep in the woods. He winked at it, and when he opened his eye and could see again, the buck winked back.

"We will meet another day," Popoford said with a casual salute and walked back to his truck.

They drove west towards Claramon College, a private school nestled in a wooded wash at the western foot of the Sierras where the great flatland of water-starved farmland fed the world when allowed to drink, and ages-old citrus, walnut, fig, and almond acres were daily uprooted for pistachio trees to feed the rising masses in China. It was a school for students of breeding, not born of royal or sainted roots, but of stock cultivated in the ways of darkness, for the spawn not only rejected God but embraced the prince of the world as well. The students, teachers, and administrators of Claramon College were a testament to the adage that training perpetuates the past and failure to teach the truths dooms the future. This is where Millie would go to school with her father tailing her, while Popoford, suddenly having mixed feelings about Mille's honey trap, would procure private space nearby.

They checked into a motel attached to an Easy Get Going truck stop in Merced and got a sandwich to go followed by a walk back to their rooms for some much-needed sleep. They were weary, and all of them, except for Popoford, slept soundly through the night. He dreamed of heroic deeds and flying above his Whimsy woods, his cape fluttering in the wind then snapping taut as he soared like an owl: silent, deadly. Finally, just as day broke, he dreamed of a young, naked woman with long auburn hair. He woke up grouchy, thinking of Millie and wishing he'd taken the job of watching after her at Claramon.

He left the motel to search for an out-of-the-way rental house in the country they could use to process Dean Wrenbutt when Millie lured the Dean into their web. He would text the address when they had it. In the meantime, Millie and Contlerust drove to the Claramon College campus and put their plan into action.

CHAPTER ELEVEN

Sarah's gut still ached as she was pushed onto a gurney and strapped down. A needle was inserted into her arm and a saline drip was started. Next, a dose of Midazolam was administered and Lamia's patronizing voice swam in Sarah's head.

"You're incredibly lucky, my dear. Soon your life will have a purpose. You're about to become a skilled leader who will focus your nascent and still erratically fascist principles on wayward, fundamentalist university students. While the student body is small and mostly a result of public schooling and the nose-ring guidance of new-school parents, we cannot allow any student not fully indoctrinated in the Brilliance in Basics program to thrive.

"In a few minutes, you will receive a dose of the most recent iteration of the memory control agent commonly called the Resurrection Runner Protocol. Your whole life will be erased leaving you without memories. But don't worry, I'll give you new memories; new thoughts that will transform you into a modern professor striving to purge the past to make way for the glorious future."

Sarah was swooning as Lamia's last words echoed in her head. She was staring at Lamia's cold smile and drifted into a sedated consciousness while someone adjusted her head and she gazed at moving images dancing on the ceiling near her bed.

At first, the images were just random, swirling colors. She was as a baby, newborn, a nearly clean slate except that her academic and professional achievements were intact. Soon the colors resolved into a confluence of dream-like scenes racing along so fast that she couldn't think of what they were and could only surrender to the litany of her new and invented life.

She knew that she had hardships aplenty, maintained raging anger against pernicious molestation, and embodied a deep loathing for the injustice imposed by the racist, privileged conservative bloodsuckers piled upon her and all the downtrodden of America.

After a couple of hours, her mind was embedded with state-of-the-art malevolence, infused with a notion of systemic unfairness, and ripe with hatred for capitalism, the concept of natural law, the Constitution, and the rule of law. She was a carefully crafted, useful idiot, with all her true experiences and considered decisions, those which had molded her into a savvy and exceptional citizen and teacher, altered, perverted, or erased.

Sarah awoke slowly from the indoctrination with her beautiful mind wasted. In its place was another world and life. To her, it was her only life, and she embodied all the sadness and joy, the dying and living, the lies and truth that her indoctrination provided. Old loyalties never were, and the woman she was, the girl that became the woman, the family and friends, schools, church, and romances she once remembered, never happened. The history that until two hours earlier was the meaning of her life was gone. In its place was Sarah S. Tufftang, a juvenile delinquent who had scrambled out of poverty and had ridden herself of her wretched, slovenly family only to excel in school supported by an anonymous donor she had yet to meet.

In Sarah S. Tufftang's new memory her success in school had caught the eye of that anonymous donor, an upperclassman who took her under his wing in many ways, not the least of which was her admittance into a secret society of radical activists, bent on correcting the mistakes the privileged class referred to as American

Exceptionalism. She was a well-placed and eager student, one without a desire to question what she heard nor to seek other sources to confirm what she was taught. Her sense of self was wrapped in unquestioning loyalty to the society, a loyalty that like all else she remembered was an alien attitude she'd never have embraced without Lamia's adroit assistance.

Charged with ever more challenging assignments, Sarah excelled, moving up the organizational ladder with astounding rapidity. Indeed, she thought herself a prodigy as she slowly sat up and swung her legs over the side of the bed.

"Slowly," Lamia said. "Take your time. You've had a fall and a severe concussion. You need to take it easy for a while and get some rest. Are you hungry?"

"No. I have a headache," Sarah said, gingerly touching a bump on the left side of her head.

"Yes. That's to be expected. Here, take these. They should help."

Sarah swallowed the pills and tried to stand up.

"Slowly," Lamia said. "It may take a couple of days for you to recover. I'm just so happy you didn't break any bones."

"What happened. I don't remember a thing after I entered the sheriff's jail and they locked the jail door."

"It seems that someone was waiting for you. They knocked you out and dragged you into the alley. Albert came for you when you didn't signal for him to drive to the back door. There was no one around when he got there, but you were lying outside the cell and the door was locked again. He brought you to me. He's waiting in the other room if you feel up to seeing him."

"I'm feeling drowsy all of a sudden. Can I see him after I rest for a while?"

"Of course," Lamia said, and helped Sarah lie down again.

When Sarah had fallen into a deep sleep induced by the injections and the pills Lamia had given her, Albert was called into the room so Lamia could talk to him.

"How did it go?" he asked.

"It looks to be a perfect process, but I'll have to do some testing tomorrow to be certain she has all the information she needs for her assignment. I need to know if there are any remnants of her previous memory that could be troublesome. I also want to dig out details of the crew she was running with so she can recognize them and handle them herself without having to contact us. It will take as many as five days to be certain that she's ready for her mission. I plan on having her back on campus this coming Monday, five days from today. Have you made all the arrangements?"

"Everything's in place," Albert said. "Her Merced house is ready. She'll be right at home when she walks through the front door."

"Is the Master Class broadcast set up properly and secure?"

"Yes. It's ready to go."

"Wonderful. The techniques I'm perfecting with Sarah will be of great interest to our leader and our worldwide associates. My disciples will go forth and multiply. It's a new and promising day ahead for we who were born to greatness."

CHAPTER TWELVE

Claramon College was founded in 1936 with major funding provided by private equity groups whose principals are anonymous and motives concealed, a practice shared by many colleges. No one questions the money sources since many think it is no one's business, even though they enjoy considerable tax relief as non-profit corporations. In truth, the several foundations are money-laundering entities for instruments of foreign governments. The primary *quid pro quo* in the arrangement encourages Claramon's directors to ensure that these countries are presented in a favorable light both in public and in the classroom. Certain stipends and other generous remunerations help to seal mouths and keep eyes off activities related to the college, its faculty, and the student body. Parents, whose darlings are finally out of the nest, are pleased with the comparatively low tuition and the announced quality of the education provided. Had some of these parents paid more attention to their children, they might have found many ways to differ with their dear one's newly-found one-world views; been astonished at how their offspring hated America; encouraged delightful conversations which may have provided abundant corrective opportunities even in their imperfect way. Most of the parents, however, would be pleased that their children conformed to their own cult's standards.

So it was that Millie Contlerust's explosive slamming of her father's car door and her stomping walk-away towards the history department building raised no one's eyebrows. What notice was made of her tantrum was smiled upon by the dean of the history department who was walking to his office as Millie began her march. Dean Wrenbutt relished her feisty attitude and licked his purplish lips at the swing of her rear end and the bareness of her long legs. The atheist that he was, he thought it grand humor to quietly sing a verse of "Going My Way." In his lust, he kept pace with Millie and was pleased when he had the opportunity to catch up and open the door for her. To his continued pleasure, she smiled at him and said thank you.

"Are you new to the campus?" he asked, surprised that she hadn't berated him for treating her like a second-class citizen incapable of opening her own door.

"Why, yes. How did you know?"

"Well, it's a small campus and I've never seen you before."

"Are you sure? I've been here since the first of the year."

"I don't know how I could have missed you," he said with a lurid smile. "Where are you headed?"

"I have to see the dean about a scheduling problem. My professor was fired or something, and the grad student taking over for her is an idiot. I need permission to move to another class. I hope he can help me."

"He's always a great help to the student body. He's an extremely considerate man."

"Oh, you know him well?"

"I should say so."

"Well, maybe you'll put in a good word for me."

"I certainly will," he said trying to get a look down her dress. "I have an appointment with him myself. Maybe he'll see you when I'm through."

"Oh," she squealed. "Would you do that for me?"

"I'd be happy to. Here's the dean's office now. Why don't you wait out here for a few minutes before going in? That way no one will think that I have a personal interest in your situation."

"Okay. I'll just sit on this bench for a while. Then I'll come in just like we'd never met."

As he turned to open his office door, Millie added "I sure owe you big time for this. I'll be grateful for what you're doing for me."

Wrenbutt nearly swooned as the blood left his head for parts un-named.

Millie sat down as she said she would. She was smiling broadly for the notion she'd put into Wrenbutt's head. She looked down the hall at a similar bench and, catching her father's eye, she signaled a thumbs up which he returned without expression.

After five minutes, a text arrived on her cell phone. It was from Popoford and indicated that he had found a furnished farmhouse a few miles from the college. He gave her the address and said he was going there now to prepare for Wrenbutt's arrival. She glanced at Contlerust who was reading the same message.

As she waited, she considered entering the Dean's office right away, but knowing better than to seem anxious, she stayed where she was for a full fifteen minutes. As she finally stood, she glanced again at her father who then stood himself and walked out of the building without a word. He would be waiting for her when she needed him. Millie opened the door and stepped inside.

A woman sitting at a desk looked up from her reading.

"May I help you?"

"Yes, please. I've come to see the dean about a problem I'm having in class. I was told to stop around and maybe see what he could do."

"Take a seat, please. He has another student in with him now. It shouldn't be long."

"Okay. Thanks," Millie said and sat down in a chair to wait.

It wasn't five minutes before the door to Dean Wrenbutt's office was opened and a young man in his twenties walked out.

"Thank you, again, Dean Wrenbutt. I'll do as you say and let you know how it goes."

The boy closed the door behind him, whereupon the young woman at the desk picked up her phone and spoke to the dean.

"You have a student here to see you. She says she was told to come by this morning. Yes. Of course, sir.

"You can go in now, Miss," she told Millie.

"Thank you."

Millie stood and opened the dean's door. She stepped in and closed it behind her. There he was: all smiles and not a lick of caution about him.

Millie returned his smile and took a seat in front of his desk. She didn't cross her legs but leaned forward to reveal what he had hoped to see.

"You're a sly fox, Dean Wrenbutt. If I didn't know better, I'd think you were having fun with me."

"No harm in a little amusement is there? It was serendipity to meet as we did, and I thought you'd like to know that I can keep a secret."

"Well, dean, I can keep a secret as well, but right now, I don't have any to keep. I just guess I owe you one."

Wrenbutt nearly stumbled over himself as he came out from behind his desk and sat on it.

"I'm sure happy you could fit me into your busy schedule. I really need to get my problem straightened out."

"Well, my dear, That's why I'm here."

"So you see, when Professor Tufftang left, the Grad student who's covering her American History class started making unwanted advances towards me and some of the other students.

Women and men alike. His comments in class are patronizing and embarrassing. And, as if that's not enough, he threw out her curriculum and is teaching some sort of twisted new version of history.

"Really," Wrenbutt said.

"I should know. I've taken the class two times already, and I was sure I could pass it this time, but I don't know now. All of what he's teaching is just plain different. I feel like I'm starting all over again. And anyway, he's too young and bratty. He's not my type."

"And what is your type, Ms.… What is your name, anyway? We haven't been properly introduced."

"Well, I'm Millie. Millie Lockhart. You can call me Millie if you like."

"I'll just do that when we're alone. Otherwise, I think a bit of formality is required when others are around. Don't you?"

"Well, of course, Dean Wrenbutt. But we're alone now. What should I call you when we're alone?"

"My name is Thornton, but you can call me Tom."

"Oh, I like Thornton just fine. Just saying it kind of makes my tongue curl."

Wrenbutt sputtered his next question. "If this grad student is too young, just what sort of man do you like?

"Oh, Thornton. A girl must never tell her secrets. Perhaps you can guess."

Wrenbutt couldn't control himself and put his fat hand on her thigh.

"Now, now Thornton," Millie purred while removing his hand. "This is no place to have fun. Anyway, I want to know what you can do to fix my problem."

"Don't you worry your pretty self about that. There's another history class I can get you enrolled in and the best news is you don't even have to attend the sessions to pass."

"Why, what do you mean?"

"You just leave it to me and I'll take care of everything."

Millie popped her eyes in amazement. "Oh, you are a darling, Thornton. How can I say thank you so you know I truly mean it." Her smile dissolved his meager resistance.

"What are you doing for lunch?"

"Nothing I can't change."

"Well, how about spending some time with me. It won't be fattening."

'Oh, you are a silly boy, Thornton. What am I going to do with you."

"I can give you a few ideas," he said.

"I think I have a few of my own. Why don't you just let me surprise you? It could be fun."

"Is there someplace we could meet? You know, somewhere we wouldn't be seen?"

"Well, there's my place. It's a small farmhouse, and it's a couple of miles down the road, but you could meet me there in an hour or so."

"What about the man who dropped you off this morning?"

"Oh, that's my uncle. He's a grumpy guy and all he wants to do is fish. He won't be back here to pick me up until four o'clock."

"I'm parked in the lot on the east side of the campus," he said, as he removed his keys and pulled an extra car key from his ring. "Here. You take this key. It's almost eleven now. My parking spot is marked with my name. You get in my car at noon and get down in the back seat. I'll be there at about ten after. How's that sound?"

"Clandestine."

"Right. Now, get along before my secretary gets any big ideas, and I'll see you in a little while."

"Yes, Thornton," she whispered. "Whatever you say."

With that, they both stood up and Millie paused for an extra, tantalizing beat and then turned and left his office.

As she passed the secretary she had a sorrowful look about her as if nothing good had come of her meeting with the dean.

"Is everything okay?" Miss Shlenterby asked.

"Sure, if getting nothing for my efforts is okay."

Millie left the room and walked out of the building. With each step, her smile grew a little wider until she was beaming. She walked toward the parking lot and then found a bench under a shade tree and sent her father and Popoford a text.

"I hope you can be there by noon. I'm bringing him in."

The response was a picture of a small house sitting well off the road with a message "Enter through the back door. Be sure he comes in behind you."

As she slipped the phone back into her purse she heard the sound of distant thunder. There was a storm brewing and a cool breeze was just starting to pick up.

At noon, Millie approached the dean's car, a light brown Jeep Gladiator pickup. She gave it a once over and figured that Thornton Wrenbutt had a nifty bank account. Maybe he was on the largesse end of foreign country money, one of the many things her father, Sarah, and the dead members of their crumbled team suspected. Whether this was true in the dean's case or not, the truck was a beauty and brand new. It still had temporary plates and the smell of new upholstery made her jealous as she slipped into the back seat.

No more than five minutes had passed when the driver's door opened and Dean Thornton Wrenbutt slid his wide rear into place.

"I hate to have you in the back seat all the way, but it's best if we aren't seen together," he said.

"Never you mind," Millie said and proceeded to massage his shoulders as he drove out of the parking lot.

"Which way do I go?" he asked.

"Just turn left and stay on the road. It's a farmhouse a couple of miles straight ahead. 2796. On the right."

Wrenbutt reached into his pocket and pulling something out, handed it to Millie.

"Light this for me, will you? Take a toke yourself."

Millie took the joint and lit it with the matches he provided.

"It's party time, Thornton," she whispered in his ear and passed the joint forward without taking a hit.

They drove for about three minutes when Wrenbutt said, "That must be it."

"Yeah, that's it," she said. She was checking addresses on mailboxes along the road. "You better park around back. Anybody spotting your beautiful Jeep from the road will know it's yours."

Wrenbutt did as she wished, and soon they were at the backdoor with Millie fumbling for a non-existent key in her purse. Wrenbutt was behind her and couldn't see her pretending to unlock the door. When she opened it and went inside, the dean was right behind her, the joint in his mouth and his eyes only on Millie's backside.

Dean Thornton Wrenbutt's lascivious, privileged world turned to lightning as Popoford discharged a Taser charge into his neck. Contlerust pulled a black bag over the man's head as he dropped to the floor with his expected romp with Millie collapsing with him.

CHAPTER THIRTEEN

Lamia was pleased with herself. Just a few days before, she'd lost favor with Vladdrac. But now, she'd demonstrate her skill in transforming Sarah into the revolution's most potent weapon. Sarah Tufftang, the outspoken adversary of the collective and the reordering of natural law: a hardheaded believer in the privileged reading of history and a formidable opponent was sitting next to her and the interview would soon begin. Turning Sarah around and making her a leader for the revolution would bring great honor to Lamia and outstanding propaganda value for the cause.

Lamia dressed for the occasion in a black cape wrapped around her shoulders. She sat in a darkened room, her head bowed slightly, her eyes open wide staring into the camera, a soft light isolating her pale face, the surrounding black shadow framing her cruel beauty.

Lamia's raven hair, her stark-white skin, and her bright red lipstick produced a compelling contrast. As the red light announced the broadcast had begun, she straightened to her full, statuesque height. Her moment of mastery had come, and she'd make a show of it. Vladdrac and all her fellow leaders would be astounded by her advancement over the original and unreliable first Resurrection Runner serum. Today, she'd rise to the seat at the right hand of Vladdrac himself. Her day had come!

"Leader Vladdrac, my esteemed associates, I have asked you to join me in this presentation to demonstrate the great advancements I have made in the mind-altering serum which was employed by Home Office to program their Resurrection

Runners. It was an effective agent for persuading their operatives that they were more talented than they were, but it is a weak formula that can be defeated. I have developed a process that is more effective, more stable, and more secure. Today's demonstration will highlight the effectiveness of my work and illustrate the value of my new serum's potential.

"The subject I'll interview today is Sarah Tufftang, a professor of history. Until recently she was the enemy. Her crimes against the people came to my attention when she went to the newspapers with a story of interference with her class curriculum and her eventual firing for insubordination, the striking of a student, and threats to the Dean of the department. The Dean, by the way, is one of our valued, unsuspecting foot soldiers.

"You will see that she's perfectly healthy. I injected her with a dose of my improved mind-altering formula and the results are phenomenal. Unlike the original formula, mine works rapidly. Sarah's memories were erased to a deep enough level that she has no notion that she's a patriot. I altered her fundamental beliefs: her family's politics are reconstructed, her education and personal experiences modified, and, in some cases, reconceived. In short, Sarah is one of us now, true blue, onboard, and trustworthy.

"All this was accomplished in five days. The old serum could take weeks. The effects are lasting and will stay in place until I alter them. The old serum unintentionally allowed the subject's subconscious to creep into his awareness causing doubt to disrupt the subject's programming. When this happened, the subject would have to be reprogrammed or eliminated.

"The new serum does not allow such waste. It requires but one procedure to end them all.

"In a minute, I'll bring Sarah on camera for an interview. She'll listen to herself giving a lecture, and then I'll ask her some questions.

"You are all familiar with this sort of drivel," Lamia said. "I only present it as a contrast to what you will hear from Sarah herself, the new Sarah, the revolutionary who has struggled with us for many years. She's a tough, in your face, bring it all down, baby, Marxist operative. Make no mistake. This is the same woman who relished natural law. But this is a completely different woman because her mind is reformed. She looks the same, but her foundational views and her skills are completely different. "I give you Professor Sarah S. Tufftang, the Eric Hoffer version."

As Lamia finished her introduction, the lights came up revealing an entirely white room and Sarah Tufftang sitting calmly in the chair next to Lamia.

"Good morning, Sarah. How do you feel?"

"Marvelous, Lamia. Thank you for having me on your show today."

"Sarah, let me begin by playing a recording of a person you may have met. Her voice was altered to assure that you don't guess her name. She's a teacher lecturing her class, presenting her views concerning natural law. Please listen carefully to what she says. I'll ask you to respond in a minute."

"Okay," Sarah said, and Lamia played the clip.

"Therefore, knowledge of the founder's dedication to natural law is necessary to a proper understanding of the founding itself. For in no way, under the precepts of natural law as promulgated by Socrates and codified by Cicero and others, can a law devised by man simultaneously invalidate the nature of man and the law of God and be judged to be true and in keeping with the design of the universe. This concept and deeply-held belief emboldened the founders to take great offense in the indenturing decrees imposed on the multitude in the new world by those benighted few in their old and distant motherland.

"It was beyond question that those who sat in princely seats of power knew little of the coarse necessities of the New World. None had earned the right of taxation without representation for they had not experienced the harsh winters, the rugged land, and the enmity of both indigenous and old-world conqueror's warrior nations. And, more to the point, such destructive laws from afar that hampered life, liberty, and the pursuit of happiness, were in and by themselves abhorrent to God the Father. By this truth alone, the founders were righteous in their Declaration and justified in suffering the calamity that such a claim had on most of the signers of the Declaration. They knew they enjoyed the grace of God in their actions and were prepared to suffer their own passion in defense of its truth."

The clip ended and Lamia, rather than jumping right to the question sat quietly so as not to influence Sarah's response. A couple of beats later she continued.

"So, Sarah, tell me in your own words what you think of this lecture. Please be frank. My associates need complete honesty to evaluate the situation."

Sarah was champing to get her answer out of her mouth even before Lamia had started asking for her response.

"Whoa! This can't be real. Where did you get such a backward, racist hag? This fascist notion is revolting. And to think that anyone could believe that any law or government could be based on a notion so absurd. These natural law idiots can't see that each person has their unique understanding of the world. Each is a special creature who must find its unique deity. Science has disavowed the notion of god as a figment of fascist enslavement and white man's racism. This is the same servitude that shackled women and drove black men to drugs. This is the same self-righteousness that is the Ku Klux Klan, the Nazis, and the Knights of Columbus. The United States was founded on a slavery economy that remains today powerfully gripping white men's hearts.

"There is no one law for all. Not until there's justice for all and reparation for the oppressed. I want to know who that bitch is so I can lead the action to have her canceled!"

"That won't be necessary, Sarah," Lamia said. "We've already taken care of her."

"Well, I'm ready to serve in any way I can. These ultra-right-wing pigs haven't gotten the message. I want to be the one to give it to them. With both barrels!"

"Sarah, have patience. We need to play the long game. Your time will come. Every program we've established and all the new ones that we'll introduce are but tiny building blocks. Each soldier in the field has an important task. You'll be assigned to an appropriate mission soon. You're just the loyal operative we need, and soon many more operatives will join with you organizing in communities across the land. Thank you for participating in this interview. I expect great things from you."

Lamia lowered the room's fill lights and adjusted the camera for a tight headshot. She spoke to the TAP members huddled in their secret warrens, but her words were aimed directly at Vladdrac.

"My work is a triumph for you, Dear Leader, and for the Master of All, yet to be revealed. With this new serum, thousands of committed operatives can be produced in a fraction of the time it takes us to program them now. Once employed, there will be nothing that will stop our glorious revolution. Instead of wasting time and energy creating propaganda education for our schools, we can mandate a vaccination protocol for all students starting as early as kindergarten.

"We will implement the program in all public institutions. We will mandate the program in private schools and universities with a threat of defunding for those who resist. The few schools that refuse to accept government funding will be crushed by public opinion while their campuses are burned to the ground.

"In a matter of months if not weeks, our army of patriots will fulfill the truth that Comrade Khrushchev delivered to the west: 'Your children's children will live under Communism. You Americans are so gullible. No, you won't accept Communism outright; but we will keep feeding you small doses of socialism until you will finally wake up and find you already have Communism.'

"My work," Lamia concluded, "is the realization of our goals and the cornerstone of our impending triumph. I recommend that factories around the country gear up for serum production at once. And each of us must enhance our programs to focus all attention on our final triumph."

Sitting in the glow of her self-assessment and unable to see any of the other participants including Vladdrac, Lamia didn't see Junko Abrams leaning close to Vladdrac whispering in his ear. When Vladdrac finally spoke, Lamia was devastated.

"Well done, Lamia. However, I must caution you once again. The tone you have taken in reporting your good news reveals an unfortunate attitude and a self-serving presumption. You're an important part of my organization just as are the other three of your associates. However, your discoveries, inventions, and improvements belong to the cause and not to one person, save for me. Your reward is continued life and wealth. You know what failure would mean. If you think there's room to sit next to me, you are misguided. If you presume to sit in my chair, you will be expunged. Do you understand your place?"

"I understand completely," Lamia said. She wanted to scream. She'd done the work that no one else could do and had accelerated Vladdrac's revolutionary plan by years. Now she was to sit down, shut up, and be a good little girl. Vladdrac would take credit for her work, and she would get nothing. As she seethed, Lamia knew that compliance meant her career was thwarted. She was a slave beholden not to her country's mighty cause but to the arrogant man. Knowing her career was over unless she unseated him, she began to formulate a counter-attack. Little did Vladdrac know that she had other plans for him.

CHAPTER FOURTEEN

Contlerust helped Popoford lift Dean Wrenbutt and carry him to a ground-floor bedroom, one of two. There, with Millie's help, they tied him hand and foot to the bed. Turning the light low, they removed his hood and Popoford prepped a syringe.

He knew full well the ramifications of what he was doing. His decision grated on his moral code: the arrogance of it was a grave sin. He prayed that God would understand that the stakes were so high he had to subject Wrenbutt to the same humiliating treatment that he, himself, had suffered for so long. He prayed that the results would conform with God's plan and benefit Wrenbutt.

He said a prayer for mercy and professed his trust in God even as his actions smacked of pride. On top of it, he was going to give himself up to the same manipulation. But he knew his impending Resurrection Runner experience wouldn't accord him the same trauma as it would Wrenbutt's. Thus he argued with the Holy Spirit who whispered to his soul, "You have strayed. Return to the path that Jesus showed you," and ignored this wiser advice acting on the poison that the dark voice hissed in his head. Action was required. He couldn't sit this one out. Popoford was too resolute for his own good.

When Wrenbutt regained consciousness, he was in a fog. Already the serum had cleared his memory of his past. He lay still, unaware of fear or hope, nor of any pressing need to do anything but to be still.

Popoford placed a headset over the helpless dean's ears and then turned on a projector that displayed a multitude of images flashing in one-second intervals. These were the foundational images that were meant to instill patriotism, love of family, and morality in the professor. They were the same images that Popoford's former handler, Hendricks, had used on him, Contlerust, and all the original Resurrection Runners. Popoford had found the slides and many other brainwashing images in the files he'd removed from Home Office headquarters years ago.

He let the slideshow continually repeat as he instructed the others on the required procedures for Wrenbutt's resurrection and his rejuvenation.

"Let these slides continue to cycle for the next ten hours. Don't worry if he falls asleep. Just be sure that they're still running when he awakens. You must keep him hydrated and offer him food, but don't force him to stay awake. Sleep is necessary so that his mind has a chance to absorb what he's seeing and review it in his dreams. This will establish the emotions evoked in the pictures as familiar memories.

"After ten hours, switch the slide-set and give him another ten hours of American history and the Founding. I should be ready to rejoin the efforts by then, and I'll bring him into his new world ready to astound his colleagues with his transformation. Is this clear?"

They both nodded.

Popoford continued for a while with medical instructions and gave them a bottle of eye drops that he told them to use liberally.

"And what are we to do with you?" Millie asked.

"You will be my handler," Popoford replied as he opened the briefcase he had set at his feet. "Here is my file from Home Office. It includes all the times I was resurrected and the exact procedure used for each re-training. The top folder is the only one you need. It's the one that details how Hendricks made me think I was such a great agent: the best in the world. You will use it to convince me that I'm ten years younger and suffer no arthritis, no fatigue, no slowing down of any kind."

"No offense," Contlerust said, "but how in the world are you going to turn back time?"

"I'm not. Millie is. All a man needs is a good woman to love him and tell him he's the greatest. She can be most convincing. The serum used at a minimum dose and the enhancing drugs are all my brain needs to make me think that I'm more athletic and skilled than I am. The suggestive language that Hendricks used can be modified to make me think I'm up to the task. The results don't need to convince me that I'm a superhero. I just need to become arrogant enough to think I can do things I'm currently incapable of. Mind over matter as they say."

Millie smiled. "Maybe I should take the serum. Why let you have all the fun?"

"There's not enough of it for both of us. And there's a downside to it. When it wears off or I'm brought back to my current consciousness, I'll be disappointed knowing I've lost the stamina I'll soon have. I don't want you to suffer. You'll have enough on your hands just getting me to fly right without having to straighten yourself out."

"Then I don't think it's worth it," she said.

"Listen to me. It's not going to be easy but it's worth the try. I can't just watch what's happening without doing something. It's going to be okay. Come on, Contlerust. Let's get this done."

Popoford preceded Contlerust into the second bedroom and set up a second projector with appropriate videos that Hendricks had used. Then he laid down on the bed and rolled up his sleeve.

Contlerust sat in a bedside chair and administered the serum and watched Popoford as he gradually fell into a hypnotic spell.

With Popoford's eyes open and glazed, Millie took over and projected the videos on the ceiling near his bed. Then she removed the file from the Home Office folder and began to recite the extended reinforcing dialog that Hendricks had used to pump up his agents.

It was a love poem for it waxed adoration upon the subject about how physically fit he looked, how magnificent were his deeds, and how effortlessly he completed every challenging task put before him.

The accompanying videos showed a man who appeared to be about twenty-five as he climbed rock walls, lifted great weights, and leaped across wide chasms. The actor performing these marvelous deeds on the ceiling resembled Popoford as a younger man. It wasn't him, but the resemblance was striking.

And so it went through the night, though Millie sometimes nodded off for a while only to wake and continue her monolog for an hour or two. At sunrise, with the rain coming to a drizzly halt, Popoford turned his head towards the window, smiled, and fell into a deep sleep.

A few hours later, Popoford was on his feet ready to test his confidence. He was ready for the fight ahead. He hoped the opportunity would come soon.

When he came out to the kitchen, he caught up with Contlerust and Millie's activities.

Wrenbutt had slipped into a shallow sleep several times during the night, but he always awoke soon after and continued to stare at the ceiling slide show. They had to take care to manage the drool from his mouth and to regularly apply eye drops to keep his eyes from drying out. He was fascinated with the colorful show and watched it like a newborn would watch a dancing ball suspended above its crib. Likewise, his cooing and gurgling were reminiscent of an infant or a psychopath after a prefrontal lobotomy.

Over a light breakfast, Popoford told them that everything was going according to plan. Today was the day they'd begin rebuilding Wrenbutt's memory. It was Friday, and they hoped to have him back in his office ready for work on Monday. They were all ready to take on the task of reprogramming Wrenbutt into a God-fearing constitutionalist.

CHAPTER FIFTEEN

Popoford joined Contlerust and Millie in Wrenbutt's room where the dean lay on a bed by a window.

"How is he?" Popoford asked.

"He's learning to talk. At first, he sounded like he had the vocabulary of a five-year-old, but he's steadily improved and I'd say that he's almost back to normal."

"Simon and I know as well as anyone," Popoford said, "that Resurrection Runner subjects don't lose their motor skills or their speaking ability. In truth, Wrenbutt hasn't lost any memory, but the entirety of it is suppressed, allowing us or anyone else who would happen to find him in this state to overlay any part of the blank whole with a new section of fabricated memory. It's time to give this misguided soul a passionate love of country, the Founders, and the Constitution.

"You're welcome to listen in if you like" Popoford continued. "I have an intercom set up so you can listen from the front room. I'll need to be alone with him so he can feel comfortable and we can bond."

Millie and her father left the room and closed the door leaving Popoford and Wrenbutt alone. Sitting down, Popoford addressed Wrenbutt.

"Thornton. Are you awake?"

After a few seconds, Wrenbutt inhaled deeply. "Yes. Who's there?"

"My name is Steven. I'm a friend. You look like you could use a friend, Thornton. Am I right?"

"Yes, I guess so."

"I'm told that you prefer to be called Tom. Is that true? Would you like me to call you Tom?"

"Yes, please."

"Okay, Tom it is. Friends call friends by the names they want. So, tell me, Tom. Who was the first person who called you Tom, the name you prefer?"

Tom thought a while and finally said "It was my third-grade teacher, Mrs. Bell."

"You must have liked her a lot."

"She was nice to me. She called me Tom and she kept the bullies away from me, too."

"So, was she the first friend you ever had?"

"No, but she was the first grownup who thought I was pretty smart. And she told me so. That I was smart, I mean."

"And she was right. Just look at you now. You're the dean of the history department at Claramon College. You've got to have brains to have that position."

"I'm what?" Wrenbutt said. "What are you talking about?"

"You don't remember, do you?"

"Remember what?"

"That you're the dean of the history department. That you received your Ph.D. from John Hopkins and your Masters from Hillsdale. You did your undergraduate work at the University of Nebraska, Omaha, and before that, you were a Captain in the United States Army. You've had a distinguished career, Tom. Distinguished and honorable. A true patriot and a renowned expert on America's founding."

Wrenbutt was at a loss for words.

"Don't you remember, Tom? Doesn't any of it spark a memory?"

"No," he said, hesitantly.

"Well, I'm not surprised. After all, the accident you were in would have killed most men. You were lucky."

"I don't remember any accident."

"No, I expect not. You see, Tom, you've lost your memory. Well, a big chunk of it. I should know. I've worked with many cases like yours. I'm a doctor, Tom. I specialize in memory loss, particularly amnesia caused by catastrophic accidents. I know this whole thing is bewildering, but here's the good news. I believe I can get you back on your feet and back to work none the worse for wear in the next few days. But I can't do it without your help. What do you say, Tom? Are you willing to help me cure you?"

Wrenbutt was bewildered. "I don't know what to say. I don't remember any of what you say I am. Nothing. What happened to me? How did I get like this?"

"Revealing all that is the beginning of your recovery, Tom, but first I need your pledge that you will give your best effort to help me help you. I'm your friend, Tom. Will you give me your pledge? Would you give your pledge to your friend, Mrs. Bell? I know you would if she were here. Just give me your promise that you will do everything in your power to get well, my friend, and we can get started. What do you say?"

"My friend," Wrenbutt said as a tear came to his eye. "Yes, my friend, I promise."

"Very good, Tom. Very good indeed. Now let's get started with how this all began."

Popoford described a bizarre accident that involved a near-miss collision on the backroads outside of Fresno when a hay wagon pulled onto the road between Tom and the setting sun. He had noticed the wagon when he was only feet away from a collision that should have killed him and the farmhand who was driving the rig. The miracle was that neither Tom, the hay wagon nor his car suffered any damage. The tragedy was that the trauma Tom suffered caused a series of minor strokes that confused his mind and temporarily wiped out his memory. The good news, according to Popoford, was that Tom's condition was reversible and would leave no ill effects.

As Popoford told the story, it had happened the day before when, thanks to Divine Providence, he was visiting the college and was able to respond to Tom's needs. Tom accepted Popoford's telling of the tale without question.

"Are you feeling okay, Tom?"

Wrenbutt nodded. "Yes, Steven,"

"Then let's get started with you taking a look at the slides and videos I'll be projecting on the ceiling while I establish a foundation of knowledge you must already have, given your credentials. This should jumpstart your mind again. You won't have any pain, but the experience may be emotional. Please remember that we are friends and I'm your doctor. I know you may not be comfortable expressing your emotions, but this is a safe space. Nothing that happens between us here will ever get out.

"Are you all right with this, Tom?"

"I guess."

"Okay. Let's get going."

And so Popoford proceeded to project stills and clips of American history in all its remarkable depth: tribulations, struggles, and triumphs. As they passed in front of Tom's eyes, he heard the brotherly tones of Popoford's narration weave the story of an impossible dream made real in "blood, sweat, toil, and tears." A tale of simple men and women, heroic in their audacity and humble in their devotion to God's will. It was not a story of perfect people incapable of error, but one of exceptional souls striving to gain and maintain liberty, a story of success and failure which, when diverted from the nation's founding virtues, always found a way back to the Republic's roots.

Popoford left out none of the wrong turns that complicated the lives of many and destroyed the souls of many more. But neither did he leave out who the culprits were and who they were said to be now. He made Tom's history rehabilitation a faithful rendition, one which would mark Tom as a troglodyte worthy of cancellation at Claramon College unless he maintained a circumspect posture.

With this in mind, Popoford did some role-playing with Tom to get him used to the kind of encounters he might expect from teachers and students alike.

"Tom, I'm going to pretend to be one of the college's students and make some statements about what is taught in my history class. I want you to tell me what the truth is. Okay?"

After working at it for most of the day, Wrenbutt was getting progressively more fluent and concise.

"So, the Ku Klux Klan was and still is a bunch of southern white republicans who wanted to keep blacks in chains," Popoford offered.

"In truth, they were democrats," Wrenbutt countered. "Republicans were considered to be almost as low as the blacks. You should do some research on the subject yourself. Go to the original documents if you want the truth."

"Yes, Tom," Popoford said. "How about this corollary? It took the Democrats to break the color barrier in the South so desegregation could proceed and black kids could ride up front in buses."

"Again, you have it backwards. You're too young to remember, but it was Governor Orville Faubus, a Democrat, who called up the Arkansas National Guard to prevent black students from entering a de-segregated school. President Eisenhower, a Republican, sent in federal troops to escort the students to class."

"That's not true, you fascist! What do you know? Your White Privilege is showing. You're trying to corrupt me! I feel violated! This is harassment!"

"Well, that's absurd. Have you ever gone to the library and read the original papers? Or do you rely on government textbooks and search engines to inform your life?"

"Help! He's molesting me! Someone help me! Rape! Help!"

"Oh, for pity's sake. Grow up and be a man."

"Ah, I don't think that last bit is helpful, Tom."

"But you're playing the fool, Steven. The kid's a dolt!"

"No doubt, but if you're going to survive, you'll have to remember how you handled these situations before the accident. You'll have to be a bit more judicious and let a lot slide if you want to keep your job and your pension. Try to remember your days in the Army. Imagine you're behind enemy lines, a spy, and you don't want to be discovered. Your job is to nudge, not to push. Make suggestions but don't degrade. Remember, emotions are the truth and facts are disturbing. If you mess with someone's feelings, you will be destroyed. Put them at ease and shift their emotions gradually. As some imagined guru might have said, be a feather, never a stone."

"That's beautiful, Steven."

Popoford had to suppress a laugh. Wrenbutt had some work to do in identifying sarcasm.

"Okay. You're doing great. Let's try another one. I'm a teacher or a student coming to you and saying this. "I've got to talk to you about a concern I have and I want to make sure this is a private conversation. You know, off the record."

"Okay," Wrenbutt countered. "but I can't have conversations in my office and have the door closed."

"I know. Why don't we take a walk to the cafeteria for coffee, and we can talk on the way?"

"Okay."

"So now you're walking to the cafeteria with this person and they say, "I'm having a problem with the new Brilliance in Basics history curriculum."

"Really. Like what?"

"Like the notion that the English were the first people to bring slavery to America."

"What's your objection to that?"

"Only that the native tribes practiced slavery and kidnapping as part of their warrior culture long before the English brought slaves here. And the Spanish were slavers in the New World before the colonists."

"Those are radical ideas. Perhaps you should keep them to yourself. If it got out that you believed these things, the College couldn't protect you. Your career would be over."

"I know. I just feel so trapped."

"Well, perhaps I have a solution."

"Like what?" Popoford asked, staying in character.

"Well, there's a rumor that a discussion group is being formed. If I hear anything, I'll let you know."

"Bravo!" Popoford said. "You nailed it! No promises just in case this person's a plant. No details about a meeting or other participants. Nothing specific, just an offer to be considered. Well done, Tom!"

"Thank you, Steven. I think I'm getting my head on straight again."

"Your recovery is going even better than I thought it would. Let's take a break."

"Sure, I could use some fresh air."

"Okay. You get dressed, and I'll get a pot of coffee going."

Hearing this on the intercom, Contlerust and Millie were already stepping out the back door and heading to the barn when Popoford entered the kitchen. They had already cleared their dishes and straightened up leaving no sign of their presence. He gave them a thumbs-up as he opened the refrigerator door and took out the coffee. The seed of rebellion was planted and the enemy would eventually be destroyed from within.

Popoford and Wrenbutt spent all day Saturday and part of Sunday in the bedroom. Wrenbutt continued to study the images and concepts of American history he had once rejected. He was a willing student who devoured the information he was discovering and enjoyed a new sense of purpose of a sort that he had never known: a personal commitment to a positive set of ideas that honored God and all His creations under the banner of Natural Law.

Wrenbutt was humbled and overjoyed that he had found a true friend in Steven and that he had regained what he thought was his former self.

On Sunday, just after noon, Popoford made an announcement.

"Tom, my friend, you have made faster progress than any of my previous patients. It's only halfway through Sunday, and I'm going to release you from my care and send you back to work tomorrow. How does that sound?"

Wrenbutt was surprised and disappointed. He had never had such a stimulating experience, and he didn't want it to end.

"Can't we just finish out the day?"

"I'm afraid not, Tom. We both need some time for ourselves. Anyway, I'll be on campus tomorrow hanging in the background just in case you need a safety net. But I want you to pretend I'm not there. Just get back in the swing of things. You can do this, Tom. And remember, I'm your friend."

With that, Wrenbutt burst into tears and Popoford escorted him out of the farmhouse and to his car. The keys were in the ignition and Wrenbutt started the car while wiping his eyes with his left hand.

"I don't know how to thank you, Steven," he said. "I feel like a new man."

"You are a new man, Tom. Go forth and multiply!"

CHAPTER SIXTEEN

With Lamia in the passenger seat, Sarah drove away from the warehouse, her re-education home. It was a pedestrian, ramshackle shed tucked away behind a gas station and some fast-food franchises that catered to the Claramon College crowd. Unusual thunder from the high Sierras was rolling over the Central Valley and a storm was gathering close upon the Merced River basin. Sarah counted the seconds between a lightning bolt and the next thunderclap. Three seconds. The storm was about a mile away and bearing down on them. She could see the torrent sheeting from the rain-laden clouds just to the northeast. By the time they arrived at the college and parked, they had to run to the nearest building for cover. As they removed their rain gear, Lamia reminded Sarah of the plan for the day.

"One last time. What is your approach?"

"Humble."

"And what is your desire?

"To be forgiven."

"Why?"

"To get back in Dean Wrenbutt's good graces."

"And how will you do that?"

"I will confess my errors and prove my allegiance to the new order."

"Great. I'll be nearby in case anything goes wrong."

"Don't worry. I've got this. He'll believe me because I'm telling the truth. And if that doesn't work, I'll suggest a little taste of flesh. He's an egotistical hound dog; a pushover."

"Anything for the cause?"

"You got that straight."

With their plan confirmed, they went down the stairs to the storm tunnels that connected the campus buildings and walked among the students and faculty who were beginning their day. When they got to the History Building, Sarah took the stairs to the second floor, and Lamia followed behind though she stopped at the ground-level rotunda where she found a copy of the Merced Sun-Star newspaper which she pretended to read.

Upstairs, Sarah entered Dean Wrenbutt's front office.

"May I help you?" his secretary said, dumbfounded by Sarah's return.

"Yes, please. I don't have an appointment, but I must see Dean Wrenbutt. I owe him an apology."

With "I should think so" written on her face, Wrenbutt's secretary rose from her desk as she instructed Sarah to wait where she was. She went into the dean's office, closing the door behind her.

Sarah could hear a muffled discussion coming from the room, and though she couldn't make out any specifics, it was apparent that the secretary was upset and Wrenbutt was trying to calm her down. After a few minutes, the secretary came out of the office. She looked defeated.

"You may go in," she snarled under her breath.

"Thank you," Sarah replied and turned toward the office where she found Wrenbutt standing at the door, a pleasant smile on his face.

"Please come in, Sarah. It's a pleasure to see you again."

Sarah was instantly on her guard. He was setting some kind of trap for her. She could feel it. He'd never said a pleasant thing to her until now. Something was up.

"Thank you," she replied, keeping a close eye on him.

When she came to the chair in front of his desk, Wrenbutt pulled it out for her to be seated. This made Sarah even more nervous. What was going on?

"I thought we might never see each other again after the troubles over the curriculum and the student body president. The lawsuit was hurtful, I must say, but I'm willing to put all that aside. At least for now. What brings you back to Claramon?"

"Well, I've had a change of opinion. I'm willing to come back on good terms and adhere to the department's curriculum."

Wrenbutt was silent and just stared at her for a long time. Finally, he leaned back in his chair, crossed his arms in a protective gesture, and spoke.

"I'm flabbergasted, Sarah. This is unbelievable. What has happened to you?"

"I just wised up and saw what was going on around me."

"But you were always such a strong defender of traditional practices. How can you have changed your ideas so dramatically in such a short time?"

"I guess that once I started thinking about the other side's arguments I couldn't stop agreeing with them. I've wasted so much time that I want to get back in the classroom so I can correct what I've done."

"Well," Wrenbutt replied. "That won't be possible, I'm sorry to say."

"What do you mean? I'm one of you now. I can prove it."

"That won't be necessary," he said.

"Well, what is it then? How about a roll in the hay? I happen to know that you're always ready for that. What will it take for me to get back to work?"

"Nothing. Nothing at all will get you back to work in my department."

"What do you mean? I'm just the kind of teacher you need."

"No, Sarah, you aren't. Ironically, because of you, or at least the way you were, I have changed my mind about many things. For one, I'm about to remove the entire BIB program from my department. It's a travesty and unworthy of the college's reputation. I'm also going to monitor all instructors for subversive attitudes and fire those who condone the bastardization of history. In your present flight of fancy, you would be out on the street your first day back. But you're not coming back because you and your fellow travelers are a blight upon the land. I will not allow the poisoning of our students to continue. Furthermore, your offer to sell your favors for your job is objectionable and unwelcome.

"I'm disappointed in you, Sarah. I hope you get your feet on the ground someday and settle on your core beliefs. Yet even if that were to come to pass, you would not be welcome here. Now, please leave my office and the Claramon campus. I will instruct security to keep an eye out for you if you ever decide to return. Don't forget. You are unwelcome here, now and forever."

Sarah was floored and an unfamiliar rage burst forth from her and engulfed Wrenbutt's office spilling out into the outer office and the building's hallways. Even the sudden slap of a lightning bolt that struck the History Building's lightning rod could not overwhelm her rage. Nor could the thunder echoing throughout the campus mask her tirade.

Below, in the rotunda, Lamia calmly folded her newspaper and went down the stairs to the storm tunnels. She'd collect Sarah later after the storm subsided. A man bundled in a long, hooded raincoat had descended the same stairs in silent pursuit.

Wrenbutt's secretary picked up her phone as soon as Sarah's screeching voice filled the room. She was told that security would be there ASAP. That done, she grabbed her purse, but instead of running into the hall, she pulled her Taurus 85 from its soft holster and made ready. She was determined to stand her ground against the wild woman railing against her boss. When Wrenbutt's door burst open, her front sights were trained on the first person that moved into her line of sight. Unfamiliar with combat or police work and in her panic, she pulled the trigger rapidly three times before she saw that it was Wrenbutt standing there. It wasn't luck but poor trigger control that sent her rounds slamming off-center, down, and left into the doorpost. She nearly vomited but held back and in her shame quickly returned her revolver to its holster and put her purse away.

Sarah, oblivious to the shooting, continued to rage even after the security guards cautiously entered the dean's office, their pepper-spray cans at the ready. Wrenbutt's secretary had her hands up in surrender, but the guards ignored her and grabbed Wrenbutt, yanking him out of his office doorway and subduing Sarah whose shrill vitriol was turned to a barking cough by the pepper cloud.

Chaos reigned supreme until Dean Wrenbutt took charge.

"Officers, let's have no rough stuff. Just remove professor Tufftang from the campus. After this episode, I trust you will do a better job of keeping fired employees off the grounds."

"Dean, there were shots fired. We need to call the police in cases like this."

"Boys, listen, the shots were fired in self-defense by my secretary. No one was hurt. There was only a bit of damage to my doorjamb. Can't we let this pass? For the good of Claramon?"

"How can we do that? There was a crime committed here."

"I don't see it that way. There was an act of heroism. That's what I think. And, the professor, here, was unruly but did no harm. Why make something out of nothing? Let's keep it in-house and out of the newspapers. Okay?"

After a hesitation, the senior security guard nodded. "You'll have to make a statement for the record, Dean."

"Of course. I'd be happy to. Now let's clear everyone out so I can get back to work."

The curious in the hallway drew back from the office door as the security team escorted Sarah out and down the stairs. In the back of the crowd, her head lowered and turned slightly away, Millie waited until the security team reached the rotunda before she quietly joined a gaggle of students descending the stairs. Keeping her distance, she watched the guards take Sarah down into the tunnel. Then she closed her raincoat and tightened its belt. She raised her umbrella against the storm and made her way toward the building closest to the college entrance. She waited there in a protected bus stop enclosure, keeping her face partially covered as Sarah was marched out of a nearby building toward the parking lot.

As the guards and Sarah neared the curb, a car pulled up and the driver reached over and opened the passenger door.

"That's my ride!" Sarah yelled.

The guards were only too happy to release the shrew and even helped her in the car.

"Get your pig-hands off of me!" she screamed and slammed the door while still glaring at them.

As Lamia pulled the car away, Sarah continued her hysterics, not because of the guards, but because of the face she saw at the curb peering out from under a raincoat hood: a girl with a face she thought she remembered.

"Millie!" Sarah screamed as her car drove away. "You bitch!"

CHAPTER SEVENTEEN

Popoford was driving with Contlerust in the back as they picked up Millie and followed Lamia's car. He wasn't worried about losing her so he let her clear the campus, allowing plenty of space between him and Lamia.

While he'd been sitting in the rotunda waiting to see if Wrenbutt could have a quiet reintroduction to Claramon College, Contlerust had stayed with the truck and Millie had gone to the second floor to see what might happen. She had to duck away for a minute when she got a message in her earpiece from Popoford, who had equipped his whole team with communications.

"Old friend coming up the stairs," is all he said, but Millie kept a sharp eye on the stairwell and was surprised to see their kidnapped team member, Sarah Tufftang, appear in the hallway and then enter Wrenbutt's office.

"Friend with Dean," she reported.

"Copy."

Popoford expected that Sarah was not alone. Somewhere, her handler was waiting and it was obvious that the dark-haired woman across the way was the one. She was turned away from him and didn't seem to have a care in the world until gunfire was heard. At the sound, she stood up and calmly walked to the tunnel's entrance and left.

"Target two on the move."

"Copy," Millie replied.

Popoford waited an appropriate time and then followed Lamia. He thought it odd that she never bothered to check her six for a tail. It was easy to keep her in view and easier to follow her to her car, especially in the pouring rain. Once she got into her car, Popoford slipped up close and deftly attached a magnetized tracking device to her back bumper. Then he went to his truck and joined the others to wait for Millie.

"Old friend in custody."

"Copy."

"Old friend on a cellphone. Guards taking her out.

"On her."

"Old friend has a ride."

"On her from here. Picking you up."

"At the bus stop."

"Roger."

Now the three crusaders rode silently as Popoford monitored the tracking blip on his screen.

The scene in Lamia's car was far from quiet. The rabid monster that Lamia had created continued to spew screaming bile. She insisted that Lamia turn around and find Millie. She pleaded with Lamia telling her she was afraid that her life's work to expose America's systemic cruelty would collapse if Millie wasn't destroyed.

Lamia was a bit more sensible than Sarah and beamed with pride at her raging experiment turning purple next to her. Finally, she'd had enough and slapped Sarah's face with a hard right.

"Shut up!" Lamia shouted. "Get a grip! There's no reason to go after her, if it was her, to begin with. Where did you see her last?"

Sarah was mortified by Lamia's slap and sat scrunched up against her door, whimpering. "I don't know," she said.

"Think, damn it! Where was it?"

"I guess it was at the house we were burglarizing. She was there with her father, I think."

"And was she there later in jail?"

"What jail?"

"In Whimsy. The one in Whimsy. Do you remember it?"

"No. I don't think so."

"Okay. It's better that way," Lamia said. "So tell me what you know about her."

"About whom?"

"Oh, come on! Stop this bullshit. Either you remember her or you don't. Which is it?"

"I don't know. The whole thing is fuzzy."

"Good. I was hoping you'd say that because it never happened. Whatever made you think you saw a girl you knew; it was only a trick your mind is playing on you. There was no girl and there was no Whimsy for that matter. I want you to settle down and see if you can't get some rest. We're going to catch a flight out of Fresno and I want you to relax and forget all about what has happened. We'll talk about it when we get to where we're going. Okay? We'll talk about it."

Sarah felt her tension pass when she heard the phrase "We'll talk about it." Her heart rate slowed and her breathing deepened. When she tried to remember what they were talking about, there was nothing to remember. Soon she fell into a peaceful sleep and dreamed dreams of things that had never happened.

Lamia, however, was concerned. It was obvious that Millie had visited the college. That meant that her father, Simon Contlerust, was probably there as well. Lamia would let the whole episode be until she could interrogate her further and find out what had happened in Dean Wrenbutt's office.

When they arrived at the Fresno Airport, Lamia dropped her car off at the rental garage. Then she and Sarah boarded a shuttle to the terminal. She bought a pair of tickets on a plane to Dulles International Airport which would be boarding in an hour and a half, checked the bag she had stowed in the rental car's trunk, and then went through security with Sarah. They found the boarding area and a small restaurant and ordered lunch while they waited for the boarding announcement. Lamia chose a table by the railing and kept a sharp eye out for any suspicious characters who might be on their trail. There was no need for conversation because the phrase "We'll talk about it," had not only quieted Sarah but had made her incapable of curiosity unless someone asked her a direct question or Lamia broke the spell by saying "We've talked too much."

When Contlerust, Popoford, and Millie arrived at the airport and located the rental car, Contlerust parked in the short-term parking lot. For Popoford it was decision time.

"They may be flying somewhere, but they might have rented another car and they're going to stay in the area. If they're not taking a plane, we've lost them for now. But I think they want to get out of here and back to wherever they came from. I believe they'll take Sarah with them. That means we have to find out where they're going and catch a flight to the same place preferably landing before them."

The others were in agreement and all of them wanted to go after Sarah and her captors. But Popoford stepped in with his decision.

"Simon, you and Millie should stay here. Sarah will recognize you and that would jeopardize her recovery. Anyway, I want Wrenbutt interviewed to see just what's going on with Sarah. It's important to know what happened in his office. I'll go after Sarah. They won't recognize me and I don't look like a threat."

"Little do they know," Millie smiled.

Popoford got out of the truck and Millie followed him. He turned to her and had an urge to hug her but thought better of it. Mille had no such compunction and threw her arms around him. She gave him a quick kiss and let him go.

"I'm going with you," she said.

"No. This will be over soon, and…"

She touched his lips and he fell silent.

"Hold your thoughts, Steven. You can tell me no later."

He looked at her ready to put his foot down, yet all he did was nod. Her wide grin was enough to confirm that he was a fool who couldn't say no. He grabbed two carry-on bags from the truck bed and they walked through the parking lot and into the terminal together. Contlerust watched them as they went out of sight.

Popoford found an electronic flight schedule board and studied it for a few minutes trying to decide which flight they'd catch.

He made an assumption which if wrong would ruin all chances of getting Sarah back in the fold, at least for now. Several flights were leaving in the next two hours. Four of them were heading south, one north, and three east. He ruled out north on a hunch, and south on a mental coin flip with the east. It was a crapshoot, based on a coin flip, derived from an assumption: a flat-out guess. He had no choice. Quitting was never part of his decisions. East it was, and Popoford saw that the first flight out was close to an hour away. It was a flight to Dulles International Airport with one stop in Chicago. Another airline had a direct flight to Dulles as well, leaving a half-hour earlier and was a direct flight that would land forty-five minutes before Lamia's flight. God was shining upon him, he thought as he led Millie to the ticket counter. The line was short and there was plenty of room on the 747 so he was able to get two seats together on the flight.

Passenger travel was light and they got through TSP security in a matter of minutes. It was a great relief for Popoford as they walked to the boarding area and spotted Sarah and the black-haired woman sitting at a restaurant table. They were sitting near the boarding area of the flight that he had guessed they'd take.

Pleased with himself, he was at once reminded of literary devices and signs from God when a lightning flash lit up the world outside followed immediately by a thunderous crash that shook the entire terminal. At once, he reflected on who was in charge.

Just after he spotted the women, Popoford ducked his head in case the dark-haired one might recognize him from the college's rotunda. Just to be sure, he intentionally let his carry-on handle fall to the floor. He hid behind Millie's legs and bent over to pick up the handle, snatching another look at the women. The dark-haired one had her head down, earnestly typing on her laptop. Sarah sat quietly gazing at nothing much.

CHAPTER EIGHTEEN

Lamia's fingers raced around her keyboard entering bursts of text in response to the unexpected reaction she was getting.

"With all respect," she lied. "You don't seem to understand what I'm saying. The dean is acting like another person. It appears that he's had a complete personality change and has become an impediment. He needs to be eliminated."

The response she received was terse. "No!"

"I don't agree."

"Yours is not to reason why…"

Lamia stewed for a while and finally typed: "As you wish."

"Of course."

But there was more for Lamia to tell.

"You should know that I was followed to the airport. A man that I saw at the college just passed my location in the airport terminal. He made a clumsy attempt to check on me after he passed. I'm certain it's the same man. He's traveling with a woman and he moves like he's had training. I've sent a photo. He passed my terminal, so I don't know if he'll be on my flight. It would be good to be aware of him when we land."

Moments later, she received a response.

"Will research and advise. Weekly meeting postponed until tomorrow, usual time."

"Understood."

Lamia logged out and ordered a double Beefeater on the rocks. They wouldn't start boarding for about thirty-five minutes, and she needed time to decompress and regroup.

Meanwhile, Popoford and Millie had boarded their flight and the jetway had been removed. They settled in for an easy flight to D. C. confident that they could pick up Sarah's tail and her kidnapper in just a few hours.

As their plane lifted off, Lamia's phone flashed a notice of an incoming private message.

She logged in to the secure service and was presented with an image of a man who appeared to be in his mid-twenties. The caption noted his name as Steven Popoford, cover name, George Mixer, an assassin for the defunct Home Office agency, and the original agent in the Resurrection Runner mind enhancement program.

Lamia smiled to herself. She'd soon capture a wonderful prize, for she'd bring Steven Popoford under her wing and demonstrate once again just how valuable to the cause she was. A brilliant notion was formulating in her head and the gin only helped her run wild with it. She concocted a fanciful storyline and created a delicious plan that would eliminate all obstacles to her reaching the top of her game. And Steven Popoford was the key to it all. He would be her tool to remove the ladder rungs above her so that she wouldn't have to climb at all to reach the top.

"Life is good," she thought. "It's so sweet when the stars align and a plan is born."

CHAPTER NINETEEN

Popoford and Millie disembarked at Dulles and found a bathroom. They put on Clarus XPR headsets. These single-sided PCI communications units were ideal radio solutions that would keep them clandestinely connected even if separated. When ready, they followed the other passengers to baggage claim though they had no checked luggage. They had about thirty minutes to wait for Lamia and Sarah, so Popoford asked Millie to mingle among various packs of passengers who were picking up their luggage while he rented a car.

When he drove up to the curb, he called her on her headset and checked on the situation. "Any sign of them?"

"Not yet, but there's a new bunch of travelers beginning to collect around the carousel."

"Okay, stay back and watch for them," he said. "I'll be out here in the car. I want you to tail them and get a fix on their ride. If they take a cab, break off and jump in our car. It's a blue Expedition parked to the left of the door as you come out."

"Got it," she said. "They just passed me, but they're not stopping for bags. They're exiting the terminal now."

"Copy," Popoford said. "Keep your distance. I see them now. They're hailing a cab. Get over here as fast as you can without drawing any attention to yourself."

"On my way," Millie said and quickened her pace. She was just getting into the Expedition when Lamia's cab pulled away from the curb.

Popoford followed at a distance as the cab left Dulles International and headed south on Sully Road taking US-50 East toward Fairfax. After traveling about six miles, the cab took the Fair Oaks Mall exit then turned left. Lamia's cab followed the road for a while then made a couple of turns and finally turned into a small parking lot in front of a building called the Fair Oaks Metro Condominiums.

Popoford drove past the building and continued down the street for two blocks. Then he pulled a u-turn and slowly drove in front of the building again.

"Looks like we're going to do some camping tonight.

"Why not," Millie said. "We can pretend we're on vacation."

Popoford laughed. "One heck of a messed-up vacation. Give me Whimsy instead. At least I could relax there."

"Sure," she replied. "Like, when do you relax?"

"Oh, come on. Everyday."

"Yeah, sure," she said.

Popoford laughed again and parked the Expedition across the street from the condos. It was a four-lane street with a landscaped median. They had a direct view of the building's front entrance and Popoford told Millie that he would take the first watch while she took a nap. She was tired and snuggled into her seat without complaint while Popoford reached into his carry-on bag and pulled out a pair of binoculars.

He spent his time searching the landscaping for places to hide, treating the scene as a possible burglary prospect. He found adequate cover on both sides of the entrance where a person could crouch down and not be seen. It was also possible to hide behind one of the cars in the parking lot, but someone might see him from the street and raise an alarm, so he dismissed that option.

Next, he turned his binoculars on the windows at the front of the building. He slowly panned from one window to the next, then from one floor to the next until he finished looking at each window. Once finished, he pulled the binos away from his eyes and looked at the whole structure. To his surprise, one of the curtains on the sixth floor was opened, and someone was just stepping away from it walking back into the room. It appeared to be a woman with dark hair, but he couldn't tell if it was black.

He waited for many long minutes and was finally rewarded when a woman with blond hair stepped to the window and looked out on the world. The blond matched the picture of Sarah he found in Sheriff Florter's arrest file. She was talking to someone but he didn't see a phone in her hand. It was obvious that there was another person in the room. Not five minutes later he hit the jackpot. The woman with black hair joined the blond at the window.

They engaged in what appeared to be an animated discussion, based on their gesturing and expressions. But suddenly, Sarah dropped her hands to her sides and calmly stood there while it appeared that the black-haired woman berated her. In another minute, Sarah still stood at the window while the other woman left. She stood without moving for ten full minutes, and Popoford knew she was hypnotized or drugged. Sarah just stood there doing nothing. His interest was raised even higher by her behavior.

Sarah was in danger. He had to get her away from her kidnapper soon. He decided he needed to get inside the condo to see what the setup was. He was unarmed, so this would be more difficult than he wanted it to be, but that didn't bother him much. This would be a close combat mission and he excelled at hand-to-hand action. It was one of the self-defense courses he taught at the Whimsy Gun Range. It was time to get Sarah back.

Popoford woke Millie and told her what he was planning to do. She insisted on going with him as his backup, but he convinced her to wait in the car. If the black-haired woman escaped, Millie would have to follow her.

As the sun was setting, Popoford slipped out of the car and walked up the road a couple of blocks. He then crossed the street and made his way to the condos. He waited there for only a few minutes until one of the owners arrived and unlocked the front door. Popoford hurriedly caught up to the man and wrapped his hand around the closing door just in time to keep it open and enter himself. The other man was startled.

"Sorry for that," Popoford said. "I thought I could catch the door before it closed. How's it going?"

"Ah, fine," the man said. "Are you new to the building?"

"Yeah, my wife and I are moving in soon. I'm alone until she can get out here from California. My name's, Joe."

"Hi, Joe. I'm Jake. You must have taken the unit on the fifth floor." Nice to meet you."

"Same here, Jake."

"Well, I'm on the ground floor, myself. I hope you and your wife like it here. It's a quiet place. Not much happens here at all."

"Well, that's what I've been told. Suits me."

"Great. Well, I'll see you later."

"Okay. Take care," Popoford said and walked down the hall to the elevator.

He rode to the fifth floor, got out, and took the emergency stairs up to the sixth. There he found the door to the condo whose window he'd looked through. His plan was simple: knock on the door, take down the black-haired woman, and grab Sarah. If she was still as wild as she was at Claramon College, he'd coldcock her and then get Millie upstairs to help him take her down to the

Expedition. Simple and slick, he thought and knocked three times on the door.

He heard someone coming and when they reached the door, they asked, “What is it?”

“Western Union,” Popoford grabbed from thin air. “You have a telegram.”

“Just a minute,” came the reply and he heard the locks turning and the door chain sliding in its channel. Then the door opened slowly and Sarah was standing in front of him, dazed.

“Sarah? Are you Sarah Tufftang, Jack Singleton’s granddaughter?”

“Who?” Sarah answered.

“Sarah Tufftang?” Popoford repeated.

“I don’t know. Maybe.”

“Are you alone?”

“Alone?”

“Is anyone else in there with you?”

“I don’t think so.”

‘Okay,” Popoford said as gently as he could. “Come with me. I’ll take care of you. Come along.”

Sarah looked at him with deadened eyes. “Take care of me?”

“Yes, my girlfriend is waiting in the car,” he said, surprising himself. “I knew your grandfather. Come along.”

Sarah allowed him to lead her out of the condo. They took the elevator down to the main floor and walked together out into the evening air. There was a soft breeze blowing and Sarah let a smile cross her face. They went directly through the parking lot and crossed the street together, going behind the Expedition so he could open the passenger door for her.

“Millie,” he said as he opened it. “Say hello to an old friend, Sarah Tufftang.”

But Millie didn't say a word. She wasn't in the car.

Popoford raced to the driver's door and opened it. The note he found taped to the steering wheel told Millie's story.

"Steven Popoford, 'George Mixer,' I have your friend. No harm will come to her if you follow the directions on the back of this note. Fail to do so, and she'll end up in the river. Comply or she dies!"

CHAPTER TWENTY

Popoford could barely move he was in such shock. He tore the note from the steering wheel and slowly slid into the driver's seat. Sarah sat quietly gazing out the window.

"There's a bottle of water in the door pocket," he said, his mind in a fog. "Will you open it and give it to me?"

Sarah looked at him without expression but finally reached for the bottle and handed it to him without opening it. Popoford took it and held it in his left hand as he turned the note over and read.

"There's a red car parked in the condominium lot. It's facing your position. Find it and flash your lights twice. When the red car leaves the lot, follow it. Other vehicles will follow you at a distance. Do not attempt to make contact with anyone. I'll know if you do. I can see and hear you. Now, get started."

Popoford had a vision of Millie gagged and unconscious lying in the trunk of the red car. He felt sick, but he would do what he had to do to save her. He started the Expedition and flashed the high beams twice.

The lights from a car in the parking lot flashed. Without a response, it left the lot and proceeded to the street where it led Popoford on a long and circuitous route through Fairfax and finally out into the countryside. It wasn't until they were free of city traffic that Popoford noticed a truck following him. From what he could see by the streetlights, it was a twenty-six-foot semi. He thought that odd.

After another twenty minutes of driving, the red car pulled into a lot vacant except for a light pole with a single floodlamp illuminating the gravel-covered property. There was a razor-wire fence enclosing the space and a similar gate. Next to the pole in the middle of the half-acre lot, there was a shed wide enough to be the front end of a state-fair rifle range. The car pulled up to the shed and the truck swung around the Expedition and parked in front of the car. Popoford pulled to a stop and waited for instructions. Sarah just looked vacant. He nearly jumped through the roof when he heard a woman's voice purring in his ear. She had Millie's coms radio.

"Well done, Steven. I can see we'll get along just swell. Now, be a good boy and park on the other side of the truck so you can't be seen from the road. Stay in your car until I come to get you. No mistakes, Steven. Just obedience."

He did what he was told to do and sat waiting. He saw activity in his rearview mirror as the trailer's liftgate was lowered. A dim light was switched on and by the rays it cast, he saw the trailer's back door was open and the light was coming from within the truck's trailer. Soon the floodlight on the pole was extinguished, and immediately he was blinded by a flashlight aimed at him from the front of the Expedition. In his blindness, he heard his door swing open and someone unsnapped his seatbelt and roughly yanked him from the car. A bag was pulled over his head that stank like an unwashed skunk hide, and he was unceremoniously led to the back of the truck and walked onto the liftgate. Someone raised the gate and he was led to a chair four paces inside the box.

The gate was lowered and raised a second time and then the truck's rear door was rolled down. By the footsteps, he counted four people walking toward him: the truck driver, the black-haired woman, Sarah, and Millie.

The truck driver walked behind him and roughly handcuffed him. Then another person, obviously the woman in charge, slipped up to him and whispered in his ear.

"Good job, Steven. You kept your side of the bargain just fine. The only problem for you is that I never seem to be as steadfast as my enemies. You see, I never keep promises if I can help it."

Popoford remained silent, but he wriggled in his chair enough to know that it was bolted to the floor.

"Your girlfriend told me her name is Millie. You have five seconds to say goodbye to her."

Lamia started counting.

Popoford yelled. "Millie!"

"Two…Three…"

"I love you! I Pray for you!"

"Four…Five".

A gunshot blasted in the close quarters and the sound of Millie's body thumped with a bounce on the trailer floor. Popoford's ears rang and he could barely hear his own screaming voice crying out for her. As his hearing gradually returned, he heard Millie being dragged past him toward the front of the trailer. Only one person remained: the black-haired monster who had murdered her.

His loss and rage, his sorrow and hatred, mingled in a damning stew that encouraged madness. Then Lamia injected him with her improved Resurrection Runner serum and the hell of a new confusion swirled in his brain.

"Now we can be alone," Lamia said. "Now we can become friends. Now I can help you find out just who is trying to mess up this beloved country of yours. Not the local fools, not even the top actors you suspect, but the one who rules them all. You and I will bring him down. What a sweet notion. What a glorious day.

And I won't even get my hands dirty because you will be my champion, my assassin."

Popoford heard her words, but they sloshed into a pool of lost hours and flowed away. Peace of a sort came to him when the drug took him completely and provided a black emptiness. He awoke suddenly to a blazing light. His lids were taped open.

"Easy does it. Take a deep breath and let it out slowly."

Instead, Popoford gulped the air and expelled it in a panicked series of gasps.

"Easy, Steven. You did a good job. Just breathe slowly and steadily and you can avoid a headache and a rush to the porcelain. There, that's it. Yes. You're going to be quite fine."

She removed the tape from his eyes and they watered profusely. He batted his eyelids over and over as his eyes began to adjust to the light and he dared a furtive look about the room. It was a long and narrow room with white walls and ceiling. At one of the narrow ends, there was a rollup door, also painted white. At the other end, there was a closed door that presumably led to another room or a hallway. The room was lit by a row of bare neon bays. It was a cool light and seemed antiseptic.

"Where am I?"

"With me," the woman said, her long black hair falling over her shoulders as she leaned over him. Her motherly smile put him at ease, and he exhaled a lung-full of air he was unconsciously holding.

"There. That's better, Steven. Are you hungry?"

He shook his head.

"Come on, Steven. You can talk. Use your words. Okay?"

He nodded.

"I'm not going to talk to you again unless you do your part and speak to me. There's a good boy. Give it a try."

"Who am I?"

The woman, Lamia, burst out laughing. "That's a good one. You've always been so funny, Steven."

"But who am I?" he repeated.

"You're kidding. You're Steven Popoford. The extraordinary Home Office agent who's working on the Normalcy Project to assassinate the head of TAP. The leader of the effort to destroy America. He was the man that P.Y Mous and Hendricks reported to, the man behind the curtain. You must remember that. Right?"

"Yes," Popoford said, hesitantly. "I remember."

"Great. Now, can you sit up? I have to run some tests on you. You've had a stroke and we must be sure you're ready to return to the field. We can't afford to put our top agent at risk. Come on. See if you can sit up."

It took a bit of effort for Popoford to comply. He was experiencing some vertigo and was having a little trouble holding the horizon. For a moment he thought he would fall off the bed, but he caught himself and concentrated on overcoming the dizziness.

"Take it easy, Steven. Don't rush it. Here, let me help you to the chair."

Popoford accepted Lamia's help and sat in a chair that was bolted to the floor. He had a sense of Deja vu but rejected it.

"Who are you?" he asked.

"My name is Lamia," she said as she took a seat herself. "I'm the agency's head of operations. Together we are going to get you back into the game. Your assignment was compromised, but we rescued you. Your rehabilitation is nearly complete. All that's needed now is for you to recite your mission. Then I'll read you in on the status of the operation. There is little time left for success, so let's get right down to it. What is your mission? March in lockstep, Steven."

With these words, Popoford's psyche reacted as if by magic. From the restrictions that Lamia had placed on his brain, the number of synapses provided for his use increased exponentially. In seconds he was transformed into a steely assassin who spit out his mission without hesitation.

"My mission is to eliminate Vladdrac, the leader of TAP, "*to anótato pénte,*" The Supreme Five, with prejudice. His location is unknown. Time is of the essence."

"Correct. As our most senior Resurrection Runner, you will succeed or die."

"As always," Popoford said, but there was a queer hesitation in his answer that only he noticed. Something was wrong with his answer, but he let it pass.

"The status of the operation is as you say, but now that you're back to form, the agency expects that to change. In just a few minutes I'll be joining a weekly meeting of TAP. As you know, I'm working in deep cover as one of the Five and will be reporting to them on my weekly activities."

Popoford knew this, but, again, he was of two minds for an instant. Again, something seemed wrong, but he tried to ignore it.

"You'll be able to monitor the meeting from behind my camera. There is no computer monitor since there isn't a video feed from the director's location. But I want you to listen carefully to what is said and see if you can get a clue as to where he's located. With luck, you can be after him before the day is out. Do you understand?"

"Yes. Completely," Popoford said.

"Marvelous. How do you feel?"

"Just fine," Popoford replied, still concerned with an off-putting feeling that something was wrong.

"Excellent," Lamia said. "When did you last eat? You must be hungry."

"I am."

"Well, I don't have much here, but I'll give you a candy bar. We'll get you something more when the meeting is over. Okay?"

"Sure."

"Good. The meeting will start in three minutes and we need to get you set up before then. Just stay where you are and I'll bring everything to you."

"Okay. I'm ready," he said, not thoroughly believing what he said.

Lamia went to the wall behind his chair and pushed a hidden button. A panel opened and she withdrew a computer cart, rolling it to a position between her chair and Popoford. She sat down and plugged the devices into a floor socket and booted the computer. Then she put her headset on and gave Popoford his, after which she tested the volume.

"You can adjust your volume with the small slide on your cable. Your microphone is dead, but you must remain completely silent. Any hint that someone is with me will result in my death. Security is a top priority for TAP. Do you understand this?"

"Of course. Don't concern yourself."

But Lamia wasn't going to take any chances. She couldn't afford any breach of security, so she invoked Popoford's unique silencing phase: "Stop the talking, Steven."

At once he had no need for speech and his mind concentrated only on the sounds he heard on his headset.

CHAPTER TWENTY-ONE

"All present, I see. Even Lamia. Well done."

Lamia bridled at Vladdrac's slight and he noticed a twitch of her eyelids.

"Touchy, aren't we, Lamia?"

She didn't respond to his rhetorical question, but his keen observation rattled her, and she felt she may have made a mortal error in having Popoford present on the call. The attendant's every emotion was monitored by highly accurate algorithms that identified fluctuations in mood that even the participants weren't aware of.

"Let's begin with you, Lamia. Please report on our latest recruit."

Lamia let the remark, meant to relegate her accomplishments to those of a lackey's, slide and began her report.

Popoford was intently listening for any sounds that might indicate where Vladdrac was located.

"Sarah Tufftang was reintroduced into the Claramon College environment as planned. She went directly to Dean Wrenbutt's office to persuade him of her changed worldview. She was a completely prepared supplicant who, unfortunately, met with an altered creature in Wrenbutt."

"Meaning what, exactly. Certainly not a surprise."

"Well, yes. A bizarre surprise. He was a completely transformed man. While he was one of ours, a fully indoctrinated Runner with a sterling history of obedience, something or someone turned him against us. He wasn't violent or raging, just maddeningly parochial and seemingly tied to unapproved accounts of history. Sarah, sadly, did not respond to him as I wished. Instead of turning the situation to our advantage, she became irrational and will need to be reassigned to street conflicts. It's a setback, but a small one."

"You're too close to the subject to assess your failure," Vladdrac said. "When this meeting is over, stay connected to learn my decision concerning your future."

Lamia nearly fainted at the prospect, but steeled herself enough to say, "As you wish, Lord Vladdrac."

Before continuing, Junko Abrams spoke in a low whisper, but Popoford was able to hear what was said thanks to the Erythropoietin he'd given himself days before.

"Perhaps you can invite her to join us here at the mountain chateau. You could use the entertainment instead of having an underling handle her."

Vladdrac smiled and nodded. It would be done.

The meeting continued for another forty minutes without further disappointments. Then Vladdrac dismissed his TAP generals except for Lamia who sat calmly in her chair, her hands in her lap, waiting for her punishment to be laid down.

"You're on a path that crosses mine, Lamia. I'm disappointed in you. I continue to think you believe you could take me down."

Lamia remained as quiet as she could, but she knew that her emotions were sending Vladdrac insistent proof of her fears.

"You will come to me at once so that I can deliver your fate face to face. It's time we met in person, time to correct mistakes."

"A time to die," Lamia thought.

"Junko will arrange for your travel. You will receive your flight details soon. In the meantime, kill Sarah Tufftang. I can't afford for your mistakes to fester while you're away."

With that, Vladdrac cut the connection.

Lamia was all action. She would follow Vladdrac's orders but only on the surface. Sarah would be sacrificed, but she would not go to Vladdrac by herself. She shut her computer down and placed it in a lead-lined attache to keep Vladdrac or Junko from observing her. She then spoke her chosen words to awaken Popoford.

"March in lockstep Steven," she said, and Popoford's face immediately relaxed.

"Yes. What is it?" he answered, now able to speak.

"Are you ready for your mission?"

"Ready and willing."

"Good. The first step is to kill Sarah Tufftang as Vladdrac ordered."

"Where can I find her?"

"I'll show you the way. When you see her, say 'Talk to me.' That will rejuvenate her so you'll be killing an enemy, not a manikin."

CHAPTER TWENTY-TWO

Sarah sat comfortably in a chair musing on trifles, her mind in stasis just waiting for whatever came. She was shut down by Lamia's words and was perfectly calm even when the person who was lying at her feet began to stir and stand.

It was Millie who rose. She had been knocked out just after the man holding her put a round through the truck's floor. She didn't know where she was, but she recognized Sarah sitting in the chair, a placid smile on her face.

"Sarah? Thank God you're alive! Talk to me! Sarah!"

But Sarah dismissed Millie's command and smiled more contentedly.

Seeing that no help would come from Sarah, Millie looked around the small, rectangular room. There was one door on the long wall and another door on the short wall. There were no windows and only a single neon tube illuminated the space. But it was not a nearly silent environment. An AC system was blowing cool air into the room. Daylight also filtered through a crack in the air duct.

Millie heard a woman's voice and put her ear to the wall. She could barely understand the conversation, but it was obvious they were in danger. She immediately began to plan their escape.

First, she checked both doors. They were locked. That wouldn't be a problem since she was well-trained and prepared by her father to pick locks, and the shim she had hidden in the heel of her shoe would be put to good use.

"Sarah," she said. "Can you stand up?"

Sarah didn't answer but demonstrated that she understood by standing.

"That's good. We have to leave here. Just you and me. Okay?"

Sarah's smile broadened.

"Alright. Come over here by the door. That's it. I'm going to open the door and step outside. I want you to follow right behind me. Don't worry. I'll help you."

Millie removed her shoe and turned her heel on a swivel exposing a cutout hiding place. She removed the shim, returned her heel to its proper place, and deftly popped the lock, opening the door. She was standing about four feet above the ground but there was a ladder leading partway to the ground. She turned around and backed down the first two rungs then told Sarah to turn and come down with her.

When Sarah was safely on the ground, Millie climbed back up the ladder to close and lock the door. Just as the door was closing, she heard the interior door swing open and someone entered the small room.

Millie slammed her door closed and jumped back to the ground. Just as she hit the dirt, she heard a man's voice calling "Talk to me!"

She knew it was Steven, but she was startled when two bullets blew through the truck-box door and Sarah, suddenly fully aware, screamed at Millie, "You bitch! What are you doing to me?"

Millie was a calm soul yet steeled for action.

She turned on Sarah and punched her twice in the face, nearly breaking her nose and defeating her programmed hysteria. She then grabbed Sarah by the arm and dragged her toward the truck's tractor. She was pleased to see that the tractor was unhitched from the trailer.

Millie let go of Sarah for a second as she stepped up to peer inside the cab. A man was sitting behind the wheel, his eyes closed and his fingers tapping out a cacophonous beat to the noise blasting from his headphones.

In a series of quick moves, Millie took a step down, yanked the truck door open, and pulled the driver out. Even as he was hitting the dirt, she was on top of him delivering a sequence of blows to his throat and eyes. She kneed him in the crotch three times for good measure and then hurriedly grabbed Sarah and made her climb the truck stairs.

Millie followed right behind and pushed Sarah across the bench seat to the passenger side of the cab. She locked the doors, started the engine, and drove away.

Much to her amazement and wonder, she saw Popoford in her rearview mirror standing on the ground, a gun in his hand, firing rounds at her as she picked up speed and pulled onto the highway. The tractor's back window shattered but was held in place by its safety film. She lost sight of him as she shifted through the gears as quickly as she could. She could not imagine what had happened to him. She was afraid for him and needed some answers from Sarah. It was now her job to save Sarah and the man who said he loved her.

CHAPTER TWENTY-THREE

"Where do you live?" Millie asked Sarah. She received nothing but a steady glare in answer.

"Listen, you're confused. You think you're a radical activist fighting to correct all the evils of mankind and making a difference in the international struggle against the downtrodden. You're no such thing. You're a walking lie, a phantom who has had her memories destroyed and replaced by a zombie mind. Your entire life has been canceled. You used to speak fluently of uncensored history, now you recite Marx, charged with false anger. Your entire life was stolen from you and I intend to get it back. If you refuse to help me, I will force you to comply. You've already shown yourself willing and able to be someone's fool. Now tell me where you live!"

Sarah scowled at Millie but finally thought better of pouting and dragged an address up from her freshly reconstituted memory.

"6836 Old River Road."

"Where? In Merced?"

"Yes. I live there with my boyfriend."

"Okay, but we're not in Merced. What about the condominium in Fairfax where we found you?"

"I don't know. It's not mine."

Millie racked her brain and finally came up with the name of the place: the Fairoaks Metro Condominiums.

She pulled over to the side of the road for a minute and set the truck's GPS. She then followed the talking-box's direction and drove to the condominium.

Millie parked the semi-tractor a block away. In this neighborhood, it was an eyesore, out of place, and would attract attention soon enough.

She put her arm around Sarah and guided her to the condos. Sarah's nose had stopped bleeding, but her clothes were a red-splotched mess. Millie covered her as best she could. There was no foot traffic so, employing her lock-picking skills again, Millie got them into the condo building unnoticed. Once in, Millie encouraged Sarah to lead the way to the apartment where Popoford had abducted her. Once there, Millie picked that lock and they entered and closed the door.

A chill ran through Millie and she froze when a man called out.

"Is that you darling?"

She was more astonished when Sarah answered.

"Yeah. I'm home."

Millie stepped in front of Sarah. "Who is that?"

"My boyfriend, Albert."

"You told me you lived with your boyfriend in Merced."

"No, I didn't."

Millie just looked at her and realized that Sarah was far worse off than she had expected.

As Millie turned around, she was met by a middle-aged man standing in the hall. He was holding a baseball bat in his hand and had a snarky smile on his face.

"Hello, Albert," Millie said. "I see you were expecting us."

"I thought you might bring Sarah here after your gallant escape, and when I heard the semi-tractor in the street, I knew I was going to have a fun-filled day. And here you both are where I can score two kills in one place. So convenient. So easy. I might even get a raise."

Millie judged the man's strength by his stature and unconsciously considered the leverage she could wield against his lanky frame. He was about a foot taller than her but appeared to need some upper-body work. He was cocky and twirled the bat passing it back and forth between his hands. He even spun the bat behind his back and retrieved it with his other hand like an adolescent baton twirler. As he displayed his expertise, Millie slowly but steadily moved forward, and her actions broadened his grin.

"Come and get it, Kiddo. First you and then the history bitch. Orders are orders, but this is going to be fun."

Sarah was covering her mouth in astonishment. Albert had never acted like this for as long as she had known him. But just as quickly as that thought came to her another followed: How long had she known him? Confusion turned to fear and she put her hand over her mouth to keep from screaming. It was an ineffective move because she let out a scream which her hand could not quiet.

Albert, seeing Millie taking short, unbalanced steps toward him, ceased his commentary and swung the bat to drive her head over the left-field wall. As the bat head neared Millie, she ducked gracefully and stepped to the side towards Albert's hands, grabbing the bat right above his grip, helping Albert complete his swing. The effect of their combined efforts, the increased momentum, and distinct course adjustment brought the head of the bat to bear with a concussive force to Albert's left temple and dropped him cold. Millie was breathing easy when she removed the bat from his hands and confirmed his condition by smacking his right temple with a similar blow. She kept the bat in her hands as she turned back to Sarah.

Sarah staggered toward Millie. She was distraught: her eyes were wide, her mouth agape. When Sarah reached her, she wrapped her arms around Millie and broke into a sobbing, gasping cry.

"There, there," Millie said. "It's all over for now. No one's going to hurt you now. Whatever they've done to you can be fixed. You have to start by realizing that this man is not your boyfriend. I bet you've never seen him before tonight."

Sarah continued to hold Millie and sob.

"Come on. Let's go in and see if there's anything to drink. I could use a good belt."

Millie took Sarah into the kitchen and sat her in a chair. The whisky was on the counter, so she found two glasses and poured two fingers into each one then brought the glasses to the table and put one down.

Sarah looked like hell, she needed a shower and a change of clothes. Then, if possible, she needed a long nap so she would be fresh for the questions Millie needed her to answer.

"Here's to prep and training, and a good day at the office," Millie said with a small laugh, and she took a deep sip. "Go ahead, it'll do you good. We have a few things to talk about, and I have a call to make. Just let's sit here and you try your best to relax. If you remember anything about when you were a history professor, you know, from before you were fired, hang onto the thought. I'll want to know all about it. When you're done with the whisky, we'll get you cleaned up and rested. Okay?"

Sarah gazed at the drink and sniffed. Its pungent odor made her scrunch up her nose, and she let out a small cry of pain. As if to counter that, she downed the two fingers in one long gulp and slumped in her chair exhausted.

With Sarah sitting quietly, Millie checked on Albert, and finding some wire in a drawer she hogtied him where he lay. Then she withdrew her cell phone and made a call. It rang several times and an answering machine picked up and she left a message.

"Dad," she said. "Millie here. If you're there please pick up."

In a second, Contlerust answered.

"Millie, how's it going?" he said.

"Just swell. We recovered Sarah, but Steven was captured and he appears to be working with the other side. I've got to get Sarah back to Claramon. How about you?"

"All's good here. There's no report of charges against anyone involved in the dustup at Claramon. But it sounds like you need help."

"Yes, I do. Can you talk to Wrenbutt just to see if his conversion is holding together? I've got to find out where Steven is and get him back. I don't know what's happened to him. But something's gotten into his head. I know because he tried to kill me."

"Wow. That's too crazy!"

"Tell me about it. On top of that, Sarah's still whacked out. I'd like to know if Wrenbutt would take her back if she had her head on straight. I just need some encouragement at this point."

"I can get that done."

"Okay."

Deep dread entered her. She was dealing with a deeply evil enemy.

She went to Sarah and roused her enough to lead her to the bedroom where she put her to bed. And then, checking the door and stuffing socks into Albert's mouth, she popped him gently with the bat and settled down on the living room couch for a nap. It was nearing dark when she was awakened by a new text. She checked her phone but couldn't find the new message, yet she heard a second text landing.

She looked around the room and then checked in the kitchen. There, she found a phone she hadn't noticed. It had to be Sarah's. But when she tried to turn it on, she couldn't. It was password protected. Certain that she should get the password, she went to Sarah and woke her.

"What is it?" Sarah asked, bleary-eyed.

"What's your phone's password?"

"Password? I don't tell anyone what my password is."

"Listen, Sarah. I don't have any time to mess around with you. Either give me the password, or I'll leave you here with the killer you think is your boyfriend. I'm sure he'll have fun with you before he breaks your neck. What's it going to be?"

"Alright, give me the phone."

"No. You give me the password."

Sarah thought for a minute and finally, the number came to her. "It's 6892."

Millie tried it but it didn't work. She tried it again, this time slower, and the phone came to life.

There were three messages, one more than expected.

"Have Albert call me. -L"

The second was "Kill the bitch! -L"

The third was "Sorry it didn't work out for you. -L"

"Looks like your friend Lamia is sentimental."

"What do you mean?"

"Nothing much, just that you're nothing to her. She messed up your mind and now she wants you dead. She wants me dead, too. I guess Albert made that clear. I'm just not sure that you understand what's happening here. It's time to get up. We can't stay here. It won't be long and she'll realize that Albert's unavailable.

I don't know what she's done to Steven, but I can guess. Come on. Get up. We have to find a ride before Lamia figures out where we're going. She's probably on her way here now and we better be long gone if that's the case."

Sarah stood up. She held her head for a minute and nearly fell back on the bed, but Millie caught her.

"Come on, let's get you to the bathroom and get you cleaned up. You can't go out looking like that."

It only took fifteen minutes for Millie to get Sarah's face washed and to have her in a new outfit. She was banged up but wouldn't draw a lot of attention in public.

They packed a suitcase and Millie slipped Sarah's phone into her pocket. Then she checked on Albert. He was conscious but could do nothing but growl through his gag while she searched his pockets. He had a couple hundred in his billfold and he also had a cell phone and a set of car keys. It was time to go.

Downstairs, Millie cautiously checked the condo's street-side view. Seeing nothing suspicious she led Sarah out the door. They found Albert's grey Kia in the parking lot and drove onto the street, but instead of driving away, Millie spotted a nearby parking place and pulled in. She shut off the car while observing another car pulling into a second entrance to the condo's parking lot, and her gut told her she needed to know who was in it.

The car parked and a man she knew got out of the driver's side. Lamia got out of the other door. Millie wanted to cry out to Popoford, but if it was as she expected, he was under Lamia's spell and would try to kill her again. She watched him go into the condo building as she said a prayer for his safe return and drove away. She had a job to do and it needed doing right away.

In ten minutes Millie and Sarah were back in the same curbside parking space, but Millie was behind the wheel of an old

Ford F-150, a ride she was more familiar with than with Albert's Kia.

They waited there for an hour. No one left the condos and no one drove Lamia's car away. Millie gave up on her surveillance and pulled onto the street and drove until she found a darker street with few streetlamps. She parked and told Sarah to get in the back seat and get some rest.

When Millie could hear Sarah snoozing, she turned on Albert's phone and was pleased to find it unlocked. The man was a narcissist leaving his phone unprotected, she thought, especially with the jackpot it held. There in his unencrypted emails and text messages was all the information Millie could wish for. Most important of all, she discovered that Popoford and Lamia were about to fly out of Dulles and would be picked up at Sacramento International. The flight was scheduled for the next morning at 8:00 and would land at 12:54 with a stop in Denver. She immediately booked a morning flight for herself and Sarah.

CHAPTER TWENTY-FOUR

Contlerust was on the phone trying to report his findings first. But Millie stepped in and redirected the conversation.

"Dad, hold your report for a minute. Sarah and I are flying to Sacramento through Denver in the morning, arriving at 11:42. I need you to meet us there with my carry gun and grab some binoculars for me."

"I'll be there," Contlerust said.

"Thanks, Dad. Now, what did you find out about Wrenbutt?"

"First of all," Contlerust said. "He has no idea why everyone around him is acting like idiots. Teachers, students, and administrators are publicly railing at him all day long. They include some who have quietly had private conversations with him to say that his turn-around is a breath of fresh air. Of course, they won't publicly side with him 'Because of job security.' You understand."

"He has no memory of anti-anything, no understanding why he's so hated. It's wearing him down fast."

"You better get him alone for a while," Millie said. "He needs some counseling on how to blend in. He needs to understand the long game and to appreciate that he's an undercover operator behind enemy lines. He should probably make a public apology claiming some kind of drug combination as the reason. He needs to pick his friends with care."

"Okay. I'll take him under my wing. He'll soon have a grip on himself."

"Make it happen before he gets fired. We can't change minds as effectively from the outside as from within," Millie said. "And he'll be an important part of Sarah's rehabilitation. I'll see you tomorrow."

Millie hung up and did a quick check outside and then closed her eyes. Her sleep was fitful and full of devilishly concocted scenes that were perversions of her normal thoughts. She woke in a start just as Sarah was quietly closing the truck's backdoor in an apparent attempt to escape.

Millie was out of the truck in a flash racing around the front of the truck while she barked orders in bizarrely hushed tones.

"Stop!" she hissed. "Stay where you are! Do not move!"

As she rounded the truck's bumper, she was surprised to see Sarah standing by the open door with her mouth agape and her eyes bulging.

"What did I do?" she asked. "I'm just getting in the front seat again. You must be nuts."

"You may be right," Millie said and helped Sarah into the truck.

Millie knew she needed rest. She was all nerves and had few constraints. She had to calm down or she would become her own worst enemy.

"Can I trust you, Sarah?" she said. "I mean, are you just waiting to take me out?"

Sarah turned toward Millie. "I don't think either one of us can trust the other completely, but I think I'm better off with you than with Alfred or Lamia. You and I are in the same boat with the same enemies, but it seems a friend of yours has joined up with them. I don't know. I'm confused about everything. Maybe your friend feels the same way."

"I hope so. In the meantime, I need some sleep. We're flying to Sacramento in the morning and I don't want to miss the flight. Let's both get some sleep. Okay?"

"Sure," Sarah said, tilting her seat back and closing her eyes. "Will you set an alarm?"

"Already done. I'll wake you up in the morning."

They slept dreamlessly until the alarm rang whereupon Millie drove them to Dulles. There, she parked the stolen truck and they entered the terminal together, boarding their flight on time. Lamia and Popoford wouldn't arrive at Dulles for another hour and a half.

The flight to Sacramento was quiet. Most of the passengers slept the whole way. When they landed, they walked directly to the pickup curb. Millie checked her text messages once again and was relieved to see her father's message.

"Arriving airport. There soon."

When Contlerust pulled up to the curb, Millie helped Sarah get into his car then got in herself and they drove away.

"Where to, ladies?" Contlerust asked.

"Take us to a car rental counter."

"Sarah, do you remember my father?"

"Maybe," Sarah said weakly.

Contlerust gave her an inquisitive look and let it drop. "What's next," he asked when Millie opened her car door.

"Give me my gun, then we'll get out of here and find a place to park. Just after their landing time, we'll start driving in a loop through the pickup area checking for Lamia as she boards a rental car tram. I'll start first and let you know when I'm halfway around. Then you start the loop. With any luck, we can follow the tram and then pick her up as she drives onto Airport Boulevard. Then I can follow them wherever they're headed."

"It's worth a try," Contlerust said.

Millie rented a car, drove it to where Contlerust was parked, and got out. She squatted at Contlerust's passenger window and he opened it. Then she looked at Sarah with a concerned expression.

"Sarah, I need you to do me a favor."

"Such as?" Sarah said, suspicious.

"You need to go with my father. Can you do that for me?"

"I thought you were going to help me."

"I am, Sarah. This is the best way right now. You know Lamia wants you dead. You also know that I'm going after Lamia to get Steven back. You can't afford to go with me. It's too dangerous. Go with Dad so that you can get back to Merced. You'll be safe there with him until I finish my work. I trust him. So should you."

Sarah nodded and looked at Contlerust.

"How long's the drive?"

"About two hours. Maybe longer since we need gas and something to eat along the way. So, we should get you home in the early afternoon."

Sarah's smile became more relaxed. "You sound like a cowboy."

"Really? Well, I don't know about that, but I was a farmer for many years. Maybe that's it. I used to work for the same people Popoford was with."

"Well," she replied, "As you said. Nice to meet you." It seemed that there was no need for secret phrases to get Sarah talking to Contlerust.

With Sarah in good hands, Millie had a last word with them.

"It's time to start our loop," she said. She called Contlerust's phone and they both put their phones on speaker. "Give me those binoculars, Dad."

"Here you go. They might come in handy. I'll be worried about you until you get back."

"Thanks, Dad, but you'd best pay attention to Sarah. She needs to get her feet under her right away, and I'm trusting you to see that it gets done."

"Okay. Be safe and bring Popoford home."

"I'll do my best," Millie said and returned to her car. At the last minute, she settled into her observer's role and started the airport loop. In half an hour, Contlerust's voice broke through her concentration.

"There they are! We got them. They just came out of the terminal and are standing in the rental car tram line. I'll keep them in my sights until you catch up."

"Here we go," Millie said as she began the tail. "Thanks for your help, Dad. And Sarah, please take care of yourself. You're too important to lose.

CHAPTER TWENTY-FIVE

Lamia and Popoford headed south and soon picked up highway 50 east towards South Lake Tahoe. They would take highway 89, a winding road, to 395 south past Mono Lake. Their destination was on a mountain peak northwest of Silver Lake which was only accessible by a privately maintained one-lane road not found on most maps. They followed the GPS coordinates that Vladdrac had provided and had no assurances of what they'd find at the end of the trail except trouble. Of that, they could be sure.

Lamia was certain that she was invited to her own death. Popoford was certain he would save her. She thought survival was a long shot. They were unarmed and she would have to present herself to Vladdrac alone. The challenge was for Popoford to get into wherever they were going unmolested. They also needed to buy a knife and whatever else they needed.

Popoford found a Sportsman's Warehouse in Rancho Cordova. They could shop there first and then follow the GPS to TAP headquarters.

They turned off the road at the North Gate exit and turned left. They could see the outfitter's building on the right as they cleared the overpass. They pulled into a parking space and went in together.

When they'd been in the store for a minute, Millie parked her car and retrieved a magnetic homing device Contlerust had handed her for the trip. She walked to Lamia's Ford rental and slipped the device up in the front wheel well. She kept walking without looking back and got back into the car and drove away more relaxed now that she could follow at a greater distance.

When Lamia and Popoford returned to their rental car, Popoford noticed something on the pavement near the front tire. In a smooth motion that Lamia didn't notice, Popoford bent down and swooped the object into his palm and then into his pocket. He knew what it was but wasn't sure who had tried to put it on the car. They might have tried planting it weeks ago, or maybe it was only minutes, but he scanned the parking lot as Lamia resumed their trip to Vladdrac's. A flash of recognition sparkled in his eyes at the sight of a driver leaving the lot before them who bore a strong resemblance to Millie, presumed dead.

CHAPTER TWENTY-SIX

The drive to Vladdrac's command center took them over the Sierras. At June Lake Junction, they took road 158 to the west. When their GPS led them to a road marked only by a small sign that read "Private Road. No Entrance Without Permission," Lamia told Popoford to climb into the back seat and lay low.

Popoford lowered his window and allowed the sweet, clean air to rush in unfiltered. Lamia didn't seem to care one way or the other, but Popoford felt that he was close to his own country in Whimsy surrounded by nature's beasts and foliage. The air was cool in the early afternoon, the sun brilliant, and as they slowed at every turn on the narrow road he could hear the buzzing of insects and the singing Robins and Goldfinches; the screeching red-tailed Hawks. He even imagined he heard elk bugling deep in the woods. The sweet ride came to an end soon when Lamia turned the car onto a gravel road and the crunching of crushed rock covered the song of the wild.

A mile up the road, the thick forest opened onto a broad, cleared expanse, dominated by a natural hill topped with a magnificent building. It radiated the nature of the mountain surroundings yet was built as if for ancient gods. Windows soared to the rooftops on all sides providing sunlight for lofty halls suitable for the gods of Valhalla. Here then was the center of corruption and deceit, the stronghold of the man who would rule the world and was remarkably close to accomplishing his domination. Here within was the throne of the king to whom politicians and tyrants of all stripes bowed. But this adulation was done from afar since the king himself was untouchable, unidentifiable, and enthroned in the American calculus through school curriculums, demeaning social strictures, mob pressures, and the denigration of history. This castle was America's Burg Frankenstein.

Lamia slowed to a stop while she marveled at what she still hoped would be her new home as queen.

Popoford took the opportunity to slip out of the car and slide into the woods surrounding the mansion. He checked the road behind him but saw no sign that anyone was coming up the hill. Another step into the woods and he disappeared.

Lamia only noticed he was gone when she looked at the empty seat behind her. She smiled with the knowledge he had her back and proceeded up the road to the grand entrance.

When she stopped the car, a man who appeared to be a butler came from the house and opened her door. He took her hand in a gracious gesture of chivalry and then escorted her through the front door into the grand, domed foyer. There, he asked her to take a seat for a moment and wished to know what sort of refreshment he could provide when she was shown into the presence of Lord Vladdrac.

"Just some sparkling water would be refreshing," She said. "And what shall I call you?"

"You may call me by my name for now," He said. "Junko."

"How extraordinary," she replied.

Junko left the room and soon returned with news that Vladdrac would receive her. As they walked to the elevator, he described Vladdrac's physical condition so as not to have her surprised by their first meeting. Lamia wasn't concerned with what she heard. But what she saw when she entered the enormous room with the panoramic view of Silver Lake to the east, and the expanse of the rolling hills and the Sierras beyond appearing so close in the pristine air, made her heart rise. Then the thrill in her heart turned to a distasteful chill at the sight of Vladdrac, his psoriatic body bathed to the neck in tar water. This man of many cruelties was a vision of his soul, and even though Lamia might be as deeply flawed as he, she was repulsed by the sight of him. Yet she steeled herself against showing any distaste, for Lord Vladdrac owned her life.

"My dear Lamia," he said. "Forgive me for not rising. please take a seat here in front of me."

The chair he offered was neither elegant nor elaborate. It was a simple folding card table chair without padding of any kind: bare, uncomfortable, and demeaning. As she gracefully sat down, Junko handed her a glass of sparkling water.

"You're the first of my generals to enter these royal walls. I do not need human connection except that which my man Junko offers. I do hope, however, you understand that my accommodations suit the situation perfectly. You're on trial, the condemned who must show her master some reason to spare her life. But you must know this. Am I correct?"

"Without contradicting you, Lord Vladdrac, I'm bewildered that you should think me guilty of any transgression. I have served you loyally for many years, and my recent work in the advancement of your cause is certainly worthy of your praise."

"How conceited you are," he replied. "And how you lust for power that is not yours to have. Your 'advancement of the cause' as you put it, is an abject failure. Furthermore, you have demonstrated by your self-centered notion of achievement, that you wish to take credit for what is doubtless mine to have. Do you wish to make a statement before I pass sentence on you?"

"I am guilty of nothing against you, Lord Vladdrac."

"For crimes against me and my rightful position on the throne, I sentence you to death by drowning. Your execution will be performed in thirty minutes right here in this soothing bath which is my prison. Junko, take her away and prepare her for death."

"You can't do this!" Lamia cried as Junko lifted her bodily from the cheap chair. "I'm innocent!"

"Silence!" Junko said calmly. "Do not demean yourself or it could go much harder on you."

Lamia was flabbergasted to think of anything worse that might happen. But when Junko had removed her from Vladdrac's presence, he set her on her feet and, putting a finger to his lips, bid her to be silent and to follow him.

She did as he wished and he led her to a room down a hall where he made her enter one of the many doors there to ask her a few questions.

"What did you expect to happen here? Didn't you know you were coming to your death?"

"I suspected as much, but I thought I might be able to persuade him that I have value."

"First of all, You're the first and only person to meet him other than me. That in and of itself requires your death. Second, your experiments on the new serum were reported as successful before they were proven effective. Third, it seems that the woman, Sarah Tufftang, has not been eliminated. All of these are capital offenses. Would you not take the same action as Lord Vladdrac if you were in his position?"

"No. My experiments represent a great leap forward. Against my better judgment, I attempted to destroy Sarah. I failed, but I can still get it done. And it wasn't my idea to come here. Laying eyes on Lord Vladdrac is a pretense for a foregone conclusion. How does he expect to replace me, anyway?"

"That will be my problem," Junko said.

He talked with her a while longer telling her things that might better prepare her for what was coming.

"I'll leave you now and return when the time comes."

The door closed on Lamia's cell and her mind swarmed with the ravings of the unjustly condemned. But she was disciplined and knew that Popoford was nearby and might already be breaching the building. She was certain that she would survive.

CHAPTER TWENTY-SEVEN

Popoford skirted the property just deep enough into the woods that he could not be seen. Not only did he keep an eye out for humans, guard dogs, tripwires, and sensing devices, but he also kept track of where he was about to place his feet so that each step would land and be withdrawn without the slightest sound. Years of stalking game in his Whimsy woods had taught him well the woodcraft of the hunter.

He made his way around the right side of the house, skipping the front for fear that multiple warning devices were installed there. When he came to the back of the house, he paused a moment to marvel at the expanse of glass rising from the foundation to the peak of the steeply pitched roof. It appeared that a single piece of glass was crafted to create the house's entire back wall. But it was a sophisticated illusion made possible by joints sealed with a transparent bonding material, itself made of glass. Somewhere in the back of Popoford's mind, he remembered an article he'd read about experiments on such a product conducted at Alfred University in New York. He was fascinated by what he saw and had to consciously shake himself to get back on track. He scanned the entire back of the building and the grounds and gave up on that point of entry.

Next, he retraced his steps in the forest and surveyed the other side of the building. It was the spitting image of the first side. The structure was designed to discourage any entrance except from the front. As he was studying his best line of approach, he was startled to hear the faint sound of a person advancing on foot towards him. He found cover in a shallow drainage ditch and waited. When the person finally appeared, it was too late for him to escape. She was only ten feet from his position and her gun was aimed right at him.

"Freeze!" Millie said. "Don't you move a muscle."

Popoford wasn't about to disobey her order. The tone of her voice made it clear she meant business.

"Do you mind lowering your muzzle?" Popoford asked. "You seem upset and you might get a twitchy finger."

"Now, why do you think I'm upset? Is it because you tried to kill me? Could that be it?"

"Sure it could if it'd happened like that. But it didn't"

"Don't try to fool me, Steven Popoford. You put three rounds right through the back window of the semi I was driving; put it right between me and Sarah Tufftang. Couldn't you make up that confused mind of yours?"

"What confused mind? The bullet went right where I aimed."

"Don't give me that," Millie said.

"I never miss at that distance." He was a ten-ring shooter out to twenty-five yards in bullseye local competition, and out to one hundred yards in precision handgun shooting.

"Then what were you doing?"

"Getting a nasty worm out of my head," he said. "When I thought they'd killed you, I was devastated and open to all Lamia's fiction. But when she discovered my history with Home Office, I snapped to. I knew she'd drugged me, though I wasn't sure what the drug was. When I woke up, I realized she was treating me like a child and fabricating a story about needing me back in the game. She claimed to be an undercover agent inserted into TAP leadership. Something didn't ring true, and all my past struggles with the Runner program came back in a flash that insulated me from her wicked intent. In other words, I spotted her crap and didn't buy it even though her drug was trying to dissolve my reason. I beat her at her own game."

Millie gazed at him with eyes of hope and doubt. "You're kidding, right?"

"Not at all. I'm serious. Here, take your tracking device back. It's served its purpose. I wanted you to follow me. I'm here to take down this bunch of crazies, and I could use your help. I'm playing Lamia's patsy to destroy her and her organization."

Millie's expression warmed rapidly as she lowered her gun and rushed to him, throwing her arms around him. "I'm so relieved!" she cried and kissed him. What's our plan?"

"I'd love to hold you like this until it all goes away," he said. "But we both know better than that. Lamia is inside and probably in danger. I'm supposed to get in there to keep her alive and then take her place on their leadership team. I need you to get me into the house so I can play my part. I'm probably going to need you to be there for my extraction. I don't know how many people are in there, but my job is to kill the ringleader, a guy they call Lord Vladdrac. If Lamia is going to make that easy, I'd be a fool to pass up her help."

"How do you plan to do that?"

"I don't know, yet."

"Maybe I could be a distraction."

"How?"

"I could ring the front doorbell and wait for someone to open the door. You could get inside in the confusion."

Popoford smiled at her. "From the mouths of babes."

"Thanks for the compliment," she said, knowing full well that he was referring to babies. "But they aren't going to just let me walk away. I'll be captured, too."

"And we'll both be inside. We can't do anything if we stay out here. Once inside, we might be helpful. I haven't noticed any security cameras, but they must be somewhere," Popoford said.

"I'll go straight to the front door from here," Millie said. "You go back to the side of the house and then work your way to the front door. Together, we should be able to get you inside."

"I'll need a gun."

"You're in luck," she said and gave him a handgun."

"Thanks," Popoford said. "Let's go."

Millie gave it a couple of beats as Popoford slipped through the woods, and then walked onto the gravel turnaround and went right past Lamia's rental car to the front door. By the time she got there, Popoford had inched his way around to the front of the mansion. Millie concealed her pistol, took a deep breath, and pressed the doorbell.

CHAPTER TWENTY-EIGHT

Junko was returning to Vladdrac in the great hall when he heard the doorbell. It was something that he would normally ignore, but not this time. He was fully expecting something unusual to happen. After all, he was the one who had given Lamia the information about who Popoford was. He had seen the photo that she had sent along with her inquiry and was able to report back to her without any research. His knowledge came from experience, and he knew Steven Popoford well. He was probably the one at the door.

In days past, in an earlier assignment, Junko Abrams' name was John, and he was the butler of P. Y. Mous, the gun-trafficking industrialist. The last time he saw Popoford was when Junko closed the elevator door on him in an attempt to crush him against the oncoming ceiling, and he remembered him clearly as the one who had nearly crippled their cause so many years ago. He wasn't sure what Lamia was planning to do with Popoford, but he rolled the irony of this Resurrection Runner rejoining their efforts around and considered how to use him himself.

Junko went to the front door and peered through the spyhole. A woman he had never seen stood there, smiling.

As he opened the door, Millie stepped back a few paces. "Hello," she said.

"What can I do for you?" Junko asked in a perfunctory tone.

"I'm with Prestigious Homes of Mammoth Lakes. I'm here to inquire about representing your magnificent property."

"I'm sorry, Miss, but the property is not for sale."

"But you haven't heard what your expected sales price would be."

"The owner is not interested in selling."

"But…," Millie started.

"Not under any circumstances," Junko replied and began to close the door.

Popoford wasted no time taking the last two steps to the door, gun in hand, and pressed Junko back into the house. Millie followed and closed the door behind them. To Popoford's surprise, Junko smiled as if he had no concerns.

"I wondered how you'd get in, Steven. I knew it must be you as soon as the bell rang. Aren't you going to introduce me to your friend?"

"How do you know my name?"

"I'll let you turn that over in your mind for a while. If you figure it out too soon, it'll spoil the fun."

"Knock off the BS. Where is Vladdrac?"

"What is your business with him?"

"I have the gun. I do the asking, you answer. That's the way this game is played."

"As you wish. Follow me."

Junko led the way up the circular staircase to the top where he opened the door onto Vladdrac's great hall. Popoford and Millie followed, gazing at the wondrous view and the bizarre arrangement in the center of the room. Expecting Popoford's amazement, Junko executed an astonishing Taekwondo back kick knocking Popoford's gun out of his hand and snatching it in midair. Millie instantly drew her gun, but before she could get it on target, Junko pressed his gun against Popoford's head.

"Looks like I'll be making the rules of the game, my dear. Drop your mag and rack your slide. No foolishness or the incompetent spy dies. Now, please place your weapon on the table next to you. That's right. Now, come here and join Steven. It's time for introductions."

Popoford was mystified. He hadn't expected such skill from the butler. It embarrassed him to know he was still as careless as he'd been as a Resurrection Runner.

Now they were captives, but he didn't lose hope for there in front of him was his target, the abominable master of tyranny.

Junko directed them to a place near Vladdrac's bathing command post and told them to remain standing, leaving the fold-up chair, where Lamia had been questioned, empty.

They stood in front of Vladdrac but Popoford looked at Junko for some hint of who he was. Vladdrac spoke first.

"Lamia sent you to execute me. Is this true?"

Popoford stared at the creature before him whose head and shoulders protruded from the coal-oil bath.

Vladdrac laughed. "Do you think you can protect her? Do you think I don't already know the answer to every question I ask? I was told you're a clever man. Perhaps my information is faulty. Why are you here?"

"You say you already know," Popoford said, maintaining a cool temperament.

"You will die in a few minutes along with Lamia, your creator."

"If you expect me to deny my Creator in favor of your toady, Lamia, you're mistaken. My God expects my loyalty."

"Ah, a man of faith. Spare me. You're on the wrong side of history."

"There is no history in eternity, but there is Hell. Your kind of place, I hear."

Vladdrac erupted into a bellowing laugh and bubbles floated to his bath's surface.

"Enough of this! Bring Lamia to me. It's time to end this farce."

Junko moved Millie's gun to the pool edge within Vladdrac's reach. He bowed and left the room.

"By the look on your face, Popoford, you're about to say something even more stupid, like "You can't get away with this." Well, hold your breath. you're about to see justice done and then you will be put to death like every fool who crosses me."

"With an inferiority complex like yours, it's a wonder that anyone is alive."

"Again with the jokes. Where's Henny Youngman when you need him?"

"He's with Milton Berle waiting to call you a schmuck and slam the gates of Hell closed on you."

"Silence!" Vladdrac erupted.

"What are you going to do, kill me?"

"He won't have to if I get to him first," Millie interjected.

Vladrrac calmly looked at Millie. His scorn wrinkled every inch of his face and malice infused his reply.

"Little woman, tell me why you imagine I care anything about you? All I need to do is raise an eyebrow and my butler will cut your throat. You are nothing. Shut up and remember your place!"

Popoford bridled at this but instantly recovered his cool demeanor.

"You can forget about them," he snapped. "I'm the one who came to kill you."

Vladdrac's eyes calmly shifted to Popoford.

"It doesn't matter. They'll die with you. It's been a trying week, and I need a change of pace."

With that, Junko returned with Lamia.

"Ah," Vladdrac snarled. "The cast is complete. Let the games begin."

"What is your preferred form of execution, my lord?" Junko said as he put Lamia in front of the two other captives.

"Let's begin with strangulation. It's so slow a death that it gives a criminal time to consider his sins," Vladdrac said. "But first, you must recite the charges against these three. Stand here beside me, Junko. Deliver the indictment!"

Junko obeyed Vladdrac and began his speech as ordered.

"I, Junko Abrams, once known as John, hereby declare the transgressions of these defendants."

At once, Popoford remembered where he had met Junko. He glowered at the man as he continued.

"Lamia, general in charge of TAP educational reforms, you are accused of conspiring to overthrow your natural leader, Master Vladdrac, by assassination, having manipulated one Steven Popoford by employing the serum you created, but which is the property of TAP's leader. How do you plead?"

"Based solely on the advice Junko gave me as he brought me to this farce, I plead guilty and throw myself on the mercy of this court for leniency."

Vladdrac smirked and shook his head in amazement at such an ignorant expectation.

"Hearing the defendant's plea and noting the plaintiff's disbelief," Junko said. "I now report the judgment of this court: for mutinous aspirations, arrogant individualism, and the theft of TAP systems for personal advancement, you are condemned to death by strangulation."

"Let the execution begin," Vladdrac smiled, all the while holding Lamia's bewildered gaze as Junko bowed to him and proceeded.

Popoford and Millie were embroiled in their rage and mortification, but none were so astonished by Junko's next act than Vladdrac himself.

Reaching his long arms out Junko snatched Vladdrac's neck in both his hands and began to squeeze. As he gradually tightened his grip on the Leader's scrawny throat, he also pulled his wretched body from the therapeutic pool.

"Observe, if you will, how the servant and the master have changed roles."

Vladdrac's thrashing grew more frantic and his gurgling protests more urgent as the seconds passed.

"You will be forgiven for thinking this, of course, because I have misdirected you and all the TAP members. There is no role change here, for I am and have long been the Master of my domain. See how the arrogance of this petty slave to assume favor from his master has brought him to accounts. It is not his management of TAP that condemns him, but his assumed inheritance of my master's kingdom. He condemned himself when he uttered these words: 'I'm their creator, Junko. It's as if I am the son of the dark leader himself.' Look, he recognizes his error and pleads with his eyes. He'll be damned forever and cursed by eternally unfulfilled hope for my sire's mercy."

Twisting his hands so that Vladdrac's popping eyes were staring into his, Junko delivered the last earthly words Vladdrac would ever hear.

"I am, by your acquiescence and my master's will, your eternal overseer. It's such a pity, isn't it, that I never have been nor ever will be merciful. That quality is found in the Other One. The One my master refuses to follow."

Vladdrac's last thoughts were smothered in self-pity. All he had given, all his suffering, all the greatness he had provided, the ideas, the leadership, the donations of time and talent, his loyalty, his commitment, his sacrifice, all diminished by ingratitude. But aside from his outstanding service, he cared infinitely more for what he had surrendered to his master. It was dismay that flooded his soul and remorse for having committed to a faithless idol. At his end, Vladdrac took no responsibility for his execution but died with hatred for his master stuck in his craw.

Junko snapped Vladdrac's neck and let his decrepit body slide into the viscous pool.

CHAPTER TWENTY-NINE

Lamia, forewarned of Vladdrac's execution, was the embodiment of calm. She stood with her hands clasped in front of her, her eyes downturned as if in prayer.

There was a self-satisfied smile on her face as she marveled at the quality of justice meted out to hapless Vladdrac, the arrogant bastard who had given no credit for the world-changing work she had done for the cause. He was a pitiful fool, unable to judge her accomplishments or the power of his servant. Committed to the secular world of nihilism, she misunderstood the gravity of Junko's proclamations. She was alone in her error, for not only were Junko's statements truthful but Popoford and Millie shuddered to think they were in the presence of the damned. Even as Junko bowed deeply to Lamia and invited her to follow him to an area of the great hall nearer the window and away from Vladdrac's bath, they noticed a distinct change in his attitude and manner. He was a servant, again, as he demonstrated how a hidden workstation, a duplication of the one which stood within Vladdrac's bath, could be made to rise from the floor. There was one luxurious chair that Junko offered her, and when she sat, he bowed again and spoke to her.

"You are master of all you survey, Lamia. TAP is yours to do as I have directed. You have a striving heart. For this reason, I suggest you direct your efforts to the perversion of the many and abandon any notion of rising above your penultimate status. I'm your servant for as long as you behave."

With that, he bowed again and took a step back.

"Thank you, Junko, for your confidence in my skills. I will not disappoint. Now, bring Popoford to me, and lock that girl up. I'll decide what to do with her later. When I'm done with Popoford, I'll want a meeting of The Five."

"Do you have someone in mind to take your place, Junko asked."

"Yes, in good time. For now, I'll keep my decision to myself. I want to be certain of my choice."

"Of course," Junko said and turned back to the two who were still standing transfixed in front of Vladdrac's body which had bobbed up to the dark surface.

With Popoford's gun in his hand, Junko moved him and Millie to where Lamia waited. Then he herded Millie out of the hall leaving Lamia alone with Popoford.

"You failed, Popoford. You were supposed to kill Vladdrac. But I forgive you. I had no idea who was in charge, but it seems my work came to his attention at the right time. Now, you must take on a new role for Section 33. You're the best agent Home Office ever had, and you're my best agent as well. Are you willing to go to the next level with me in charge? I have work for you to do."

Popoford's mind raced to understand what was happening. Was Lamia saying that she was truly an undercover agent, or was it something else? His only chance to find out was to accept the work she offered.

"Yes, if it's in the line of duty, of course."

"It most certainly is in the line of duty. I want you to take over my TAP position. You need more training, but you'll work in a pinch. What do you say?"

"So, you want me to continue your work in guiding the education imperative. For the agency. Is that it? "

"In a manner of speaking, yes."

"I have no idea how to do it."

"You'll learn. It won't take long to get your brain working on accelerating my work and making the schools produce the best little robots that were ever created. Just one good session with you and you will be great."

"I'm flattered," he said, encouraged by her words that she was ignorant of the mind-altering training not affecting him. He smiled to himself.

"I'm calling a meeting of my TAP generals, General Popoford. When the meeting is done, I'll tell you what I want you to do with Millie. She will be your first test."

"As you wish," Popoford said.

"Go now and find Junko. Tell him I want you to stay here tonight. Ask him to show you to a room. The meeting will be this evening. Get some rest because I want to have a training session with you before then. Understood?"

"Yes. Understood."

"Good. Now leave me."

Popoford did as he was told as Lamia stayed where she was and scanned the beauty of her new view. The lake beyond was still and reflected the vast Nevada sky for miles to the east. It was a brilliant day and the pines that topped the high canyon ridges were bending to a wind not felt in the protected flatland below.

Lamia scanned the instruments collected on the command station where she sat. Aside from several computer monitors and tv sets, there was a bank of gauges and clocks which informed her of many things: the current time in many parts of the world and the weather in these places as well, the various financial markets, and the locations of the three remaining TAP generals. She made a mental note to have her tracking capsule removed. Then she realized there were five locations displayed and one of them was for Vladdrac himself and realized she'd be obliged to retain her capsule to satisfy Junko's need to know.

She checked the local weather and noted the falling barometer. There was a radar image displayed on a small screen above the readout. Though the sun was shining now, a storm, represented by the dark-green image on the screen, was bearing down on them from the north. It was still several hours away, but it promised to bring rain and thunderstorms in the night.

Lamia was marveling at the rapid change in her prospects when Junko softly announced his presence.

"May we speak?" he said.

Lamia nearly jumped out of her chair she was so startled by his silent approach. She gathered her wits quickly.

"Of course. I was expecting we would talk soon," she smiled. "Are you in the habit of walking silently?"

"Yes, I am. It's a skill that you should master yourself. It's a wonder what you can discover if you can come upon a conversation without being noticed. I'll teach you. It may come in handy one day."

"I look forward to learning all you can teach me. What is it you wish to discuss?"

"Steven Popoford. I know him well. You brought him with you."

It was a statement delivered in a dispassionate tone, almost too softly spoken, as one might imagine a prosecuting attorney's leading attack in the cross-examination of a psychopathic killer. Having seen enough of Junko to know that resistance would be futile, Lamia was candid.

"I did, and with malice aforethought. When you identified him after I kidnapped the Tufftang woman, I decided to inject him with my new serum. I made him believe I'm an undercover federal agent working inside TAP to bring it all down. He now believes he has returned to Government duty. I sent him here to kill Vladdrac."

"I see. Most interesting. I like the way you work. I believe we will make great strides together. Where Vladdrac merely ambled, you will run at my side. This is your show and I'm your servant."

"As long as I know my place?"

"Exactly," Junko said. "Without doubt."

CHAPTER THIRTY

Popoford noticed that Junko had reverted to his butler role when he opened the door. His placid countenance announced that he was no longer TAP's interim leader.

"Leader Lamia requests your presence in the upper room," he said and gestured for Popoford to follow him.

Popoford looked forward to the meeting. Qualifying for the TAP leadership team would put him in a position to take them all down. When Junko left them together Popoford was a bit surprised at Lamia's familiarity and frankness, but not at her continued sham undercover agent persona.

"Steven, we're still on the job," she said after Junko left. "Remember that and observe everything that happens. You never know what will make a difference in the future.

"Also," she continued. "You and Millie must leave here tonight. Junko tells me there's a car parked at the bottom of the driveway. Is that so?"

"I don't know, but I expect there is. She had to get here somehow."

"Do you know what happened to Sarah Tufftang?"

"No."

"I want you to find out all you can about Sarah and Millie and their movements. Report your findings as soon as you can. Explain that you're working with me undercover for the government. The truth will be easier than fiction. As soon as the call is over, you are to get Millie and get out of here. In the meantime, let me explain how this upcoming call will work."

"Of course," Popoford said.

"It's easy for you because you'll have nothing to say. You're the new boy, and no one expects anything from you. I'll report on the education program myself. Next week it will be your responsibility."

"I understand."

"Good. Just one thing more. No one in this conversation can see me or the other participants. Imagine you're in the same boat. That way, you won't reveal where you are and who you're with. Let's begin."

Lamia directed Popoford to sit in front of a computer monitor and told him to put on the headset. Then she logged into the group discussion software and, seeing that the others were there, she made her presence known.

"Good evening everyone. You are undoubtedly surprised to hear my voice at the beginning of this meeting. There is no reason to be concerned and also no reason for you to know anything more than TAP's leadership has changed. Lord Vladdrac is no longer with us. I, Lamia, am now your leader. Comments and discussions concerning this matter are forbidden.

"I have selected a new Number Four to take over my former activities. He's called Farrago. He's one of us. Enough said on the subject. That is my report for the week.

"Diomed, your report."

"Thank you, Lady Lamia. We summarily put down the expected anti-Brilliance in Basics conversation on various opposition channels. All who have raised a dissenting question about the program suffered cancellation, and boycotting action is underway to ruin their contributors and advertisers. The press is in line with our talking points and our opposition talking heads are following the perfectly balanced formula of understanding and conciliation. I'll leave it to Number Five to report on the suppression of the rabble at your pleasure, My Lady."

"Thank you, Diomed. In next week's report, I expect you to bring a one-year plan detailing the next stage of defaming the faithful, especially the Jews, Catholics, and Bible thumpers. Leave Islam out of this plan for now. Let them continue to believe they're protected. You will work with others to employ your plan in all segments of society. Are there questions"?

"None whatsoever."

"Good. Now, Tamisra. Your report."

"Lady Lamia, The Senate is aggressively confirming federal judges sympathetic to our cause and trained in our schools as activists forming a bulwark against opposing future president's efforts to thwart our progress. Our funding partners, both private and nation-state, are compromising state and local politicians with campaign financing linked to supporting our desired outcomes. Furthermore, the Senate is lining up votes to pack the Supreme Court with at least four more justices. As soon as we have the White House again and a majority in both houses, we will control the third legislative branch, the Supreme Court of the United States. When we abolish the Electoral College and add two more states, our power will become perpetual."

"Remember everyone," Lamia warned. "Ours is the long game. Patience is essential and readiness to spring our plans in a coordinated swarm is our end game. Keep your powder dry for the coming days of the Glorious Revolution.

"And now, Blagden, for your report."

"Our Downtrodden Community Fighting Corp has completed localized intelligence surveillance for twenty cities that are rarely mentioned in national news. With our Lightning Mobility Strikeforce ready for action with four hours' notice, we can overwhelm the country with riots, looting, and murder before the sun rises again."

"Make it three hours notice, Blagden, and have the plan ready for presentation next week."

"It will be done."

"And Diomed, report next week as well on your plan to gaslight all opponents. The sheep must be made to condemn the current administration."

"Of course."

"Now, I'll give my last report to this committee. It is a condemnation of our former leader Vladdrac. His dethroning became necessary when he became the Cause and forgot his soldiers who engage in the daily struggle. Vladdrac allowed the Cause to be about his aggrandizement; indeed, he fostered a tyrant's privilege which I will not condone. Under my leadership, you can expect to receive credit for your achievements. I will not co-opt your efforts. Do not make the mistake of thinking I will rule with anything but an iron hand. I will. But credit will go to you when it is deserved. That is all until next week."

Lamia cut the connection and was pleased to still see and hear her staff even after they had shut down their computers. She scoffed at the smiles and clapping that they indulged in. If they only knew how much worse punishment could be with Vladdrac replaced, they'd drop a cyanide cap right now, knowing all hope was lost.

"What do you think, Popoford?"

"That I need to get to work so I can have something positive to report next week."

"I'm happy you feel that way, but I've changed my mind. Here's what I expect you to get done. You're to leave here and take Millie with you as I said. No one is to know about our special arrangement. You are to convince them and anyone else who was looking for me to give it up. Tell them that you killed me and that the problem is resolved. Find Sarah Tufftang and hold her for me. I'll deal with her personally.

"As you wish," Popoford said.

"As far as next week's call is concerned, you will be on it, but I'll send you the information to report. No need for you to waste your time on what I know best. When we are ready to proceed against this cabal, you will be the muscle to bring it down."

"I'll be ready when the time comes. May it be sooner rather than later. By the way, will you tell Junko to return my gun? It could come in handy."

"Of course, but Millie doesn't need hers."

Popoford rose and, with a slight bow, turned and left the room where TAP's brain trust recently self-refreshed.

Below, Millie was huddled on the floor of a small, unused pantry. She wasn't constrained in any way except by the threat that Junko had made when he locked them in. Death on the pike seemed too bizarre to be taken seriously, but given the strangulation of Vladdrac, she thought better than to just wait passively for death.

She stood up, stretched, and quietly walked to the door. As she reached out to try to turn the handle, the door opened and Popoford was standing there.

"Millie, come with me right now. We need to leave. Now!"

Millie followed him through the door as fast as her cramped legs would allow.

"What's going on?" she asked Popoford.

"No time to talk. Just head out the front door and down the driveway. We can talk when we're on the road."

"But where's my gun?"

"Forget about it. Let's move!"

Popoford put his hand on her back and hurried her on as they went through the already open front door and ran down the driveway. As they were about to disappear below the rise in the driveway, Popoford looked back and saw Junko standing in the door with a broad smile on his face waving goodbye. He stifled an urge to flip him off, realizing that the gesture would reveal his true loyalties. He figured that Lamia had explained why Popoford was there and that Junko thought he was under the serum's spell. Junko would have never let him go otherwise. Even now, Popoford knew he had to be careful.

When they got to the bottom of the hill, Millie was already down the road near her car. She was about to get in when Popoford called out to her to stop.

"Wait! Don't get in yet!" he shouted. "We need to check the car for a bomb and any tracking equipment. It's got to be clean before we go or we'll never be safe."

Agreeing, they both walked around the car putting their hands on all the metal and rubber both on the outer and underside of the body and the tires. Then they popped the hood and checked it. Popoford got under the car as well but they found nothing of interest. Finally, they checked the interior: seats, floor mats, headliner, glovebox. Nothing.

"Okay," Popoford said. "Let's roll."

CHAPTER THIRTY-ONE

Contlerust and Sarah had an easy drive from Sacramento to Merced. As she got comfortable with Contlerust, she settled into a mostly confused monolog about America's political climate. It was apparent that though she spoke fluently against the country's founding with prescribed phrases quoted from critical race theory dogma, deep memory tickled her tropes with truths still thriving within her. She would often stop in the middle of a pat argument that presumed to prove the basic racist nature of America only to blurt out an objection.

"But that's bullshit," she'd say. "No one could believe that if they just read the original documents and the histories of the founders. Why are people so lazy?"

"Seems to be a way of life. Know nothing but what someone else tells you to know. Been going on since time began. Trouble is, we used to call that childish. Now they've established a K through post-doc curriculum to maintain that norm. You're one of the valiant ones fighting to get critical thinking back in the schools and especially at Claramon. You do remember that you worked there, right?"

"Yes, but I'm confused about all this."

Contlerust decided to let the conversation drop for a while as she slipped into deep thought. He expected her to figure this whole thing out without much help from him. Time would heal all wounds, he thought, and time might also dilute the serum in her veins.

As he sat there next to her he tried to judge the difference in their ages. He was forty and he put her around thirty-five. An insignificant difference he thought. With the math out of the way, he snuck a look at her, and not for the first time. He was attracted to her when they met, but she was deep into the stress and anger of losing her job and being canceled by her students and colleagues. She was depressed and angry. When she became friends with Millie, Sarah joined them in their cause. His appeared to be a father's role.

It seemed so long ago, but it wasn't. Now he melded his thoughts into his private scheme initiated in the beginning.

By the time they reached Turlock, the sun was going down and the feed corn and young orchards appeared vibrant green against the loam. To the west, there were clouds building and the rain it would bring was a needed drink for the Central Valley. Livestock was being herded into corrals and barns. Farmers and ranchers, their daily toil nearly done, would soon sit at the table together with their families, sharing another meal from the land. Soon they'd make their nightly rounds and later settle into a cool bed to sleep until the cock crowed. These good people, stubborn, proud, and god-fearing were still the measure of America. Along with the men and women in the mines, in the fisheries, the oil and coal fields, and in the skies, at the steel mills, and on the roads; the builders, makers, and growers: these were still the heart of the land. As long as it would be true, Contlerust had hope that America would thrive. Perhaps, he thought, this is where he could find his way, for a thriving America was just the playground his dark thoughts secretly coveted.

When they got to Interstate 80 the nearly full moon had set, and Sarah was awake again and talking.

"How much longer until we get there?"

"No more than thirty minutes."

"Any chance to stop for some food? I need a bathroom, too."

Just the thought of food made his mouth water and the thought of a bathroom automatically placed his urge to go front and center.

"I've seen signs for a truck stop in a couple of miles. How about that?"

"Anything and soon," she said, giving him a smile.

Contlerust, with his recent musings, imagined hidden meaning in her words and gave her a lingering glance. To his surprise, she held his eye an extra beat then blurted out a warning.

"Look out! You're running off the road!"

Contlerust snapped his head around and gracefully returned the car to his lane.

"You need to pay attention to the road," Sarah said. "For now."

He glanced at her again. This time there was no doubt that she found him interesting. They drove the couple of miles together in warm silence, each with the other in mind.

Jimmy's Truck Stop & BBQ was an enormous complex with garages capable of handling six sets of doubles at a time. There was a motel attached conveniently called Jimmy's Rest Stop. "By the Hour or by the Day," the flashing yellow neon announced.

"I'll drop you off in front so you can use the restroom while I park. Okay?"

"I'd rather not go in alone."

"All right," Contlerust said. "But there's nothing to be afraid of."

"I'm not afraid. It's simply better for a girl to be with a man. You probably don't understand, but it's like that with me."

He knew better than to say more, so he parked and they went into Jimmy's, separated, and met again just inside the door looking relieved.

Over a Served-All-Day breakfast, they sat face-to-face for the first time.

"Simon, I get a feeling that I've known you for a long time. Do you feel that way, too?"

"Well, not a long time, but for about a year," he said. "You remember when you were looking for help to get your job back at the College? You gave Millie a call and we met with you. You two have worked together ever since to change the direction of America's educational system.

"Change? How?"

"I know you remember something about it."

"Humor me. I have conflicting memories."

Contlerust was afraid Sarah might have an emotional explosion if he wasn't careful, but he decided that he had to tell her the truth.

"You and the rest of our team were trying to rejuvenate a clandestine program once run by our government to alter and control the minds of its spies so that they'd commit unthinkable crimes without compunction. I was one of those spies. So was Popoford. We plan to use the same program now but with a different focus. We are committed to classical education. To us, students must focus on original documents and critical thinking. We believe we can still recover much of a lost generation."

Sarah gazed at him for a while and finally said. "There were more of us then, weren't there?"

"Yes. More of us, as you said."

"What happened to the others?"

"The other three members were murdered in cold blood. They were in jail for raiding Popoford's house. You were in the same cell with them and saw it all. The person responsible for their murders is Lamia. She's the one who killed them. You were kidnapped by her and your memory transformed."

"Oh, my God," she blurted and tears suddenly filled her eyes. "What have I done."

Contlerust reached out and handed her a napkin for her tears. He took her other hand in his and answered.

"You're not responsible for anything that's happened."

"I knew something was wrong. Even before Millie saved me, I had confusing thoughts. There was something wrong with what happened with Dean Wrenbutt. He wasn't the same, and neither was I. I don't know what to say except help me."

"I'm doing that right now. I'm making it my priority to help you recover all your true memories and your life."

"You are?"

"Yes, if you'll let me."

In response, Sarah squeezed his hand softly.

"Thanks," she said. "We better finish up and get going. You've got to be worn out."

"I'm a bit tired, but we don't have that far to go. Let's just get you home."

Contlerust paid the bill and they drove the rest of the way to Sarah's house in silence.

When they got there, Contlerust walked her to her door. When she stepped inside, she turned back to him.

"Don't stand out there. Come in. You can sleep in the spare room. You look exhausted. Come on. Don't be bashful. I don't bite. Much."

CHAPTER THIRTY-TWO

Millie drove the car into June Lake and headed north on Highway 395. At Lee Vining with Mono lake on the right, its shallow salinity deemed a necessary evil in the effort to water Los Angeles, they took 120 west past Priest, bypassing Old Priest's Road and its frightful grade, down to 49 south through Coulterville and Bear Valley into Mariposa. They stopped for lunch at Castillo's Mexican Restaurant where they both ordered chili Rellenos.

When the road straightened out as they descended to the flatland and they slowed at the outskirts of Planada, Popoford took a long look back towards the foothills. What he saw made him jumpy.

"Millie! Swing the car behind that bar on the right and shut it off. Be ready to pull out when we need to."

Millie was already doing what he asked when she spoke.

"Something on the road?

I'm not sure, but we may have company."

"What do you see?"

"It's a car traveling extremely fast. It's a car with flashing lights. It could be cops, but their siren's off. Either they're after an escapee or they're after us. Looks like they'll be here in two minutes."

"How would they know where we are?"

"What did you do with the tracker I gave you? The one you put on Lamia's car."

"Damn. It's in my pocket."

"Well, grab it and give it to me. I'm going to get rid of it."

Millie snagged the tracker and tossed it to Popoford who was already out the door. He ran across the street and up to an intersection about twenty yards away and then he casually crossed back to the other side again. As he did, he placed the magnetic tracker on the bumper of a car waiting at the stoplight. He rejoined Millie but remained outside the car with his pistol in his hand. Peeking around the corner of the bar, he watched, and soon a car without police markings slowed as it neared the edge of town. Their flashing lights were turned off as they cruised toward the intersection. When they were about two blocks away, the light turned green and the car that had the tracking device on it turned left while the other cars continued on their way. The cop car followed the pack.

Popoford got back into the car and told Millie to follow the police.

"I guess they weren't tracking us after all. But keep a couple of cars between us if you can. If we get too close, pull over for a second. I don't know who they're after, but we need to stay on them. Lamia knows we're coming back to Merced, and Junko probably knows too. The good news is we're the cat now and they're the mouse."

Millie did as Popoford asked though sometimes she ended up behind a slow-moving truck and fell too far behind. When she finally was able to pass, it took a while to spot the car they were following. But as the sun finally set, they were helped in the chase by the flashing lights the car now employed to force vehicles ahead of them to make way and move off to the side of the road. The lights could be seen for miles across the flat landscape. Even when the road was hilly, the red lights flashed against the low clouds moving in with the advancing storm. And when the rain finally came, it was an unusual deluge that hindered visibility, yet the haloed flashing of the red lights continued to urge Millie on.

Soon, she closed in on them to a quarter-mile.

"Why don't you call my dad and warn him that he may be about to get busted? He can tell us where Sarah is, and we all can drive there without worrying about detection."

"That's a better idea, Millie. I'll call him."

"Here's my phone," she said.

Contlerust answered the call on the first ring. "Millie. What's up?"

"It's me, Steven."

"Everything okay?"

"No. We're behind a cop car we're following. They're unmarked but decked out with flashing lights. Thought you should know. Are you in contact with Sarah?"

"Ah, yes. She's right here."

"Where's that?"

"At her house. How far out are you?

"We're just turning on to Arboleda."

"Okay. We'll get ready for trouble here. How far ahead of you are they?"

"It's looking like a quarter-mile. What's the address there?" Popoford asked.

Contlerust told him to drive across town on Yosemite and then take a right on the Snelling Highway. I'll text you the address."

"Got it. We only have one handgun between us. I hope you're better prepared."

"We'll do our best. If you manage to get here before they do, pull into the driveway and keep going through the canopy next to the house. There's a barn in the back where you can park. The storm is hitting hard here, so you might want to let Millie out of the car at the side door."

"Good idea. See you soon."

Popoford hung up and entered Sarah's address into Millie's GPS. "He's with Sarah at her house. Let's see if we can get there first."

Millie increased her speed.

As she neared Snelling Highway, the police car driver put on his turn signals and slowed down. A low whistle escaped Popoford's lips as the driver pulled into a gas station and parked at the pumps. Millie passed them and turned north, slowing in the downpour as streetlights gave way to country darkness. Both she and Popoford squinted into the pounding rain, paying close attention to the ditch on the right, worried she wasn't going to find the house in the deluge. But every so often she caught the glimmer of a farmhouse porch light and finally, the GPS voice pleasantly announced that they had arrived. Millie pulled onto the driveway and under the canopy.

"Time to get out," she announced. "I'll get this thing parked in the garage." but Contlerust was opening her door as she spoke.

"Give me the keys, Millie. I have a raincoat. You and Steven get inside. Sarah has some coffee and hot cocoa waiting. Grab a gun and some ammo for yourselves. Lights out in five when I get back."

Contlerust helped his daughter out of the car and, as soon as they were all headed inside, he drove past the house and into the barn.

Sarah was waiting for them as they walked into the living room.

CHAPTER THIRTY-THREE

Millie didn't know what to expect from Sarah. She approached her smiling and they both hugged. There was a warmth about her that Millie had never seen.

"How have you been?" Millie asked. "Was it a good trip back?"

"I feel better than I have in months," Sarah said. "I've had a lot of time to sort things out and many old memories have come alive again."

"Really? That's great," Millie said.

"Like who I was before I was fired from Claramon. Like what happened in the jail in Whimsy."

"Wow! That's a huge change," Millie said.

"Yeah. Simon has helped me so much. All of you have helped."

Popoford stepped into the room and closed the door.

"Let's have this conversation later. Grab a gun and ammo and douse the lights. Two cars are coming up the road, and my guess is they're coming here."

Simon came in from parking the car.

"Simon, take up a position covering the front door. Millie, cover the back door. And Sarah, you take the side door. I'll be outside working the perimeter."

"Millie, if they get in here, do what you have to do. But if you recognize one of them. Keep him alive."

"Or her?" Millie said.

"Of course.

Everyone did as he said while he grabbed a rain jacket hanging on a mudroom peg and sneaked out the back door.

The storm was blowing full force as Popoford ran across the backyard to the surrounding oak forest. He was at home among the trees and positioned himself at the far edge of the lawn. He had eyes on the back and sides of the house, the driveway, and one side of the barn.

His wait was short. As he took up the surveillance, a black car silently rolled up to the driveway blocking an easy exodus. It cut its engine and turned its flashing lights on. It sat there for ten full minutes, apparently to cause apprehension within Sarah's house.

To an untrained ear, there was no sound except for the wind, rain, and occasional distant thunder. But Popoford had well-trained hearing and his observational talents were almost as acute as a deer's. He was a skilled tracker who could distinguish a woodland intruder's movement and sound from the wild inhabitants. Thus, even with the increasing storm, he caught the sound of two humans, both advancing through the woods from behind.

He waited, listening to the enemy's approach while keeping an eye on the house.

Popoford was standing on the far side of a large oak when the footsteps nearest him stopped. He waited in the shadows without moving. His patience paid off when he heard some words spoken in a hushed voice just a few feet from him.

"Bravo, report." It was a woman.

Popoford couldn't hear the response, but the woman's next words told the story.

"Advance." was all she said, and then she took a step out of the woods toward the house.

As she did, Popoford took one step toward her, and, reaching out his hand, he ripped the headset from her ear and then clasped his other hand over her mouth as she tried to yell a warning no one could hear. He wrapped his arms around her and squeezed hard. When she exhaled, he squeezed tighter. When she tried to inhale, he prevented it. In a few seconds, she was docile and co-operative and Popoford turned her toward him making sure she saw his pistol and putting a finger to his lips to demand quiet.

The look in Lamia's eyes was of disappointment, almost sorrow. Her posture was drooping, deflated.

"You drove a long way just to check up on me," Popoford whispered. "How many of you are there?"

"Only one," she said.

"Really? Call your partner to join you."

"You've got to listen to me," she said. "I'm here to help you. You must understand."

"I said call your partner. You can try to explain yourself to everyone at once."

Lamia gave up and raised her voice ordering the other assailant out of the woods. Soon they were at the back door. With a signal from Popoford, Millie opened it.

"What do we have here?" she said and let them pass.

"Turn on the lights," Popoford called out. "We have company. Simon, disarm and secure them. We're going to let them explain themselves before we dispose of them."

Millie helped Simon put them in straight-backed chairs. Then they handcuffed the pair and tied them to the chairs with rope.

"I must speak to you alone," Lamia said.

"We're all friends here," Popoford replied.

"My associate isn't fully read in on this operation. He must be isolated before we talk."

"Must?" Popoford said. "That's a strong word for someone in your position."

"It's because of my position that I must have privacy."

"Well, dear Leader, since you put it that way."

"What's with 'Dear Leader?" Contlerust said. "Who is this. anyway?"

Popoford gave Contlerust a slight bow of his head.

"Forgive me. I haven't properly introduced our guest. Simon, this is Lamia, the new leader of TAP, the ones that killed our friends and kidnapped Sarah. The one who injected her serum into Sarah and me. The one who will direct the downfall of America."

Contlerust's eyes narrowed. He ground his teeth together with a sound heard by all in the still room.

"I say whack her now," he hissed. "The coyotes around here are hungry and they'll need raw meat when the storm passes."

Sarah, who had joined Contlerust, gasped. "Simon. We can't do that."

Popoford looked at her and wondered what was going on in her head. He recognized an attachment to Contlerust that seemed familiar like between lovers. He looked at Millie who was looking back at him with a quizzical expression. She recognized the same thing.

"Simon," Popoford continued. "We'll save that for later if it's warranted. For now, we'll hear her out. Help me by getting a gag on this guy. We'll get him out of the way for now. We can execute our verdict later."

Popoford and Contlerust lifted the man's chair with him still roped into it.

"Millie, get the back door, will you? Our friend needs some fresh air."

They put the man, chair and all, on the back porch and wrapped another rope around him and a nearby post so he couldn't edge his way off the porch and possibly get loose. Then they returned to the living room and took their seats.

"Now, Lamia. It's your turn. Tell us your tale. It better be good, or you and your sidekick may find your rest in the Merced River before dawn."

As if God was seconding Popoford's threat, a crack of lightning struck in the front yard and, in an instant, the house shook to its foundation with a long, ultra-deep, thunderous rumble that rattled everyone to the bone.

CHAPTER THIRTY-FOUR

Lamia's answer began with a question. "Who am I? Before I answer, consider your past, each of you. Think about why you have to question your thoughts, doubt your sanity, and mistrust everything you believe?

"You, Steven and Simon, more than the others, have so many memories that aren't yours and so many others that are lost, never to be known. Sarah, you have a similarly mixed-up mind. And Millie, you have invested your life in restoring these two men who lost their lives in service to our country and its wellbeing.

"I know the story from beginning to end. That's why I'm here. That's why I got involved with the Resurrection Runner program."

"What's all this crap about?" Contlerust said. "The Resurrection Runner program ended when David Konklin killed Rosiva. Home Office was destroyed."

Lamia shook her head as if at an idiot.

"Home Office was never destroyed," she said flatly. "And the program limps on even though Steven did his best to bury it. Home Office became Section 33, and the program was, pardon the pun, resurrected."

"Somehow, I'm not surprised," Contlerust said. "But TAP is no government organization even if it's quietly supported by many in the government."

"I never said it was. What I'm saying is that I'm an agent of Section 33, and we've developed a serum that approximates the Resurrection Runner drugs."

Popoford looked at her and the others with a skeptical gaze.

"Really? Do you expect us to believe that? After what you did at the Whimsy Jail and how you messed with Sarah and me? Don't forget, I was there. I saw Junko, or John, or whatever he calls himself kill Vladdrac and put you in charge. Don't forget that I'm your new education general. What you're saying would make more sense if you just drop the crap and admit that all you are is a tool of TAP, nothing more."

Lamia was silent for a time. When she finally spoke, her voice was quieter than before but just as earnest.

"I see that you're trapped by your entrenched beliefs. How can I convince you that what I have done is for the betterment of America? I have infiltrated TAP's inner command. I have become their leader. I'm in a position to control all the deceptive, mind-tangling programs they run. I have access to all their banking partners, all their big-business stakeholders, and government acolytes. In my position, I can reverse the tragedy TAP has fomented and all I have to do is get to the three other generals and run them through the new *R*esurrection Runner program and the whole TAP structure will crumble."

"If it were true, it would be a start, but not enough of one to reverse the minds of those on the street and in the schools and the government who are true believers."

"Maybe not at first, but with patience and guts we can get it done," she said. "Doing nothing has failure attached to it. You can't stand there and tell me that you're going to give up, can you? I brought you into the new program, Steven, because I felt you'd relish a chance to crush this evil once and for all. Perhaps our means have become too harsh for you to handle in your advancing age. Perhaps I thought you were a man, when, in fact, you're not."

"You certainly are a twister of words, aren't you?" Popoford said. "Tell me, how was I able to defeat your new serum so easily?"

"I was trying to improve the drug to reverse their grip on your lives. Sure, it needs more work. But that doesn't suggest dropping the program. Don't you see that TAP is already on the way to ruling the world? They don't need drugs when they have the means to control all our minds from the womb to the tomb. If you can't understand that then I'm lost. Do with me what you will. I've failed just when it looked like victory was ours."

Popoford once again sat quietly for a while. When he finally spoke, his tone was different.

"Tell me what happened at the jail."

Lamia sighed. Her gaze was unfocused as her mind concentrated on her memories. Her expression pinched her face as if revolted by her thoughts.

"Why don't you untie me first? This is a bit overboard don't you think?"

Popoford gestured to Contlerust to do it.

"Thanks," she said and took a deep breath before continuing. "When I arrived in Whimsy, I went directly to the Sheriff's office. Someone had been there before I arrived. The sheriff was on the floor and there were four inmates. Three of them had multiple gunshot wounds, but the killer spared the fourth one. She was in shock. I took her into custody and left Whimsy. She was in my protective custody from then on."

"Protective?" Millie said. "As in beating her up? As in corrupting her mind? Putting her in danger? Siccing Albert on her."

"I needed a subject to test my serum. If I could turn her beliefs around, it would be a feather in my cap and a way to achieve more access to Vladdrac and more power in TAP's organization."

Popoford glared at her with a look earned by many wasted years serving an agency with an identically amoral philosophy.

"So, it's all's fair in love and war with you. To hell with the little victims. Focus on the bigger picture. No one who gains by your cruelty will condemn you, not if their power is increased. Why is it that the world continues to revolve on this repeating corruption?"

Sarah answered Popoford's question.

"Because of people like Lamia who falsely believe that the ends justify the means. It's an immorality continuously renewed in innocent minds by all tyrants, many of whom believe devilish plans are a holy crusade."

"Exactly," Popoford said, addressing Lamia. "Why would we throw in with you? From my experience, the clandestine government has motives that parallel TAP's."

"You have great esteem for yourself, Steven," Lamia said. "But you have neither the tools nor the funding to challenge TAP. And you minimize the importance of me being its leader. With your help, we can take them down. By yourself, you will fail. I can do it on my own, but I want to get it done as fast as possible. I need you to do that, and you need me if you hope for success. I'm offering you access. If you won't work with me, you're an egomaniac and it's all about you."

"It's about our friends who were killed and our country which is fading away."

"On that, we agree. Why don't you all figure out what you're going to do so I can get back to my job? If you reject me, so be it, but your lack of faith may defeat an otherwise certain victory."

"You tried to kill me!" Sarah countered.

Lamia raised her eyebrows and let a smile cross her face. "Yes, I did. At the time, it seemed necessary so I could prove my loyalty to Vladdrac. Luckily, Albert's a putz."

"Lucky I didn't kill him," Millie said. "Who's the bum you brought along tonight?"

"He's the Section 33 western field ops chief."

"Why did you bring him with you?"

"For backup."

"Are all your Section 33 operatives as effective as the two of you?"

"Can't you grasp what I'm saying? We're wasting time. I'm here offering you a way to make your dreams come true. Pull your heads out and take the risk. You're washed up if you don't."

Popoford looked at the others. There was no expression on his face, but he paused as he moved from one to the next, holding their eyes for as long as it took for him to count their vote. The last one he queried was Millie and she was the slowest to respond. When she finally raised her left eyebrow a fraction and curled the right side of her mouth in a "why not" expression, Popoford faced Lamia as he spoke to Contlerust.

"Get the guy out of the rain, Simon. Looks like we're taking on some partners."

Simon opened the back door, looked out, and immediately slammed it shut and locked it.

"Better tie her up again. The chair's still there but the guy's gone."

CHAPTER THIRTY-FIVE

Popoford was in action at once. "Strap her down. Take your defensive positions. Millie, you come with me. Move!" Millie grabbed a rifle and was at the door first as Popoford snatched Lamia by the hair and pulled her head back to see her eyes.

"You didn't bring enough of your thugs. You know that, right?" and he darted out the door before she could respond.

Outside, the rain had slackened but it still fell softly making its presence known just enough to be irritating. The moon was hidden behind a black cloud but its light escaped to the windward providing enough illumination for Popoford to see figures moving up the driveway. He signaled Millie to retreat into the woods and he did the same burying himself ten yards within the soaking trunks before he headed in her direction. When he found her, they moved together to the edge of the trees. There was a five-man entry team preparing an assault on the backdoor. Popoford was calm and deliberate.

"They're all zipped up in body armor. Take steady aim. I want them alive. You know the drill. Let's do this."

Millie knew nothing about "the drill" Popoford referred to, and if he wanted them alive, then why was she aiming at all? Confused but amped up and ready for action, she charged the five paramilitary operatives until she was within a few feet of their leader and then let loose with a banshee cry that stopped them dead in their tracks. Popoford kept his sights on the leader as he advanced. The man's mouth was agape.

"Freeze!" Millie yelled. "Freeze! One move and you're all dead."

The startled attackers followed her orders and froze in place, all except for the one in the lead who saw Millie but missed Popoford in the rush. Recognizing the threat he faced and seeing his duty, the man swung his rifle fifteen degrees away from the door he intended to breach and was lining up his sights between Millie's eyes when Popoford's gun butt crushed into his right temple. The attack leader, bearing the weight of his lethal steel, crumpled with a clatter. The other members of the team lowered their weapons and raised their unencumbered hands. All five men were out of the fight and were soon cinched up in their own handcuffs and hogtied on the soaking lawn.

Inside, Sarah and Contlerust maintained defensive positions, one behind a couch in the living room and the other behind the kitchen island. Millie came in from the back and called for Sarah to help her disarm their captives.

Suddenly, Popoford burst through the back door and grabbed Lamia by the throat, lifting her and the chair off the floor. His rage seemed uncontrollable as he bellowed vile curses for long seconds that seemed like minutes. It was Millie's hand raised in his face and Contlerust's arms wrapped around his chest that finally subdued the bulldog possessing him. They had to hold him back a second time when Lamia, now set back on the floor, gave him a sardonic smile, and whispered as if to herself, "Better luck next time."

"Millie, you and Simon get their cars into the barn," he said. "Be careful. There may be others skulking about. Sarah, do you have any alcohol in the house?"

She nodded, still in shock herself.

"Get a bottle of scotch, if you have it, and bring it here."

He took a seat in front of Lamia and shook off Millie's concerned glance. Drinking at a time like this was trouble.

"It's time you leveled with me, Lamia. They used to tell me that I can be so cruel. They used to remind me what a cold beast I was. All I know is what they claimed because they wiped my mind of most of my heinous crimes. Once in a while, they'd produce photographs and say that I'd done the awful things they showed me. They said that I could expertly employ Apache and Roman tortures like flaying an enemy, enjoying seeing his guts lying twisted on the floor, the man's stripped flesh draped upon my back as tribute, savoring his raw, screaming nerves. I don't know if I believe what I was told. I was lied to a lot. Still, I find it curious that I know the technique. I have the will to do that to you, Lamia. It's not too complicated and you deserve a lingering death."

Lamia held his eyes; she had overlooked his icy stare. His lunacy was different from Vladdrac's insanity. It was more like Junko's sadism. Popoford was crazy. His file hadn't revealed the depth of his depravity yet she knew the Resurrection Runner program had created this monster. She dared not provoke him.

"What do you want?" she asked without inflection.

"The hardest thing for you to give. The truth."

Her expression had turned placid, but Popoford could see her constricted pupils, and he knew she was grasping for a way out.

"You have no choice," he said as he took the bottle from Sarah and glanced at Millie, winking his good eye, the one turned away from Lamia. "Do you like scotch, Lamia?"

"Not really."

"Well, you're going to learn to love it tonight."

With that, he stood up and grabbed her jaw, forcing it open as he poured the whisky down her throat.

"There's more in the bottle and it's all yours. All for you. Maybe you'll live. Maybe not. I don't much care. I'll stop pouring when you start telling the truth. When you stop cooperating I start pouring again. Understand? Truth or consequences. The deadly version."

He started simply. "Five of your boys are out of commission. Are there any more with you or on the way?"

"No," she said, gagging.

"Where is Junko?"

"I don't know."

Popoford poured more scotch down her throat, making her swallow it, gagging and choking.

"Junko," he said.

"He's at the mansion."

"What were you supposed to do tonight?"

"You should know that," she said slurring her words.

"Tell me," he said. "Use your words."

Lamia smiled at that. "He wants you all dead."

"Including me, his newest general?"

"No. Junko knows who you are. He wants you for himself."

"You must be the last one to figure that out. We go back a long way."

Her eyes were turning red and she was having a hard time keeping her head up to look at Popoford.

"But you've got me wrong. I'm with Section 33. I really am," she slurred, collapsed, and passed out.

CHAPTER THIRTY-SIX

While Lamia slept off the first round of drinks, Contlerust and Sarah went to the bound men and forced them into the barn, leaving them strapped to a series of barn poles. It was still a few hours before dawn when they came back to the house, Lamia was passed out, but the others were talking.

"What are we going to do with the men and Lamia?" Millie said.

"It's Lamia I'm most concerned about," Contlerust replied. "If she's with the feds, we should help her. If she's not, she needs to be eliminated."

"Or turned over to the proper authorities," Sarah replied.

"What good would that do? There's no guarantee she'd be brought to justice. She'd just continue doing what she does."

"So you agree that she should be killed?" Sarah asked him.

"No. Not at this point. I'm in favor of letting her continue as the head of TAP. If she's telling the truth, it would be the best way to take them down. If she's lying, she may divulge information that would help us eliminate them anyway."

Then Millie chimed in. "Aren't we supposed to be changing the educational system by re-educating people like Wrenbutt? Why let TAP dictate our plans?"

They all sat quietly for a minute and finally Sarah spoke up.

"Millie's right. There's no reason to stop what we've already started. I'm getting my memory back more rapidly every hour, and I want to see Wrenbutt again. He should be the focus. At least for me."

Popoford nodded. "You need to contact him tomorrow. In the meantime, I'm leaning towards letting Lamia go even if she's lying about Section 33. I fear that she's not and that our government is either operating a Resurrection Runner program on their own or they're in cahoots with TAP. Both possibilities are bad. I say let her run and see what she does."

Now Contlerust returned to Millie's question about the men and their guns.

"What about them? One of them needs a doctor and all of them need to be gone."

"We'll take care of them later. It's time to rouse Lamia," Popoford said. "She needs to answer a few more questions."

With everyone gathered around, Popoford got her attention with a full glass of straight scotch under her nose. She winced at its peaty aroma and her eyes opened wider as she turned her head away.

"I take it you haven't grown fond of my favorite drink."

"Hell no. I'm going to puke."

"I wouldn't if I were you. You'd be covered with it. The rule is you clean up your own messes."

"How chivalrous you are."

"Tell us about Section 33. I'm intrigued. What about the Normalcy Project?"

"We are re-creating Resurrection Runner to accelerate an education program that will rapidly cancel the perversion that has seeped into our public school in the last sixty years."

"Interesting. I've heard of that plan."

"I suppose you have," she said. "It's similar to Contlerust's plan."

"How did you know about that?" Contlerust asked.

"I've tracked you and your group of conspirators for months. You weren't as clandestine as you thought. It was you who led me to Whimsy and Popoford. We were after the same formula. If the sheriff and your friends were alive, we'd have it now. Instead, I'm relying on my serum."

"But yours doesn't work."

"That's too harsh," she said. "It worked on you and Sarah."

"Not really. Both Sarah and I have recovered our thoughts and memories. You have no control over us."

"You have to give me credit for trying, and for the way I got you into the leadership of TAP?"

"I think Junko will have something more to say about that."

"Look, you're wasting time. I told you when you grabbed me that I wanted to talk to you alone. Get the others out of here and I'll give you some information that will prove who I am."

Popoford studied her face. He couldn't see any deception in it, but that wasn't reassuring. Whether she was the TAP leader or a Section 33 agent, she was their enemy.

"Let me have a minute alone with her," he told the others. "It can't hurt, and we might as well get past this roadblock."

Millie wasn't happy about it, but she herded the others into the kitchen.

"So, what do you have to say in private that you couldn't say to me at headquarters? What is it that's so secret?"

"Junko was at headquarters. What I have to say to you is for your ears only."

"So get on with it," Popoford said.

"March in lockstep, Steven," she replied, quietly, and Popoford clasped his hands in his lap. His expression relaxed and his head canted to his right like an expectant dog. "Who is Steven Popoford?"

"I am," he said.

"Correct. You're a Section 33 agent. Tell me what you are."

"I'm a Section 33 agent."

"Your mission is to provide the Resurrection Runner serum to Section 33. What is your mission?"

"To provide the Resurrection Runner serum to Section 33."

"Right. Are you ready to complete your mission?"

"As always," he said.

"Where's the serum?"

"In Whimsy," Popoford said.

"Okay, untie me."

Popoford did as he was told.

Once he had freed her, she took Popoford's pistol. "Call the others back in here."

Popoford did as he was told. When they entered the room, Lamia fired a round into the floor. The shot startled them all.

"Everyone be calm. Steven understands how important it is that we work together. We want the same result as you, though we have different points of view. Isn't that right, Steven?"

"Yes, it is. Lamia has convinced me to work with her to stop TAP. I hope you will all join me in this effort."

Millie was dumbfounded. Popoford's features were distorted, his expression off-kilter. His eyes were vacant and his smile apologetic. While she was in the kitchen his vitality had faded. She glared at Lamia and swore vengeance on her for his condition.

Lamia and Popoford went outside and as he turned to close the back door, he looked straight at Millie and darted his eye from her to the front of the house repeating the bizarre twitch over and over again until the door shut.

Millie grabbed her raincoat at once and as she slid into the storm, she called to her father and Sarah. "Dad, you and Sarah get in touch with Wrenbutt in the morning. We need to have a meeting with him tomorrow."

Millie slipped around the side of the house. From there she could see Popoford and Lamia entering the garage. She moved quickly, ducking her head against the unruly wind until she took cover in the barn's lee. There she snuck up to a small window and peeked in. The bare bulb swinging freely from a cord strung from the rafters cast a rhythmic shadow dance upon the walls. Lamia and Popoford were on opposite sides of her car pulling the trussed-up men out and untying them. When they were all freed, the men crammed into the back seat and Lamia got into the driver's side. Popoford took shotgun.

Millie stepped around to the barn's front corner when the car was backed out of the garage. Lamia had her head twisted around so she could see out the back window, but Popoford was looking straight at Millie. As the car backed into the darkness, he put his hand to his lips, and then he made a subtle gesture that Millie caught even through the windshield and the thrashing wipers. She blew him a kiss in return as Lamia drove away.

Millie then jumped into her car, following them running silent, running dark.

CHAPTER THIRTY-SEVEN

Following Lamia's car was treacherous. Without headlights, Millie could only squint through the mist to keep track of the road's shoulders and remain in contact with Lamia's lights. It was an effort so intense that she developed a headache within minutes. Her safety was only possible because no other drivers were crazy enough to be on the road. Millie drove too fast until Lamia finally slowed and made a turn onto a farm road. She braked and shut off her lights.

"Thank you, Lord," she prayed out loud.

Millie slowly pulled onto the farm road with her lights still off and drove slowly behind Lamia. She glimpsed a house way in the back of the property. When Lamia stopped, Millie parked her car in the middle of the road going the rest of the way on foot.

As she moved slowly closer, she kept her eyes on her quarry. Lamia and Popoford entered the house. Someone turned on a single light, and Lamia could be seen closing the curtains. Two of her raiding team entered the house supporting their injured partners. When the door closed, Millie rushed forward and took a position next to the door.

Inside, Popoford went to the fireplace and started a fire. He removed the logs that were already stacked on the grate and replaced them with a dry log to keep smoke at a minimum. He needn't have worried. The fire was roaring in minutes producing a steady updraft. Smoke rose from the chimney and into the wind swirling its scent about the roof and the house. Millie looked up as lightning from a distant bolt backlit the house. An idea came to her.

Returning to her car, she grabbed a blanket from the trunk and returned, but ran further up the drive to the garage.

She slipped around a parked car parked in the garage and found a ladder. She carried it to the back of the house where she silently set it up against the eaves.

As if he knew what was happening outside, Popoford put another couple of logs on the fire but this time they were soaking wet.

"Get comfortable, Steven," Lamia said. "Do you want something to drink?"

"Water, please."

"No scotch?" she said. When she returned with his water, she was direct.

"I need your serum as soon as possible. How much do you have and where is it?"

His answer was slow in coming as he continued to act the fool. Lamia's hypnotic phrase proved ineffective though he appeared to be under her control. He turned to her, his eyes downcast, his demeanor humble.

"There are only thirteen doses left. That's four full vials and one partially empty They're all in a freezer in my basement in Whimsy."

"Now, wasn't that easy? I knew we could work together. After all, we have the same goals."

"What goals do you mean?"

"To reset the educational structure of America. To establish a curriculum that promotes defined principles. To clean up what's wrong with this country."

"I see what you mean," Popoford said. "We must control what is taught."

"Of course. The hodgepodge of thought has become an untenable burden. And the Brilliance in Basics program is driving us to Communism. I trust you agree."

"Oh, of course," Popoford lied, her version of freedom taking a special step backward with her own totalitarian taste for censorship.

"Good. In the morning we're going to drive to Whimsy to secure the serum. Once I have the serum and all the documentation you have, I'll drive south and take up my position as head of TAP. You'll stay in Whimsy and play the role of The General of Education."

Popoford's nod was enough for her.

"Okay. My guys are getting something to eat. If you're hungry, join them in the kitchen. If not, sit down and take it easy. We'll be leaving soon."

She left the room without saying more and stopped at the kitchen door and spoke to her Ops Chief.

"Pack it in, Joc. I'm sending you boys back to D.C. I'll be taking Popoford home. He's got the motherload stashed at his place in Whimsy. I'll be upstairs. When your guys are fed and rested, give me a yell."

"Yes, Ma'am," her Section 33 field ops chief replied.

Popoford listened for Lamia's footsteps on the stairs. The men in the kitchen were talking quietly, unconcerned by him. Still, he was cautious when he rose and moved to the fireplace again. He stood listening at the chimney as if in a trance and then he heard soft footsteps above. His premonition had been correct. Millie was on the roof.

He poked the fire urging the wet wood to ignite. Steam soon turned to fire and fire to a chimney full of rising black smoke. Then he heard the sound of Millie's blanket thwacking overhead. In seconds, the blocked chimney belched its smoke into the room.

As soon as Popoford knew that the chimney was blocked, he sat down again and feigned sleep. In seconds he was back in action.

The men in the kitchen came running into the living room to see what was happening. Finding Popoford there, they grabbed him and walked him out of the soot, into the fresh air. The rain had stopped, but the rain-laden clouds blocked the stars and the moon. Presently Joe, the Section 33 field ops boss, came through the door helping Lamia while she convulsively hacked the smoke from her lungs. Someone must have called the fire department because a siren and flashing lights announced their imminent arrival. Through all this turmoil, Millie came down off the roof and ran across the field to her parked car further down the driveway.

Once in, she waited until the fire truck arrived, and when it did, Millie turned the engine over leaving her running lights off. As the truck pulled into the driveway, Millie stepped on the accelerator and raced toward the house.

Lamia and her men stood in the smoke watching the speeding car approach. They lost track of Popoford who edged to the rear of their gaggle. He was in the right place when Millie reached the house and skidded into a u-turn trailing a gravel rooster tail. She snapped her high beams on just as she came to a stop only long enough for Popoford to scramble into the front seat. He slammed the door closed as she floored it back down the driveway straight at the still-advancing fire truck. Before she crashed headlong into it, she swung into the soggy field and, with tires spewing mud, she found the driveway once more. In seconds, she was out on the road and away.

Popoford looked out the back window at the turmoil left behind. "We've got to get Simon and Sarah. Lamia will want to grab them before she heads to Whimsy."

"Why is she going there?" Millie asked.

"To get the serum I said is stashed there."

"I think we better get there first," she said.

CHAPTER THIRTY-EIGHT

The storm had passed by the time they arrived at Sarah's house and the sun rose in full radiance while the departing clouds left a sparkling southeast sky.

Sarah was dressed and ready for her Wrenbutt meeting at nine o'clock. Contlerust was finishing a cup of coffee.

"We have to go!" Popoford insisted as he came through the door. "Lamia and her boys are tied up for a while with the fire department, but they'll be here soon enough. If she catches us it's all over."

"What's happened?" Contlerust said.

"I was faking being under her control. She wanted to know about the original Resurrection Runner serum and the techniques they used on us. I told her that I have lots of it at home in Whimsy. She planned to take me there, but Millie came to the rescue before we could go."

"Well that sucks," Contlerust said.

"More than you know. Section 33 is the new Resurrection Runner. She plans to stifle free speech by inserting her mind-adjusted hacks into the education system."

"You mean like we're trying to do?" Contlerust said. "Like TAP is trying to do. Like you're trying to do."

"Not me. I want to encourage free speech. Lamia wants to do the same thing as TAP does just with a different result in mind. They both want to control acceptable speech."

"You're as much a part of it as I am," Contlerust replied.

"Look," Popoford said. "You and I both need to get to Whimsy before she does."

"That could be arranged."

"How's that?" Popoford said.

"I can fly a plane and you can't. Also, I'm retired air force and I have a few local buddies who can help. You understand?"

Popoford winced. If there was one thing he didn't like to do it was to fly in a private plane.

"What's wrong? It's the only way to get there before her. We might be able to hitch a ride with a friend of mine. I'll give him a call. He owes me, anyway."

"I hate little planes."

"Tough. We'll fly whatever he has to offer," Contlerust said.

Contlerust got his friend on the phone and they talked for a few minutes. When he hung up, he had a big smile on his face.

"Slick!" he said. He's in the air right now and only a short flight away, What he's got for us is something special."

"Not hang gliders, I hope."

"Hardly. This is a recently decommissioned AFSOC U-28. It usually takes a crew of four, but the two of us can fly it just fine. He's heading to the Merced airport now where he'll land, refuel, and complete pre-flight. It's wheels up when we get there."

"What about your meeting with Wrenbutt?" Popoford asked.

"Well, it's just the two of us going to Whimsy, Millie can be with Sarah when she meets Wrenbutt. That might be better anyway."

"Are you okay with that?" Popoford asked her.

"I can do it," was all Millie said, obviously not happy with the idea.

"Millie?" Popoford asked.

"I just hope Wrenbutt doesn't remember me."

Popoford was the only one who laughed.

"All right, I don't have any baggage, but I have a gun," he said. "Millie, will you come with us to the airport so you can drive the car back?"

"Sure," she said.

"Okay. Let's go," Contlerust said.

The three of them drove twenty minutes west to the Merced Municipal Airport. It was a well-kept landing strip with a small office. Contlerust's friend was waiting next to his plane when Popoford parked. They all got out and Contlerust walked to the waiting plane. Popoford turned to Millie.

"Keep your phone charged. I'll talk to you soon."

"Be careful, Steven," she said. "You never know what Lamia will do."

"I think you have that backwards."

With an uncontrolled impulse, he reached out and pulled her to his chest. Placing her face in both of his hands, he bent to kiss her as she rose on her tiptoes to meet his lips. The rushing release heated their souls and the inevitable words he'd been forestalling mixed with her hot breath.

"I love you," he whispered over and over again, gasping, and continually finding her lips again. It was Millie who gently pushed away, blushing, and breathing deeply.

"Wow. The giant awakes! I want to go with you."

"I want you to, but I need you here with Sarah."

"I know. How long will you be gone?"

"I don't know, but I'll make it as quick as I can."

"You promised to call," Millie said as he turned to go.

"I will. As soon as we get Lamia taken care of. I'll be thinking of you the whole time."

As Popoford took his first step towards the plane, Millie said one more thing.

"I love you, too, Steven Popoford."

He turned back quickly and grabbed her again, giving her a long, deep kiss, enough to last them both until they met again.

Then he hurried to the plane where Contlerust cast his fatherly gaze on him and introduced his friend.

"This is Steven. Steven, Jack."

"Good to meet you, Steven."

"He doesn't like to fly in small planes, Jack."

"What, like Piper Cubs? Well, this baby's a lot bigger than that. We should have a smooth ride, even over the Sierras."

"Hey, I'm ready to go," Popoford said. "Today my motto's 'the end justifies the means."

"Okay, hop aboard and I'll get the engines warmed up. Simon, give me a hand with my pre-check, will you?"

"Sure," Contlerust said.

Popoford stepped through the fuselage door and entered the stripped interior. There were only two seats in the cabin and two on the flight deck. All the equipment installed when the Draco was used for ISM missions in Iraq and other theaters of war had been stripped out. The only hint that there was once much more to the plane's capabilities was the many clipped and capped electrical wires dangling from the interior walls. There was a pair of porthole windows so Popoford could see what was going on outside. The flight deck was visible as well and he watched Jack run through his pre-flight sequence. It wasn't long until Contlerust climbed aboard and strapped in next to Jack.

"You okay back there?" he asked.

"Doing good," Popoford replied.

In a few minutes, Jack turned in his seat to look at Popoford.

"Seat belt, Steven. And keep it on until we disembark. Flight time with a headwind is about an hour."

"Give us what you can. The sooner the better."

"Roger that," Jack said, and Contlerust gave them both a thumbs up.

Popoford looked out the window at Millie who was still standing by the car, waving. In a minute they were airborne and Jack had set his course to the northeast banking away from Merced and hiding Millie's face from view. Popoford settled into his seat consumed with thoughts of her and longing he had never known.

The flight started far smoother than the private plane flight he'd made years before. He thought of those days less often now, and he dismissed them as warm weariness overtook him and he slipped to sleep.

Fair dreams were overshadowed by an overwhelming nightmare that spared him no pain for he was endlessly searching, a companion at his side, a friend at first but transforming into evil itself, keeping its arm wrapped around him as he struggled to find his way. Like a leech, it continuously drained his strength by murmuring dismal expectations to counter his every hope. And all the while it called him friend.

At times, his dementia conjured a happy ending, a trophy won at the finish line. Yet on it went, purring and muttering, hissing, and mumbling, always drawing him from the light to its darkness.

Once he was certain he had broken free as it let him run for a time in sunlight and fresh breezes. Millie was there and they held hands as they slid through the tall grasses. In love. Such a wondrous thing! But his joy faded and the way ahead finally turned miserably black. Millie let go of his hand and his crazed mind carried him to its hopeless depths, there to repeat the nightmare for eternity.

Popoford woke with a jolt, soaked in sweat and gasping for air.

Contlerust was at his side. “You’re having a panic attack. It’s just a little turbulence. Nothing to worry about. Here, have some water and take a deep breath. It’s okay, Steven. You’ll get used to it.”

“I doubt it,” Popoford said. “but thanks. How’s our time?”

“We’ll touch down as planned right about seven. We should be in Whimsy before eight. We should get something to eat.”

“We’ll wait until we get home,” Popoford said. “There’s no time to waste.”

“Okay. It’s your call.”

“ Did you make plans for a car at the airport?”

“Jack made arrangements before we left. There’s a car waiting for us.”

“Good,” Popoford said and peered out the porthole.

The foothills below were sun-drenched and the hills were green. From nearly thirty-thousand feet above, the spring foliage presented a romanticist's dabbed, verdant pallet. Endlessly varied shades of green and yellow swept towards the Sierra peaks. Blue-grey runoff filled snaking channels with late winter melt, the sun glinting off myriad rapids, and occasional falls. Beyond, the eastern slope was thick with the green shades of grey pine and blue oak. Popoford was too far up to make out the madrone, buckeye, manzanita, redbud, or red willow he knew were there for he had hiked through similar woods for years and knew what to expect on the ground below. His woodcraft and tracking abilities had allowed him to venture far from home on his hunting trips. He knew the wildlife trails around Whimsy well enough to trek them with ease in the gloaming and the day’s first light alike. He called the eastern Sierras home and he was happy to be returning to them even under duress.

They landed at the Truckee Tahoe Airport five minutes early and the car was waiting for them on the tarmac. Popoford took the wheel and Contlerust sat in the passenger seat. They both carried Sig M18s under their jackets. Popoford had a California CCW license, but Contlerust didn't. He was counting on some fake State Department ID he had just revealed to Popoford.

"How did you get that?" Popoford asked.

"Jack has his ways. He's mighty handy to have around when I need him."

" I would think so. Isn't he coming with us?"

"No. He'll stay with the plane so we can get out of here as soon as we're done."

"Right. Good thinking. Let's get going. I sure don't want to see Lamia on the road, and I don't want her to get there before we do."

It was an hour's drive to Whimsy and another ten minutes further to Popoford's house. When they arrived, Popoford stopped the car at the edge of the clearing and rolled down the window listening for any telltale sound.

It was quiet except for the chuckling squirrels and the staccato tapping of the Hairy woodpeckers. A pair of frogs croaked one to the other by the creek past the far side of the clearing. Popoford listened beyond these familiar sounds for any strange rustlings and paid close attention to the ridge that overlooked his house. Hearing and seeing nothing unusual, he drove into the clearing, swung the car around, and backed in behind the house where he switched off the engine.

"She may come in on foot," he said. Contlerust understood and didn't reply.

They worked rapidly exiting the car and grabbing their rifles and extra mags.

"She'll want to come in through the front door. I'll unlock the door so she doesn't smash it in."

Once done, he led a surprised Contlerust to the woods where he disclosed the tunnel hatch. They paused for a second and it was Contlerust who spoke first.

"Someone's coming. I can hear a car on the gravel road moving slowly,"

"I hear it," Popoford said. "It's her. She just parked. She'll come the rest of the way on foot."

Popoford entered the tunnel first and descended the ladder. Contlerust followed him lowering the hatch. When it was closed, Popoford switched on the light.

CHAPTER THIRTY-NINE

Popoford took his time as he led the way. He was attuned to every sound and wasn't about to underestimate Lamia's abilities. He moved with rhythmic purpose showing Contlerust where each footstep should be taken so they could silently move to the trapdoor hidden in his bedroom closet. At the end of the tunnel, they stopped and took up positions behind some crates. Popoford signaled Contlerust to cover the stairs in front of them as they waited. The wait wasn't long.

Popoford put his finger to his lips signaling quiet, and then he pointed to the ceiling light. Contlerust nodded and Popoford reached a switch on the wall and switched the lights off. It was so quiet they could hear Lamia approaching the front door. They waited to hear the knob turn and the door swing open. A blistering shattering startled them so much that they almost cried out as the door crashed into the house. Stifling their instincts, they listened as Lamia entered and searched the place.

They calmed themselves and waited, hearing her rummage through drawers and cupboards, searching every room. When they heard her on her hands and knees crawling around the floor, Popoford knew she'd find the trapdoor in minutes. She was more efficient than expected and instantly the trapdoor was flung open and a brilliant flashlight beam temporarily blinded the men.

Popoford and Contlerust opened fire depleting their ammunition at the same instant. As the racket reverberated and diminished deep in the tunnel, they were reaching for backup mags when Lamia stepped onto the landing. She flipped on the light and fired two rounds in the dirt next to their feet.

"Little boys shouldn't play with big girls," she said. "They might get outsmarted. Hands up, you two buffoons. Step out where I can see you."

The men stepped out as instructed.

"Turn on the light, Steven," she said and continued. "March in Lockstep, Steven."

Popoford just smiled at her.

"What is it about you, Steven?" she said. "How did you overcome my serum?"

"I don't care what you call it, it doesn't last long," Popoford said. "And what you think is hypnotism wouldn't mesmerize a chicken. I've played you since the beginning."

"Now who's got it all wrong?" she said. "I'm here to collect all the original Resurrection Runner serum you have. I'm going to get it even if it takes a little extra convincing."

"Like what? Waterboarding? I've suffered that before. I can handle it."

"No, not waterboarding. Old school torture meets the new world," she said. "Like these."

Lamia tossed a package to Popoford. He caught it.

"Open it," she ordered.

There were two thick rings inside. They were simple bands like wedding rings but the metal was dark and thick and there were two small LEDs installed close together on each of them.

"What are these for?" Popoford asked.

"I'll show you, Steven. It's something you won't like, but don't worry, they're not for you. At least not now."

"So what am I supposed to do, accept your hand in marriage?"

"You're such a dope, Steven. Here's what you're going to do. One at a time put the rings on Contlerust's thumbs."

Popoford's quizzical expression amused Lamia. "We're going to play a little game, Steven. Do what I tell you to do."

To emphasize her point, she fired a round between his legs.

Popoford turned to Contlerust who shrugged and stuck out his hands.

"Hold them with your fingers pointing straight up and your thumbs straight out," Lamia said. "Now, Steven put the rings on his thumbs."

As she said this, she placed her hand in her pocket and pulled out a small keypad all the while smiling at Contlerust.

"You understand that I can't hurt Steven, don't you Simon? He knows where the serum is and you don't. But Steven has a flaw. Do you know what it is?"

Contlerust's eyes narrowed perceptibly and a nasty smirk expanded on his face.

"He's a softy. He's a Jesus-loving guy. He hates to see any creature suffer."

"That's excellent!" Lamia said. "Yes. How did you know? Maybe we could end up working together when I'm done here."

"I doubt it," Contlerust said.

"Well, I'll be the judge of that," she responded. "For now, you're going to be the one that suffers. If I were you, I'd pray that he really does think that way, because you're about to suffer more than you can imagine and only Steven Popoford can save you."

Contlerust's smirk grew into a sneer and a growl rose from his chest much like the cry of a wild beast.

Lamia was tired of his demonstration and aimed the keypad at him while pushing one of its two buttons.

Immediately, the rings on Contlerust's thumbs began to constrict. Feeling them tighten, he grasped them with apposing hands and tried to rip them off his thumbs. His efforts failed as the rings were already too tight to be removed.

Panic crossed his face but at once was controlled. His sneer became gape-mouthed astonishment, his glare turned to steel.

Lamia continued the slowly increasing constriction and his agonizing pain. As she increased his suffering, she turned to Popoford.

"Even you must see that Simon is your responsibility. You can make the pain stop at any time. All you have to do is tell me where the serum is. Produce it and all this will be over. Refuse, and Simon's thumbs will be crushed and severed. It can take as long as you wish. I've seen these thumb screws work for a full week. Do you think he can take it? If it were you could you take it? And what do you think he'll do to you when it's over? You who let him suffer for a problem so easily solved. I'm just going to stand here on this stoop and wait for you to give me the answer I need. In the end, you'll do it. Why not do it now for Simon's sake?"

Popoford's mind raced through a dozen scenarios in an instant. They all ended in his or Contlerust's death. Lamia was right, he couldn't deal with that. He steadied himself because he knew what he was about to do could unleash an institutional hell on the country. Letting a government agency get the last of the Resurrection Runner program serum could result in liberty's death. He had agreed to help Contlerust use the serum to counter the corrupted educational system as well as to avenge his friend, Sheriff Florter. But he had to let Lamia win in the hope he could stop her later.

"Okay. Let up on Simon. I'll show you where the other vials are."

"Such sacrifice is impressive," Lamia said. "Predictable but significant. Your wish is my command."

She aimed the wand at Contlerust and pushed a button. The red light on his thumb screws turned green and the pressure was relieved. As soon as he could, he gingerly pulled the rings from his thumbs and put the torture devices in his pockets.

"Both of you take two more steps back from your guns. That's it. Now, Steven, it's your show. Where are you keeping the vials?"

"You're standing on them," he said. "The step you're on lifts up to disclose a small refrigerator. The last of the serum is inside."

"Okay. Is there a lock on it?"

"Yes, of course."

"Do you have the keys on you?"

"No."

"Where are they?"

"There are no keys."

With that, Lamia pulled her pistol's trigger. Her bullet once again hit the packed floor between Popoford and Contlerust spraying dirt and ricocheting against the cave's wall.

"Enough of this crap!" Lamia said. "How do you open it?"

"There's a series of slides like a Chinese mystery box. Move them in the correct sequence and the tread will lift off."

"Get up here and do it. Now!"

Popoford glanced at Contlerust and nodded, but his compatriot laid a death stare on him. "Understandable," he thought and climbed the stairs.

When he was able to reach the hidden box, he leaned over, and with practiced hands, he pushed and pulled the milled slats in the correct order and lifted the tread. Under it was the refrigerator box that he also opened. Then he took a step back down the stairs.

"Go all the way down, Steven," Lamia told him. "I'm not fool enough to have you within striking distance while I'm grabbing the goods."

Popoford raised his hands in surrender and retreated while Lamia came forward. She kept the gun aimed in the men's direction and her eyes on them as she blindly raised the refrigerator's lid. She reached inside and felt around for the vials, but before she could pull them out, there was a sudden snap. She was astonished and let out a quick yelp as she yanked her hand back.

"What the hell!"

Contlerust was in action at once. He drew his Sig M18 while slipping a fresh round in the chamber and pressing the slide release. Then he shot at Lamia. His aching thrumbs threw off his grip and his shot was skewed. The round grazed the outside of her right shoulder. She dropped her pistol and spun on the steps, losing her balance, tumbling over the banister to the packed-earth floor below. She lay immobile as Contlerust swung his pistol towards Popoford. He didn't fire but stood completely still while he studied the Resurrection Runner's face. Finally, a gravelly chortle emitted from his mouth, and a belittling sneer widened into a prolonged belly laugh.

"You look perplexed, Steven. How could I turn on you? Aren't we in this together? Didn't I enlighten your Catholic belief? Aren't we friends?"

Popoford remained silent.

"We are not friends and never were," he continued. "You should have suspected it from the beginning. My loyalty is elsewhere. I don't give a damn about you or this country's problems."

He paused a moment and continued.

"On second thought, that's not true. I care a great deal about all the problems that face this world. But, unlike you, I'm committed to increasing those problems and introducing more. It is my purpose for I'm the man behind the TAP curtain. TAP is my brainchild. Therefore, I care deeply about your problems, but not about you or your people. What you get you deserve. I'm only too happy to help you on your way down. With the serum in my hands, my acolytes will create a potion far greater than Lamia was aiming for. And I have no moral compunctions at all. I'll rule the world through my surrogates at TAP. You, on the other hand, will see that hopeless day when God bows before me."

The first devilish image that entered Popoford's mind was too repulsive to consider, but Contlerust seemed to read his thoughts.

"You're right, Steven. It is I. Take a knee and kiss my ring."

Popoford stared at the man who had convinced him that it was God's will and fully acceptable to Church teaching to do what he had done. Contlerust was deranged and Popoford needed to take great care dealing with him.

"I will not honor you. If you are who you think you are, you know that you can't take my free will from me. I will never kiss your ring."

Contlerust hissed and Popoford expected to see a forked tongue dart from his mouth, but instead, he smiled again.

"We'll see what you will do. I can wait an eternity for you to become mine. Now be a good boy and sit down right where you are. That's it. See, you can comply, can't you?"

Contlerust took Popoford's pistol and walked up the stairs. He grabbed the serum that was resting next to the sprung mousetrap and stood at the top of the stairs.

"I know you're still wondering what happened in the jail," Contlerust said.

Popoford intuitively knew what he was thinking. "You," he said. "You killed them."

"Yes. I'm not surprised you didn't figure that out at once. You never were the brightest light. But keep trying. Someday you might achieve something of value."

"Why did you kill them?" Popoford said.

"Masterson and Singleton were in on it and knew too much. The sheriff was a witness that had to die."

"Then Sarah has to die too?" Popoford said.

"Not yet. She wasn't read in on my true purpose and I was interrupted before I could shoot her. I have other plans for her."

"And your daughter?"

"Millie? What about her?"

"Is she in the know?"

Contlerust burst out laughing. "You've got to be kidding. She hasn't got a clue. She'll do anything I tell her to do including seducing you."

Popoford felt the pain of Contlerust's allegation. He tried to put it out of his mind, but it remained, a worm eating at his heart.

"But enough of this. Here is where we part company, Steven. At least for now. I'll leave the car for you. You're used up and walking would kill you. Don't take any wooden nickels and don't come after me. For you, the game is over. For me, it never stops." He walked up the stairs, through Popoford's closet, and out of sight.

Popoford went to Lamia at once and checked her pulse. Her breathing was rapid and her eyes were open, darting about. She was startled when she finally caught sight of him.

"Take it easy," he said. "I'll get you fixed up. Just lie still for a minute."

He got up and hurried to a section in an outer tunnel where he found the emergency equipment he needed. When he returned to Lamia, he tore her shirt away from her shoulder and cleaned the wound with alcohol. It was a minor injury, but he dressed it. She winced and cursed him under her breath, but when he was finished applying a pressure bandage to the wound and taping her up, she reached out with her left hand and patted him on the cheek.

"You'd have made a good big brother, Steven. Why did you help me?"

"Just habit, I guess," he said.

"Thank you."

"What was I supposed to do? Let you die?"

"Yes. That's what I'd have done."

"Well, you're a cold-hearted bitch, no doubt, but you make too much of it. You'd do better if you softened up."

"Putting me in my place?"

"Sure. Someone has to before you get yourself killed."

"Why do you care what happens to me?"

"I don't. I care what happens to me. I don't kill in cold blood."

"A goody two shoes, huh?"

"If you say so. Come on. Get up! I need to get going."

Popoford helped Lamia to her feet. He left her standing at the bottom of the stairs as he retrieved a set of earbud listening devices hidden in a nearby cabinet. He also added two extra fully loaded M18 magazines and strapped a sheathed straight knife to his belt. Then he ran back and helped Lamia up the stairs.

"Do you think you can drive?"

"If it's an automatic."

He led her to the car parked behind the house.

"I wonder why Contlerust didn't take the car?" she said.

"I have the key, and I think he has an accomplice hiding in the woods. I've got to go after them now before they're too far away. Do me a favor, will you?"

"Maybe."

"Drive into Whimsy and go to Sam's Bar. Tell them I sent you so they can get you medical care. Tell them to keep it quiet. There's a doctor in town who'll help you on the QT. After that, just wait for me to catch up. Okay?"

"I guess," she said and started the car. "What are you going to do to Contlerust when you catch him?"

"I'll let you know when it's over. Now get going."

Lamia drove away and Popoford switched his earbuds on. There was nothing but silence, yet he waited, listening. His eyes squinted slightly when he heard the first report.

"Subject acquired. Northeast quadrant. On foot. One-hundred meters. Erratic path."

Popoford dropped the M18's magazine and did an ammo check. He replaced the magazine and racked a round into the chamber then patted his knife to confirm its location and slipped into the woods north of the cliff to avoid crossing the clearing. There was no telling if the subject was Contlerust or Jack, who was certainly his accomplice. His suspicion was confirmed shortly after he entered the woods.

"Second subject acquired. South quadrant. Stationary."

Popoford moved toward the gravel road with practiced steps, placing his feet silently on bare earth, rocks, or freshly-fallen timber. He crossed the road examining the tire tracks and discovering fresh footprints of a large man who had walked briskly on the road's edges where the gravel was thinly dispersed and his weight had pushed the stones deep into the soft soil. Stepping into the woods again, he followed the tracks as they climbed to the clearing and then to the woods across from his house.

He stood still behind a tree that hid him from the intruder and waited. Presently, he heard the rhythmic sound of crushed leaves as someone moved slowly away from his position and deeper into the woods.

"Subject two on the move. Descending to Northeast Quadrant. Accelerating. Advancing on Subject one."

Popoford could imagine their path and decided to change his attack plan. He bolted from the trees like a spooked deer and trotted without fear of discovery down the gravel road slowing and finally stopping just twenty feet from the intersection with the main road into Whimsy. There he re-entered the woods and walked silently to a place where he could see the road without exposing himself. In seconds he was rewarded by the message in his ear.

"Subjects one and two together. Stationary. Update. Subjects moving. Standby. Subjects traveling at motorized speed west. Forty-five MPH. Accelerating."

Popoford heard the sound and looked up the road just in time to see two motorcycles racing towards Whimsy. Contlerust was riding the first cycle and Jack was following close behind.

Popoford sighed deeply, removed his earbuds, and closed his eyes. He despaired for a second, then, from a dormant cavity unexplored but somehow familiar, words of hope formed on his lips without explanation: "Lord, without you I am nothing. Help me do your will."

Strengthened in purpose, he set a determined stride and walked up the gravel road where he entered his work shed and collected one of the electric bikes Contlerust's raiders had used. He put an extra battery in a backpack and slung it over his shoulders. Then he rode away to Whimsy.

CHAPTER FORTY

Sam died in his bar. That was the only time anything changed except prices and the new owner. The tables were still made of the same rustic planks. The Miller clock with the babe dressed in shorts, and flashing a huge smile never got old. The neon beer signs were the same ones Popoford remembered from his first days in Whimsy. The payphone on the wall still worked. But Sam wasn't there and Popoford didn't frequent the place like he used to. Sam's had lost its soul.

"Ain't seen you in here forever," Cecil, the new owner said as Popoford entered. "You need a drink?"

"Just a Coke," Popoford said and sat down at the booth where Lamia was waiting.

"Got it."

"Have you had anything to eat?" he asked Lamia.

"I'm waiting for a hamburger.

"Cecil, give me the same as the lady ordered. A hamburger."

"Make that two burgers, Gillie!" Cecil yelled at the cook.

"Have you been waiting long?" Popoford said.

"For you or the hamburger?"

"The hamburger."

"Too long," Lamia said.

"Hurry up with the food, Cecil. We're hungry."

"It'll be there when it's done," he said.

Popoford ignored him. Sam's Bar died with Sam a long time ago.

"Did the doctor fix you up?"

"Sure. The bullet just grazed me. He refreshed my dressing and told me to come back tomorrow. I paid cash and left, never to return."

Popoford laughed. "Well at least one of us had a happy ending."

"You lost him?"

"Yes. The pilot who flew us into Truckee was waiting for Contlerust on the main road above where you turn onto my property. They had two motorcycles. Must've gone through town about a half-hour ago. You didn't happen to see them did you?"

"No. You must be pissed about Contlerust."

Popoford nodded but said no more as Gillie, the cook, delivered their food.

"I'm disappointed more than anything. Disappointed with myself. I was taken in by him. It's not the first time I've been fooled, but I think I'm old enough to stop being had."

"Don't feel sorry for yourself. It happens to everyone. Hell, you put one over on me with me thinking that my serum was long-lasting. They say you've got to trust your gut even if it's a liar."

"Really. I never heard that one before."

"Me either," Lamia said, and Popoford laughed. "That's better. Now, what's your plan to stop Contlerust?"

"The first thing I want to know is what do you make of what he said? Was it just a bunch of crazy talk?"

"Well," Lamia said. "He claims to be involved with TAP. Do you believe him?"

"It would explain a couple of things," Popoford said, "but not everything. He acts like he's a god or something."

"He must be nuts."

"Well let's pretend he's not. We might get to the bottom of it if we take him at his word."

"Possibly," Lamia said.

"You told me Junko was the boss of TAP. Right?"

"You misunderstood me," Lamia said. "I believe he's taking orders from someone. Vladdrac imagined himself to be the golden-haired boy, but he didn't have the brains to run TAP. I assumed there was someone above him and that Junko was a mouthpiece."

"That makes sense. When I knew Junko as John the butler, he was a hatchet-man. Based on what he did to Vladdrac, he still is."

"Do you think that Contlerust truly is the head of TAP?"

"It's looking more like it all the time," Popoford said.

"So what do you propose we do now?"

"That's a sticky question. There are three of us in this game, and none of us are willing to let someone else win. You want the serum for clandestine government manipulation of citizens, Contlerust wants it to overthrow the government, and I want it to reverse educational perversion and protect the Constitution. At least that was what I did want. Now I want to destroy the whole program."

"So, we'll remain enemies in this game," Lamia said. "That's too bad. I had hoped you'd join me at Section 33. I was sincere when I talked about the Normalcy Project. I still think that assassinating the head of TAP is an honorable task."

Popoford thought for a few minutes and finally found the words to answer.

"I can join you in getting rid of Contlerust, but you must understand: our partnership will end there. Once done, my goal will be to take your pet project down. The serum must be destroyed."

"Fair enough. It's a truce then. But you must see that someone will always want the serum or some other method to rapidly control the citizens. No matter what country you're talking about there is someone who imagines themselves to be superior to the common man. There's always someone who will cut the rungs away from those above to eliminate the vulgar climb and to draw the pinnacle closer to their mediocrity."

"Lamia, you're the perfect agent. Your heart is pure cynicism. We will be enemies again unless I can change your mind."

"Or I change yours," she interrupted.

"For now,' Popoford continued. "we are in a war against the dark side. At war with a man who thinks he's the devil himself. If you ask me, I'd say he may well be that black Archangel."

When they finished eating, Popoford paid the bill and they left.

"You didn't have to do that. I could have picked up the check."

"And leave me owing the government something? Not me."

Lamia shrugged and they went out the door. Popoford left the electric bike parked in front of Sam's bar and walked across the street to his car.

"We need to get to TAP HQ as soon as we can, but I need a few things at the house. Jump in. I'll drive."

When they got close to his house, Popoford's realized he was still wearing his earbuds. There was a crackle and then an alert.

"Two subjects in tunnel."

"We have visitors," Popoford said. "Two of them. They're in the tunnel so I can drive up and they won't hear us. If we play this right, we could have Contlerust and his pilot hogtied soon."

Popoford drove up his gravel driveway and slowly drove the car behind the house. He parked it next to the motorcycles Contlerust and Jack were riding.

Lamia and Popoford silently opened their doors, closing them again as quietly as they could.

"Subjects have breached sublevel. Descending."

"Damn!" Popoford said.

"What's up?"

"They found the lower-level tunnels. They must be stopped."

"Why?" Lamia asked. "What's down there?"

"Let's just say the BATF wouldn't approve."

"Okay. What's your plan?"

"Pull the plug and smoke them out. The problem is there are three exits: the one in the house, one that opens deep in the woods, and one that opens on top of the cliff behind the house."

"And only two of us," Lamia said, stating the obvious.

"True, but think about it. They're going to want to take all the equipment they can, right? Plus, they don't know where we are. We could be coming back for all they know. It would be a fatal guess to ignore our imminent return."

"So? We still have three exits and two of us."

"They don't know there's a car here, so even if they find the other exits they'll want to take only what they can carry now on their cycles. They'll come back later when they get a truck."

"So, we wait here, right?"

"I'm going in through the cliff entrance. I'll move on to their position and block them at the gore point where the tunnels meet. You stay here and disable their bikes. If they come out this way, you can stall them and I'll be right here with a gun trained on their backs."

"Let's get to it," Lamia said and went to the motorcycles and pulled their sparkplug wires. She was working on jimmying their tires as Popoford made his way to the cliff.

He found his seldom-used path well hidden by undergrowth and easily ascended to the top. There, in a pine copse, he opened a manhole-sized cover with the aid of a key he'd secreted in the crotch of the largest pine. As he descended the ladder, his warning system alerted him again.

"Subjects stationary. Armorer's room."

Popoford expected they were taking a quick inventory. He completed his descent and made his way towards the Armorer's room. He was carrying his Sig M18 as he advanced on Contlerust and Jack.

"Subjects exiting armorer's room. Ascending to tunnel level one."

Popoford quickened his pace and was soon climbing the same stairs as the intruders. When he reached the top, he peeked into the next tunnel and caught a glimpse of Contlerust's feet as he stepped out onto the main floor.

"Subjects exiting building west,"

Popoford hurried up the stairs. As he came to his kitchen, he froze.

"*Subjects retreating.*" his system reported too late.

Contlerust had a pistol stuck in Popoford's face before he realized they hadn't left the house.

"Why don't you just quit, Steven? You're not particularly good at this game."

"Don't be so smug," he said.

"I'll be sure to take your advice," Contlerust said. "I'll keep it tucked away in my 'how not to behave' file. You know we heard you behind us even before we came up here. We were just waiting for the right moment to grab you."

"I'm scared," Popoford smiled.

"You should be, Steven. If you were smart you actually would be. Jack, bring those cuffs. Let's get him trussed up and ready to ride. We have a ways to go. I want to be back at headquarters before sunset."

"Yes, sir," Jack replied and spun Popoford around so he could snap the handcuffs on his wrists. Then he frisked him and took his car keys. "We'll need these unless you want to ride tandem on my bike."

Popoford was wondering where Lamia was as they marched him out of his house and put him in the passenger seat. Jack got behind the wheel, and Contlerust climbed in behind his driver. As he did, Popoford adjusted his position and turned in his seat to look at Contlerust. Jack started the car.

"Say goodbye to your little home, Steven. You won't be returning. But don't worry. I'll be back to plunder your munitions."

As Contlerust was bragging, Popoford clutched the door handle and yanked it up while thrusting himself backward out the door.

"Oh, my, Steven!" Contlerust said, sarcastically. "What a tough guy you are."

It was Lamia who answered Contlerust's smear.

"Hands up! Both of you! Lock 'em behind your heads. Move and you're dead."

The two men complied. Jack wore a frown but Contlerust was wearing his semi-permanent smile.

"Come on, Steven," Lamia said. "Get on your feet."

As he stood, Jack slapped the car into reverse and gunned the engine. Gravel blasted from the rear tires up into Popoford and

Lamia's faces. By the time they were able to open their eyes again, Jack had the car screaming around the house heading for the main road.

Lamia ran after them and emptied an entire magazine in their direction but it didn't slow them down. They could be heard laying rubber as they headed to Whimsy and presumably to TAP headquarters.

Lamia returned to the back of the house where Popoford was leaning against the wall.

"There's a chisel and a hammer in the kitchen toolbox. It's under the sink. Better bring the whole thing."

When Lamia came back she busted the cuffs off Popoford's wrists.

"Thanks. At least we have their Harleys. Can you put them back in order?"

"Sure. I'll have them ready to roll in ten minutes."

"Good. Check their fuel and I'll get some water and food for the road, and a few other things as well."

Popoford returned with two duffle bags which he strapped to the cycles.

When he brought the supplies out, Lamia was just finishing up.

"They need to be topped up," she said.

"There's a gas tank in the small shed. I'm going to call Millie and see where they are. As soon as I'm off the phone, let's ride."

CHAPTER FORTY-ONE

Contlerust and Jack dumped the car at the Truckee Tahoe Airport and refueled the U-28. Then they flew back to the Merced Municipal Airport.

"What are your plans, Sir," Jack asked as they disembarked. "Will you need the plane again?"

Contlerust answered after a moment's thought. "Get it fueled."

"Yes, sir."

"Keep your phone handy. I'll call you when I'm on the way back. I should have a passenger with me. No matter what, prepare a flight plan back to Mammoth. I'll want to take off as soon as I'm on board."

Contlerust took a taxi to Lamia's farmhouse and hot-wired the car that was still parked in the garage. It was dusty, but it started up right away and there was more than enough fuel in the tank to get him to the Merced airport. When he arrived at Sarah's house. There was no answer when he rang the bell so he called her on his cell phone.

"Hey," she answered. "Where are you? How did it go?"

"I'm back. Here at your house. Things went well."

"Great," she said.

"What are you up to?"

"I'm just about to have a meeting with Dean Wrenbutt. Wish me luck."

"Sure. What if I come to the college? We could go for a ride and you could tell me how it went with the Dean."

"Sounds good to me. I'll let Millie know."

"Okay, I'll pick you up in front of the History Building."

"That's not fair," she said.

"What do you mean?"

"I'll be thinking about you during the whole meeting."

"Yeah, I know what you mean."

"Well, wish me luck."

"Sure," he said.

There was a pause and then Sarah spoke again.

"Is everything okay?"

"Why do you ask?" Contlerust said.

"I don't know. You just sound a bit distant," she said.

"Sorry. We had some problems at Popoford's house. I didn't want to mention it until we were together. I still think that's best."

"Well, okay. I hope you're alright."

"I'm fine. I'll see you in a little while."

When Sarah hung up, she put her phone back in her purse.

"That was Simon. He's back in town and coming here."

Millie reacted with a doubtfully raised eyebrow. "What did he say about Steven?"

"Only that they had some problems in Whimsy," Sarah said as they climbed the stairs to Wrenbutt's office.

Unlike her last meeting, she had an appointment with Wrenbutt, but it had taken a long time to convince him and his secretary that she was sane. Now she opened the office door and was coolly received by Miss Shlenterby.

"There you are," she began. "I was hoping I'd never see you again. After all, the dean said you were unwelcome here, now, and forever."

"Things change, don't they?" Sarah said. "For instance, I thought attempted murder was a felony, but here you are."

Miss Shlenterby abruptly punched her intercom button. "Your appointment has arrived, Sir."

"Send her right in," Wrenbutt said, and his secretary indicated his door with a rude gesture. Then she turned to Millie and pointed to a chair against the wall.

Millie, not wanting to spend time alone with Miss Shlenterby, left the office and took a seat in the hall.

"Sarah," Wrenbutt said a bit too familiarly. "I'm so happy you reached out. Come, take a seat and we can work it all out."

"Thank you, Dean. I think you'll find that I've returned to my former self. Gone are the radical notions I expressed just days ago. I don't know what got into me, but I'm okay now."

Wrenbutt looked at her for a long time and finally spoke.

"There was a time when you held convictions opposed to mine. Then, my convictions were changed in surprising ways and I feel much happier now than I once did. Indeed, before our latest contretemps, I was hoping that the two of us could come together on a plan that would transform the department by emphasizing your originalist convictions. But you had shifted your views. I was confused and disappointed."

Sarah held a concerned expression while he spoke. "I'm sorry for causing you any hardship. Will you forgive me?"

"Of course I will. Let's just put it all aside and proceed as if nothing has happened."

"Except that we're both on the same page now," Sarah said with a smile.

They spent the next hour discussing throwing out the Brilliance in Basics program and replacing it with an old curriculum that they both remembered well. It was a robust conversation and

Sarah was heartened by the courage Wrenbutt had developed in such a short time. When their meeting was over, it was decided that Sarah should report for work the coming Monday, and they parted with a handshake that sealed their deal.

Sarah left the office with a pointed smile for Miss Shlenterby. "See you soon," she said as she closed the office door.

Millie got up and walked down the stairs mimicking Sarah's lite step. "I guess that went okay?" Millie asked.

"Smooth as silk. I'm floating. It couldn't have gone better. I'm working again and my situation was much improved." Her smile was gleaming when she caught sight of Contlerust waiting at the curb. "What a great day!" she said as she opened his passenger door.

"Hey, Dad," Millie said. "Sarah says you had some trouble in Whimsy. How's Steven doing?"

"He's okay. No bruises. He's fine."

Millie didn't say anything more. Her father wasn't paying any attention to her, anyway.

"Get in, Sarah. We have to get going."

She didn't resist as Contlerust reached over and pulled her closer, kissing her like a long-lost lover.

He then pulled away from the curb leaving his daughter alone to wonder what was going on beyond the obvious. She watched the car leave campus and then walked to her car.

Contlerust was all smiles. "I take it things went well," he said.

"Swimmingly," she said. "I have no cares in the world."

When she said it, she immediately knew she shouldn't have.

"But how about you, Simon? You said there were difficulties in Whimsy."

"Lamia tried to steal all the serum Popoford had stashed. She got away. I need to get back there now. He'll need my help."

"You mean this minute?"

"Yes. I was hoping you would come with me. We're going to wrap this whole mess up and I want you there when we do."

Sarah thought for a while.

"What's the matter," Simon said.

"I'm supposed to start classes on Monday. I can't miss that."

"Don't worry. I have a private plane and can have you back here on Sunday without a problem."

She thought for a second and turned to him. "When do we leave?"

"Right away."

Contlerust phoned Jack with the news and told him to warm up the engines. Then he looked at Sarah and saw the smile he wanted to see: the indiscriminate smile of a woman in love.

CHAPTER FORTY-TWO

Millie was driving when Popoford answered her call.

"May I call you sweetheart? I'm in love with you." he sang in a tone-deaf voice.

"I like that," she said.

"Sweetheart, Sweetheart, Sweetheart,"

"I guess you're feeling good."

"I am now. It's been pretty rough here."

"What do you mean? Dad said you were all right."

"When did you talk to him?" Popoford's carefree voice had changed.

"Five minutes ago."

"Where is he?"

"He just left Claramon with Sarah."

"What? How's that possible?"

"She got in his car and they took off," Millie said.

"It's the plane! Dammit!" Popoford snapped.

"What's the matter. Why are you angry?"

"I can't talk about it now, but I want you to do something for me. Okay?"

"All right," she answered, hesitantly.

"Can you drive to the Merced Regional Airport and see if you can spot them? It's important."

"Yeah, I guess so. What's going on, Steven. Tell me."

"Millie, you have to trust me. I'll fill you in on everything when I see you. I can't talk about it now."

"It must be pretty bad," she said.

"I'll tell you later. For now, just get to the airport and call me back. I've got to go. Call me as soon as you know. I love you."

Popoford hung up and Millie was dumbfounded. What could he possibly have to tell her that had to wait? She was worried. Something bad had happened and he wanted to tell her face to face. She worried more when she drove into the Merced Regional Airport parking lot. From her car she could see a twin-engine plane sitting on the runway, its stairs extended and her father and Sarah walking smartly across the tarmac towards it. She parked her car in front of the airport building so that it was hidden from view and went inside. She walked over to the window and watched them board.

"That's a nice looking plane out there," she said to the grizzled man sitting behind the counter. "My father used to fly those when he was on active duty."

"Oh, yeah?" the attendant said without interest.

"Is it hangered here?"

"Sometimes," came the perfunctory answer.

His eyes were pink, grading to blood-red in the corners. His ectropion lower lids rolled towards his chin appearing to rest on his cheeks. His age was a question needing no answer. He was nearly dead.

"Know where it's heading?"

He scratched the bit of the thinning hair still left on his head and came away with a few long strands that drifted to the countertop.

"Yup."

"Where?"

"Mammoth-Yosemite Airport."

"Really? How nice. Do you have any planes heading to Truckee?"

"Nope," he said, getting worn out with the effort of responding.

"Is there a pilot you know who would fly me there today?"

"Maybe."

"Well get the pilot on the phone. I need a flight to Truckee as soon as possible."

"All right," he said.

Millie waited.

"Jethro? Got a lady here needs to get to Truckee right away. What? I don't know. You talk to her."

He put the receiver on the counter instead of handing it to her.

Millie smiled extravagantly as she picked it up and turned away from the taciturn coot.

"That's right. Truckee. Right away."

She listened to his response. "I don't have cash like that on me."

She listened again. "You can run my card? Okay. How soon can we be off the ground? Half an hour? You must be close. Where? In which hanger? Okay, I'm on the way."

"Thanks," she said to the counter agent.

"Think nothing of it."

Millie didn't and made a call to Popoford on her cellphone as the attendant leaned on his elbows and rubbed his temples.

"Steven, Dad and Millie boarded the plane in Merced and are flying to Mammoth Lakes. That's just south of where TAP HQ is, I think. I've got a pilot who will fly me to Truckee. Can you pick me up there?"

"When are you taking off?" he said.

"In half an hour."

"I better get going. I'll see you soon."

He hung up without saying goodbye or anything. Something was terribly wrong. She just knew it.

CHAPTER FORTY-THREE

When she disembarked in Truckee, Millie gracefully thanked her pilot even though he'd turned out to be a lecherous wretch. When she'd given him her credit card in Merced, he took it with both hands, slipping the card away with one and pressing his other on a telltale artery in her wrist. She recoiled against his creepy, slimy touch and wrenched her hands away, round-house slapping him square across his face. He'd shrugged and turned away to run her card as if her rejection was an everyday occurrence, nothing to despair since it might have brought him closer to the rare acceptance he lived for. Understanding the odds wasn't his thing.

Popoford was waiting for her on the tarmac and she rushed to his arms. They kissed and hugged again as if they'd never let go. But time enough passed and they had to leave. As Millie released him and he turned toward the terminal, she spotted a woman waiting by a Harley Davidson.

"What the hell is she doing here?" Millie spat. "You brought that bitch with you?"

"Hang on, Millie," he said wrapping his arm around her shoulders. There's a lot to tell and this is not the place."

"Why is she here? Why is Dad going to TAP HQ? What's going on!"

"The answers aren't so simple. Calm down and I'll lay it out for you. Come on, let's get out of here and find a place to talk."

Grudgingly, Millie allowed him to guide her off the tarmac and into the terminal. He led her to a seat at a small table that overlooked the runway. Several travelers were sitting nearby.

"Do you want some coffee or water?" Popoford asked.

"No. I want the truth."

He didn't reply but went to the Red Truck counter and bought three bottles of water.

The lights were too bright for a discreet meeting; not dark enough for an inquisition but that's just how Millie started the conversation as Lamia walked in the door and joined them.

"What the hell! Why are you here? Where's my father?"

Popoford jumped in fast as Lamia sat down across from Millie.

"Hang on, Millie. We're not alone here," he said indicating the several other people in the room. "Let me fill you in."

"Where's my father?" she repeated.

"We'll see him later," Popoford said, trying to calm her down.

"Why didn't you just say that to begin with?"

"Because it's not as simple as that."

"Meaning what?"

"You remember when you came to my house for the second time? The time that I showed up with Simon?"

"Sure. In your kitchen," she said with a quick smile that morphed into stern insistence. "You brought him from Whimsy where he was waiting to get the others out of jail. So what?"

Popoford drank some water. "He wasn't waiting to get the others out."

Millie's jaw clenched. "Then what was he doing?"

"He was gathering his wits when I jumped him. He had just murdered everyone in the jail except Sarah."

"Bullshit!"

"It's true. He told me himself after he shot Lamia."

Millie was flabbergasted.

"He also admitted that he's running TAP."

"That's a lie! It has to be."

"He's insane. He thinks he's the Devil; Satan."

"You're a liar. He's a God-fearing Catholic."

Popoford let that line hang in the air for a while. He looked at Millie without flinching and she knew he was telling the truth. Then he looked at Lamia and made it clear she should keep her mouth shut.

"I'm here, Millie," he said. "because Simon and you convinced me that the only just path for me was to join with you to break up TAP. You recall how the conversation went in my kitchen. It was a hard sale. I wanted nothing to do with it. Helping to subject anyone to Resurrection Runner slavery was anathema to me. But you convinced me to suspend my disgust for the program and to turn its mind-bending drugs and procedures against a greater evil. In the end, the greater evil was Simon Contlerust, your father."

Millie's face was red with rage and confusion. She shook her head slowly in denial and ran her hands through her hair over and over again. Finally, tears came to her eyes and she sobbed, pointing an accusing finger at Lamia.

"What does that bitch have to do with this? Why is she here?"

A busboy was clearing a table next to them but reconsidered and left them alone.

"Lamia is working with us for now. She wants the serum and the files for the government, something you and I oppose. But we can use her skills for the job ahead of us."

"Which is?" Millie asked.

"To get inside TAP headquarters and destroy their nerve center."

"Is my father there?"

"He might be. His pilot might be with him as well. It's hard to say. I'm guessing he is. We know his butler, Junko's there, and maybe others. We're going to find out. But no matter what we find, we have to stop their operation."

Popoford and Lamia waited for her reply. Nothing prepared them for her perfunctory question.

"When do we start?"

Popoford's gaze jotted to her eyes.

"Soon," he said. "First, I need to talk to you alone." He waved Lamia off, and she stepped out of the coffee shop. Millie composed herself as Popoford struggled to find the words.

"When we first met, you were so aggressive. I mean towards me. You know, forward."

"So? I was attracted to you from the first moment. Is that strange?"

"I don't know. It's unheard of in my world. Surprising, I guess."

"Are you suggesting that I'm playing you?" Her voice had an angry edge.

"No," he said. "I don't know. He told me that he'd ordered you to seduce me."

Millie stared at him in disbelief. "No way!"

"You're saying that he didn't do that?"

"That's right. I don't need anyone's help when it comes to you."

Popoford reached out and placed his hand on her cheek and she looked him square in the eyes.

"I had to ask," Popoford said. "He was lying, trying to rile me up."

"What else did he say?" she said still holding his gaze.

"No. I can't repeat it. It would hurt you too much."

"Nothing would hurt me more than you not telling me or lying to me. I want the truth."

Popoford studied her face and her determination moved him to speak.

"It's just how he talked about you as if you weren't his daughter."

Millie reached for his hand and removed it from her face. She held it as she gathered her composure. When she finally spoke, she had a tone of remorse but no bitterness.

"I can only tell you what I know and what I believe, Steven. Simon Contlerust may not be my father. I don't know. I didn't know him when I was a child. My mother raised me herself and told me that my father had died in combat. One day Simon approached me and claimed he was my father. He said he had been a victim of a government program called Resurrection Runner. He said that he had just recently escaped from their clutches by faking his death. He took Jack Singleton and Bill Masterson with him and they all vanished. He had been looking for me ever since as the three of them began building the team. I was skeptical at first, but he had so many details about his time with my mother and me when I was a baby that I came to believe him."

Millie and Popoford sat quietly for a moment and she continued.

"I don't know what to believe, Steven. You're the only one I can trust right now. I need to be with you when you find him. I need to know the truth."

Popoford leaned over and they hugged. She kissed him and told him to bring Lamia back inside.

When Lamia returned, they discussed what they knew about the TAP headquarters layout and their weapons inventory. Then Popoford laid out a recon plan for their advance on the building. When they were done with breakfast Lamia paid the bill.

"I'm on duty. It's on my expense report."

"You mean the taxpayers; us, we're paying for it. Right?" Millie said.

"Sure. And I'm a taxpayer too. Why don't you get that chip off your shoulder? I didn't turn your father. I had no idea he was working against us. Right now, the three of us are on the same side. *Capiche*?"

Millie turned away without a word and it appeared that she'd let it drop when she smiled and said, "As you wish."

"Good," Lamia said. "Can you ride a Harley?"

"Sure I can. Steven? Is there room on your bike?"

"Yes. Let's ride."

The time had come and they all fell naturally into a combat mindset as they started their engines.

CHAPTER FORTY-FOUR

When Popoford and Millie got to the TAP HQ clearing, he pulled his Harley off the road. Lamia followed and drove her bike up behind them. Popoford and Lamia removed the duffle bags and they gathered around and distributed their weapons and ammo.

Millie and Lamia grabbed a shotgun and Popoford took a Socom 16 and hoisted a rocket launcher. Lamia also picked up two grenades and they all made sure their guns were topped off and that they had backup ammo.

When they were all armed, Popoford gave a Clarus XPR radio and a headset to each of them.

"These will be our primary means of communication. Keep the radios on at all times but observe radio silence unless there's an emergency. If you're captured, disable the unit so our comms will not be jeopardized."

Finally, they held a brief meeting to review their plan of attack.

"I don't know how many we're up against today. It could be only Junko, or there may be nine or ten hostiles. We play it by ear, keeping our entire team updated. Any questions?"

With no questions, Popoford continued.

"When Millie and I are in place, I'll give the signal. Lamia, you ride in at top speed, drive directly to the front door and lob your grenades, then retreat. We'll wait to see the response and then we'll all breach the house."

Lamia returned to her Harley and made ready. As she did, Popoford led Millie into the woods. His experience indicated that there were no security devices on their path, but this time he expected Junko to play the game differently. Millie remained ten yards back as they advanced. Instead of walking parallel to the driveway, Popoford turned away from the house and moved along the perimeter of the trees, pausing every so often to mimic a grazing deer. Millie followed suit. No alarms were raised, but that meant nothing. Junko could well be smiling in victory even as they moved on the outskirts of the forest.

Popoford didn't care. If they were spotted, they'd be distracting Junko from the real attack. If he didn't know they were there, it only enhanced the probability of surprise.

When they were perpendicular to the side of the house, Popoford made the turn and continued their stealthy approach. They stopped just before entering the clearing and Popoford scanned the building. Seeing nothing unusual, he raised his hand to his radio's controls and was about to signal Lamia when the tree's bark just to the right of his head exploded. An instant later he heard the rifle's report.

Popoford and Millie dropped flat on the forest floor before the next round struck the tree exactly where Millie had been standing. Popoford toggled his radio.

"Under attack. Rooftop. One shooter. Advance."

They could hear the Harleys' engine roar to life and then accelerate through quick shifts up the driveway. All at once, the bike raced into the clearing with Lamia in the saddle. She screamed up to the front entrance, braking only at the last instant as one after another grenade was launched and landed right at the front door's tread. She was pulling out of a quick spin and heading back to the driveway when a shot rang out and Lamia's rear tire blew out. Her bike fishtailed and it laid down. She was scrambling away on the ground when the two grenades exploded.

At the same time, Popoford had worked his way to the front of the house with Millie close behind. He saw the shooter along the parapet and delivered suppressive fire accurate enough to force the shooter's retreat. Seeing this, he was on the radio again.

"Attack! Attack!" he shouted and shouldered his rocket launcher.

Millie jumped to his side and shoved a rocket into the tube. Turning her head away, she called "Clear," and Popoford loosed a rocket at the damaged front door, flattening it.

Popoford and Lamia were on their feet at once. They all jumped onto the porch and pressed against the brick wall. Popoford placed the rocket launcher on the porch and readied his rifle.

"All good?" Popoford asked. All were thumbs up. "Let's do this!"

At once, Millie followed Popoford into the breach, bursting through the shattered door as Lamia brought up the rear. Once inside, they spread out and found cover. Everyone's senses were sharp, searching for the slightest sound, movement, or odor to alert them to an impending attack. But nothing unusual presented itself: there were no strange sounds, nothing moved, and no odd smells aroused them. Only their breathing rose above the stillness until a bloodcurdling banshee wail reverberating from the upper floor spread throughout the house. It was followed by two more shrieks, each of them more heartrending than the last. Then all was silence.

They looked at each other for a second. Then Popoford took the lead signaling them to advance toward the staircase.

They were in a terrible shooting tunnel and moved rapidly up the stairs. Popoford maintained a focus on the upper level and Millie, who was now bringing up the rear, proceeded sideways with her shotgun in the ready position for threats approaching from below. When they reached the grand hall, Popoford peered over the top tread and was surprised to see Junko sitting in the tub that Vladdrac had habitually occupied. He was submerged in the black coal-water up to his gaping mouth, his head tilted back, his eyes bugged out and fixed on the ceiling. There was a dark stain covering his cheeks and ears testifying to his head being recently submerged. He resembled a dog howling at the moon.

Not trusting what he saw, Popoford signaled the team to split up and take defensive positions to the right and left of the staircase. As they responded, scuttling to protection, a bestial moan rose from Junko's throat like the cry of a revenant shredded by his return to life. His guttural complaint rose and shifted to a screech so penetrating that Popoford almost pulled the trigger to put him out of his misery. But he controlled himself when he heard a sinister laugh rising from behind. As he spun to confront the enemy, a shot rang out that grazed his temple and slammed into the staircase riser. The bloodshot eyes staring up at him were merciless.

"Shall I kill you, Steven, or not? Now, or later? What, no answer? Pity. I guess I have to make all the decisions around here."

Contlerust started up the stairs.

"Drop your guns, all of you. Stand up slowly. The game is up. It's time to die."

Popoford lowered his rifle but didn't drop it. He turned away and took the last steps into the main room. With his free hand above his head, he called out to the others to drop their guns as he continued walking to the psoriatic treatment tub, his eyes locked on Junko. When he got close, he was able to look over the tub's rim. He saw Junko's hands trussed up above the black liquid with Lamia's thumbscrews in place. Junko was pleading for death with his eyes.

Popoford focused on Junko as his team came forward and in an act of mercy raised his rifle and placed its reticle between Junko's eyes. As he began to press the trigger, a hand knocked his barrel off target and his shot went wide. It was Contlerust who interceded.

"Killing him's my pleasure, Steven. I won't let you take my joy from me. My man, Junko, has lost his way. He made the mistake of putting Lamia in Vladdrac's chair. Now he has assumed the throne for himself and he must suffer for his arrogance just as Vladdrac did. Step away, Steven, and let the thumbscrews do their work."

Contlerust snatched Popoford's rifle and turned his on the others.

"I'm so happy you could all be here today. I was only expecting you, Steven. I thought Lamia would be out of the fight, but I see she's tougher than I realized."

He darted his eyes from one captive to the other as he considered them.

"Lamia will become a Runner for me, the perfect irony, a touching end for such a pest.

"And you, Millie, my trusting girl, you will join Sarah as party favors for the rich and famous."

Millie's scorn faltered. "Where is she? Where's Sarah?"

"Waiting for me, unaware of her future. I'll let you explain it to her."

Millie lunged for him, her sorrow and rage propelling her through the air. She balled her fists and landed on her feet swinging. Contlerust blocked her first blow but lowered his gun as he struck. In an instant, Popoford ripped the rifle out of Contlerust's hand and slammed its butt into Contlerust's hip, throwing him off balance. The others swarmed him and wrestled him to the floor. As they held him down, he let out a guttural laugh the chilled everyone.

"You still don't understand who I am, do you?" he hissed, and in one enormous thrust, he threw Millie and Lamia off him, sending them skidding out of reach.

They were all stunned as much from the knocking of their heads as from Contlerust's astonishing strength. It was superhuman, but that was impossible except in fiction, or heaven, or hell. This wasn't fiction and it sure wasn't heaven.

Contlerust rose from the floor and straightened his jacket. He gazed at the inept gaggle strewn about and smirked. "Nothing like a little mechanical enhancement to make the day," he said and pulled his sleeve back a few inches to reveal the exoskeleton he was wearing. "I'll be leaving you now," he said, almost sorrowfully. "But before I go, I'll give you a little test, good Catholics that some of you are. See this?"

He held something in his hand which was familiar to Popoford and Lamia.

"It's Lamia's thumbscrew control. I'll leave it for you so you can help Junko out."

As he spoke he pressed one of the buttons and a shrill cry broke the quiet as the thumbscrews tightened on the hapless Junko. Contlerust laughed and tossed the control into the tarry pool.

"Find it and save him or kill him if you wish. Maybe just walk away now and be done with him. Let your conscience be your guide. I'll critique your decisions another time."

With that, he raced to the stairwell and fairly flew down it and straight out the smashed front door.

Popoford listened the best he could as they all jumped up and ran to the pool but he couldn't pick up the sound of a car or bike leaving the property.

Millie was in the water first diving into the dark water, feeling the bottom for the controller, and rising again for air, empty-handed. Meanwhile, Lamia ran to the second TAP control panel. Popoford joined her and together they gathered a series of USB hard drives. Popoford opened the computer and removed the SSDs. There was no paper to be found, but they confiscated a small server. When they had all they needed, they hurried back to the pool.

Junko's constant howling and blasphemies crippled any semblance of thought. It wasn't until Millie burst from the water with a triumphant cry that even Junko went quiet. He held his breath as she pointed the stick at him and pushed the button. Then tears of joy replaced those of pain as Millie broke his bindings and helped him to his feet.

Popoford was standing right in front of him and kept his gaze on Junko's hopeful expression. He raised his rifle once more, his mind struggling with conflicting desires battling for supremacy. Millie, seeing the conflict in his eyes quietly spoke to him.

"How precious is life, Steven? Yours, I mean. 'Thou shall not kill.' There is no conflict. You chose what to do here, right now, many years ago. Let God deal with him."

Millie's plea was framed in her insistent eyes, begging Popoford to stand down. He quietly lowered his gun and turned away and took two steps toward the stairs. Then he heard a strangled call for help. In a well-trained fluid motion requiring nothing but one good eye and a sight picture, he pivoted and was squeezing the trigger even before his feet were rooted to the floor.

Junko had Millie around the throat and was dragging her to the far edge of the pool. The shot was daring, one no sane man would take, but Popoford wasn't sane. The bullet flicked past Millie's head so close that she wound up with powder burns, but Junko wound up with only half his head. The back half was pink mist and shattered bone.

In death, Junko Abrams, aka John, P. Y. Mous's butler, completed a story told long before of a time worth forgetting, but Popoford savored the moment while others said good riddance. A dozen cliches passed through Popoford's head to describe it, yet none of them was a suitable ending. Contlerust was still at large, Sarah was in jeopardy, and Lamia would soon be released in the wild to develop a wrong-headed correction of America's path. Her intended results would be co-opted by sinister actors who would play into Contlerust's plan. The propaganda that Contlerust embraced would solidify as fact. Fact without proof. Dogma without principle.

It was the sound of a motorcycle firing up that caught Popoford's attention, and in an instant he was bolting down the stairs following in Contlerust's footsteps, raising through the front door.

He saw the Harley as it left the clearing with two onboard and raised his rifle, steadying his breathing as he focused on the tandem rider. He delivered three quick shots to the person's back and saw the bike swerve. Before it could crash, the passenger fell to the gravel road and the remaining rider gained control of the bike. It was Contlerust who sped away. It could only be Sarah who he'd killed.

CHAPTER FORTY-FIVE

"Where's Sarah? Is she here?" Millie cried as she jumped out of the bath where Junko's body floated on the tarry surface. "We have to find her."

Lamia had retrieved her shotgun and was heading downstairs by the time Millie shook off what she could of the coal-infused water. She grabbed her gun and raced after Lamia.

Reaching the main floor, Millie and Lamia worked together searching the rooms where they'd been held. They found Sarah in Junko's quarters tied to a chair, her head hanging on her chest, a gag in her mouth. They immediately untied her and moved her to the floor. Millie got a towel from the bathroom and soaked it in cool water. She knelt at her side and applied the wet towel to Sarah's head. Soon, Sarah's eyes opened in fright, but her mood improved rapidly when she recognized Millie. Her first words were sputtered in thankfulness.

"Millie. You came for me." Then she focused on Lamia and let out a moan. "Why is she here?"

"It's a long story, Sarah," Millie said. "We're working together. Don't worry about a thing. You're going to be all right."

Sarah's gaze lingered on Lamia's eyes until Millie helped her up.

"Are you feeling better now?" she said.

"I'm a bit woozy, but I'm better."

When Popoford entered the room, he was thrilled to find Sarah. "I thought I shot you just now," he said.

"Not me. I've been right here since Simon brought me here. I've been a fool, haven't I?"

"No more than the rest of us. He's been playing us for a long time. Did he hurt you?"

"I don't know. I don't think so, but my head hurts."

"Well, take it easy for a while. You should be okay."

"So what do we do now?" Millie asked.

"Let's get out of this place," Lamia said. "There's nothing more I need here."

Popoford gave her a nasty look. "If you think you're taking the hard drives and the files from the TAP computers, you're mistaken."

To show he meant it, he raised his rifle again. "Millie, collect everything she has and go through her purse. She might have stashed something there. She's not leaving the place with any TAP info."

"You can't do that. TAP is a criminal enterprise. They've committed multiple federal crimes and their entire organization needs to be taken down."

"I agree, but the government with all its made players, many of whom are entangled in TAP operations, is not the best choice to take them down. If you turn those drives over to the agencies, they'll be buried so deep that no one will find a speck of them. And you might as well plan on joining them in that deep hole. You know too much to live."

Lamia remained silent.

"You know it's true," Popoford said. "The only way to use the information we have is to keep it ourselves. Only God knows why we've been thrown into this mess. I believe that we're expected to use these gifts to right a great wrong. And I know that nothing good will happen if we walk away from our responsibilities."

"And if I say no? What then? What are you going to do if Millie and Sarah say no? Kill us all?"

"I'm not going to kill any of you," Popoford said. "What good would it do? I'd just as soon drive back to Whimsy right now and try to forget about the whole thing. But I've made my decision to handle TAP myself, and that's final. Join me if you will, but the TAP data goes with me. If you want to bring TAP to its knees, join me. Otherwise, you're out. Your choice. I've made mine."

He kept his rifle trained on her, his eyes steadfastly looking for any signs indicating her rejection. But Lamia soon spoke up.

"I choose to live another day," she said and handed the drives and her purse to Millie.

"Good. I'm not foolish enough to believe you've given up. For now, we're on the same side. But I'm warning you. One hint that you're planning to turn us or the TAP information over to the government and you're dead."

"Looks like I'm dead either way," she said.

"Not really. Play it straight with us and we'll do the same for you."

Turning his attention to Sarah, Popoford asked if she felt well enough to identify the person he'd shot. She nodded and he gave her a hand as she stood.

"Why don't we all go outside together. Bring everything. There's no reason to come back here."

"We can't just leave the place," Lamia said. "Someone will show up and find Junko. The cops will investigate and it won't be long before they're looking for all of us."

"What do you propose? To burn it to the ground?"

"Yes."

"No!" Popoford snapped. "The forest would go up in flames and the police would be on our tails even faster. We'll walk away and be done with it."

"But what about Junko?"

"What about him?" Popoford said. The coyotes and mountain lions will make short work of him. Let's go!"

Lamia relented and Popoford followed all the women out the breached front door and down the driveway to the body sprawled on the gravel.

As soon as Popoford rolled his body over he knew who it was.

"It's Jack, Contlerust's pilot."

Popoford kneeled beside him and rifled his pockets. "He doesn't have the serum. Help me drag him into the woods."

When they got him a few yards away from the driveway, they left him for nature to deal with. Then they returned to the mansion and found a door to the garage. Several vehicles were parked there, the nearest to the garage door was a Ford F-150, its keys in the ignition. Millie drove.

They found little to talk about as they drove down the mountain, their thoughts tangled in moral and inglorious arguments.

When the road straightened out, Millie reached out for Popoford's hand. Her gesture said simply that they were in this together. Her firm grip was just like his love. And he loved her the more, seeing the strength with which she bore her sorrow. Win or lose, their happiness would have to wait a while longer to consummate.

CHAPTER FORTY-SIX

The earth spun past high noon as the sun hung above the eastern Sierras. They were heading back to Claramon College, to get Sarah back to work. They dropped Lamia off empty-handed at the Mammoth Yosemite Regional Airport to catch a plane to Washington D. C. via Las Vegas. Her exit brought a sense of relief as if the all-hearing government had been struck dumb. The extra back-seat space was emblematic of freedom to freely discuss next steps.

"How are you going to take down TAP on your own?" Sarah asked Popoford. They must have an enormous operation?"

Popoford adjusted his position to look at her. "TAP itself isn't all that large. It's only three generals and Contlerust now that Lamia isn't posing as one of them. It's one reason that she didn't argue much about giving me all their data. She knows where to find the generals. She got that information after Vladdrac was killed. Once I access the hard drives, I'll know where to find them as well. The bigger problem is the system they're part of, the web that directs other cells like theirs, and the thousands of frontline troops that are positioned throughout America."

"Is that what Lamia is going to tackle?" Millie said.

"I think she'll try, but I don't think she'll get far."

"Why?" Millie said.

"Because it's so well established. It's an entrenched threat no one wants to touch."

"Sounds like a conspiracy theory," Sarah said.

"It's not a theory when it's sitting right there in front of you. If you ignore it, you mean to hide it. That can't be done unless there are many people in high places who benefit from the organization."

"You're talking about politicians," Millie said.

"And agencies, courts, big business, their stakeholders, social media, and even presidents," Popoford said. "Believe me, I know."

They rode to Lee Vining lost in their thoughts. Then they left the alpine eastern slope following Highway 120 over the mountains. Millie spoke first. "Sarah, how long has the trouble in your curriculum been going on?"

"There was already an effort to revise history long before I started teaching. I think it started with Andrew Jackson, or maybe in the Garden of Eden."

Popoford laughed at that. "Telling lies comes with breathing. Revisionism establishes control and control provides power. It's the circle of death."

"And he's a part of it," Millie said.

"Contlerust? By what he says, he's the center of it; the current alpha dog," Popoford said.

"I need to be with you when you hunt him down," she said, a fierce edge to her voice.

"You can't do that. It would only hurt you more."

"You don't understand. You can't keep me from being with you. He betrayed me. And you. He killed my friends and he was going to send me and Sarah to God-knows-what kind of slavery. He can't be my father. He's a demon."

Popoford held her gaze and nodded. The determination he saw was indisputable. He nodded again.

"So be it."

It was dark by the time they arrived at Sarah's house. They were all exhausted and shuffled inside one after the other. Sarah went straight to bed, and Millie fell into the spare bed with eyes aching and bloodshot from her hours behind the wheel. Popoford laid down beside her and fell into an unusually dreamless sleep. He awoke feeling as scruffy as he looked with the sun too bright for wide-open eyes and a visceral knowledge that he needed some toothpaste. Wobbling to the bathroom, he used his finger as a brush and at least made his mouth taste clean. Then he got the coffeemaker going and finally had his first clear thought of the day when he inhaled the coffee's aromatic steam. With his first taste, he had a decent idea for the day.

The women were stirring soon after the coffee was ready, and when they were all together in the front room, Popoford asked them a pointed question.

"If you were Simon, what would you do next?"

Everyone thought about it for a few seconds and Sarah spoke first.

"He might come back here to get me," she said.

"Yes," Popoford said. "He might. How about you, Millie?"

"He could be heading back to Whimsy to wait for us to return," she said.

"Maybe, someday. If I were him, I'd call a meeting of the three surviving TAP officers. They're the ones who could make trouble for him. They're true believers and aren't going to change stripes anytime soon, but they might have eyes on the power. Some will want to fill the vacuum. I'd want to evaluate their continued usefulness, for sure. After all, one of them could qualify as the new TAP Leader. If they all pass muster, he could be up and running rapidly. Even if he kills them all, our objective is to stop him and get our serum back."

They both agreed and Popoford filled up everyone's cup.

"So, who will he see first? Second? Last?"

"It depends on where they are," Millie said.

"That could be, or which one is the best leader."

"Well, what difference does it make if you don't know where they are?" Sarah asked.

"I think the disks can tell me that. I'll have to weigh their skills from afar and take a chance I've picked the right one. If the first choice is wrong then there will only be two left to choose from. Sooner or later they will all die."

"Well, let's get cleaned up and get over to the college," Sarah said. "You can use their computer equipment to help you figure all this out while I have another conversation with Dean Wrenbutt."

"Great," Popoford said. "Do we have time for some breakfast?"

"Sure," she said. "The eggs and bacon are in the fridge. The skillet is under the cutting board."

Popoford accepted the role of chef and soon it was scrambled eggs and bacon for three. They were ravenous and were back in their car heading for Claramon College in half an hour.

CHAPTER FORTY-SEVEN

Sarah drove Popoford onto the campus and parked in her assigned space. They walked to the History Building as Millie parked the pickup next to Sarah's. Millie got out and strolled in the opposite direction along the path that encircled the college grounds.

It was a breezy morning and many students and a few teachers were walking about the campus. The sun was shining, and only the chirping of birds and the tractor drone of a farmer disking his fields interrupted the quiet.

Suddenly, tranquility turned to screeching chaos. Many students turned and saw Popoford and Sarah near the entrance to the History building confronted by several rascals. The irate boy leading the group had his face pushed up inches from Sarah's. He was screaming vulgarities while his fellow travelers shook their fists at Professor Tufftang, loudly chanting "Die, Fascist, Die."

Millie started running across the grass directly at the assault, but she came to a stop when she saw what happened next.

Popoford was carrying the hard drives and he quietly placed them on the pavement. As he moved to defend Sarah, she put her arm up and stopped him by handing him her armful of files. Then she quickly turned on the snotty student and landed a roundhouse punch that knocked him cold. His clutch of recreant anarchists vanished like cockroaches in an abruptly lit room.

Millie allowed a cheer to rise as Sarah grabbed the dazed tyrant by the scruff of his neck and forced him to his feet. She then marched the would-be radical into the building. Popoford turned to Millie and gave her a big smile. He then followed Sarah. Millie resumed her morning stroll.

Sarah kept a firm grip on the aging brat and marshaled him up the stairs and into Dean Wrenbutt's outer office.

"Is the Dean in?" she asked his instantly flummoxed secretary.

"Well. . .What?. . .You can't. . ."

"I can and I have, Miss Shlenterby. If this is a child, he needs discipline. If he's a man, he needs jail time. Tell the Dean I'm here."

The receptionist hesitated.

"Tell him, now!" Sarah snarled, and the secretary immediately announced her arrival.

"Professor Tufftang to see you, Sir."

He came to the door at once.

"Sarah! What have you there? Has he caused a problem?"

"Nothing I can't handle, Thornton. But this one is making a bad name for Claramon. I believe his parents should take him back until he learns his manners."

"Miss Shlenterby, call security. Have this miscreant removed from campus."

"Yes, Dean," was her meek response as she obeyed.

Security called, Popoford stepped forward and took the brat off Sarah's hands.

"Thank you, Steven," She said. "When security takes him away, you can go to the library and do your research. Thornton, this is Steven. He's helping me on a project of historical significance."

"Pleased to meet you, Steven," Wrenbutt said. "What's the subject?"

"The American Revolution, part two."

"Excellent. Please make yourself at home."

"Thank you, Dean. I already feel welcome."

Wrenbutt nodded and spoke to Sarah. "Now, Sarah, come in. We have a lot of work to get done."

"Just one minute, Thornton. I need a few words with Steven first."

Wrenbutt acquiesced and went back into his office while Sarah whispered in Steven's ear.

"I suppose you'll be leaving here as soon as you can."

"Yes. As soon as I get what I need off the hard drives. We need to go."

"Then it's goodbye. Please tell Millie that I owe you both a huge debt. You've saved me. It's as simple as that."

Popoford only smiled.

"If there's ever something I can do to help you, you must let me know. Do you understand?"

"Yes, Sarah. I understand," Popoford said. "Right now, your job is to work from within to reverse the current state of affairs and to reinstate a true liberal arts curriculum at Claramon. After that, we can implement the Wrenbutt Solution, to coin a phrase, where needed. Your experience will be invaluable then."

She hugged him the best she could as he held his charge at arm's length, and then turned and entered the dean's office closing the door behind her.

After security had walked the molesting thug out of Wrenbutt's office, Popoford found his way to the library and set up at a terminal where he mounted his USB drive. In a matter of seconds, he was logged on to the drive and was searching a wealth of information about the three remaining TAP leaders. Most importantly, he obtained their bank account information. From there, he discovered their home addresses, their club affiliations, and their shopping preferences. When he left the History

Building and found Millie, he had a sequence of actions planned that would bring him into contact with Contlerust soon.

They returned to Sarah's house before Popoford said anything. When they went inside, he looked at his cell phone.

"Look at your emails," he said to Millie. "I sent you an aerial view of the place Contlerust will be meeting his minions."

When she had the image pulled up, he explained what she was looking at.

"This is a satellite shot of a posh spike camp where gentleman hunters and their guides spend their nights while on a hunt. It's in a wooded section of rolling hills west of Bootjack. As you can see, there are four structures in the camp. Three of them are small cabins for hunters. The larger building is used to house the guides and it looks big enough for a kitchen and a common room."

"What's the significance of this place?" Millie asked.

"The three remaining TAP leaders have orders to meet there tomorrow. They're to arrive on a schedule spanning one hour starting at 10:00 am."

"What's that all about?"

"Contlerust doesn't want them seeing each other while they're at the camp. And the three cabins mean they'll be isolated during their stay. See how far away from each other they are and how they sit in dells in the forest? A quick look tells me that no one in any of the cabins can see the other cabins. Contlerust will be able to meet with each of his generals without the others knowing he's done it."

"Okay, but how do we get on the property?"

"My plan is almost worked out. I'll explain it when we get there. We need a good night's sleep. I want to be on the road by 6:30 tomorrow morning."

"Are we going hunting?" Millie said.

"Yes," Popoford answered and picked up a scratchpad. But instead of finishing his plan, he only stared at the pad.

Millie gazed at him while she sipped her coffee. His complexion had taken on a ruddy cast and his eyes a doubting stare.

She put her arms around him and was instantly concerned. Every muscle in his body was flexed. Had she not felt his steady breath on her shoulder, she'd have thought he'd fallen into a catatonic fit. But as she held him, his breathing became deeper and then more rapid. She was astonished to see tears forming in his eyes. "What is it, Steven?"

Popoford opened his mouth to speak, but the words didn't come as his breath was throttled in his throat. He gave her a melancholy smile and forced his strained voice to utter "I must do this. I must destroy Contlerust and TAP even if I'm forever damned."

CHAPTER FORTY-EIGHT

They were just starting their trip when Popoford stopped for fuel then they began their push to the spike camp. They drove up to Mariposa and then headed south on Highway 49 to Bootjack. From there they wound several miles into the hills. Millie was the first to spot a sign that read "Columbia Outfitter's Spike Camp. Private Property. No Trespassing. No Hunting." He turned on the gravel road leading to higher elevations. When the road turned to dirt, Popoford noted a fresh vehicle track, its tread marks still crisp; impressed in the damp road. It had rained within the past few hours. Judging from the darkening sky, it would rain again soon. He slowed down and turned his attention to the woods.

Thick underbrush walled the road's shoulder, while beyond, low growth deeper in the shadows of the trees, shrubs, and tangles gave way to layers of grey autumn leaves moldering into rich loam. Driving further, Popoford pulled into the woods and stopped. He put on the parking brake and told Millie to get out as he opened his door and stepped into the forest. With an eye to the trees, his ears to the faintest sound, and his nose to the breeze, Popoford studied his surroundings with the focus of military science and a hunter's discipline.

There was one road up and over the hill: one road for in and out. The closest major airport was in Fresno where he expected the TAP hierarchy would land.

He wanted to get onto the spike camp property unseen, and he had to get that done before the TAP bosses were cozy in their private cabins. Deterrence. Stalling. That was what he needed: time to play the city slicks with a bit of country deception.

During the night, his plan had taken on a solid form. He walked the trees looking for one thing, and when he found it, he quickly returned to the car and grabbed a coil of rope from a bag in the trunk. Taking the rope with him, he asked Millie to follow him as he returned to a fallen tree limb, hollowed from seasons of rain, snow, worms, and beetles. He tested its weight, and though it appeared to be heavy, it was light enough that he could move it by himself. This was the limb he had hoped to find.

"This is our way into the spike camp," he said as Millie looked to him for a better explanation.

Popoford told her his plan as he quickly went to work tying the rope to the end of the limb. When the rope was snug, he grabbed a hank of it and dragged the limb out of the woods onto the road where he created a roadblock. Then he untied the rope and returned to the woods with Millie.

"They'll come one at a time so Contlerust can keep them separated. Each of them will encounter the fallen limb. They'll get out to see if they can move it. To their surprise, they'll be able to move the rotted thing enough to get around and on their way. What they won't know, is that by the time the first one returns to their car, you'll be stowed away inside. Then I'll repeat what you do with the next one. With any luck, we'll get into the spike camp undetected."

He paused for a minute hoping to be reassured, but Millie's silence told him she didn't like his idea at all.

"What's the matter?" he said. "It'll work fine."

"Until it doesn't," Millie said. "What do we do if there's trouble?"

"I'll take the driver out and whichever of us is in the trunk will take the wheel and drive the car to the campsite."

"But I don't know what we're expected to do when we get there."

"Look," Popoford said, "We both need to stop trying to figure out all the things that can screw this up and focus on executing the plan. It's not perfect. I know that. But we have our radios so we can call each other for help if needed. Now come on. Let's get back in the woods before the first one gets here."

"I have one question," Millie said. "What if someone else comes up the hill?"

"I know the target's faces. Let's move."

Understanding that he couldn't cover all the possibilities, Popoford knew his plan was weakness itself, but it was all he had. It had to be enough.

They did a radio check and then Popoford positioned Millie a little downhill from the roadblock. He gave her a tracking device and he kept one himself.

"Hide it where it won't be seen." They each had an app on their phones that kept track of the devices. "If you're captured, crush the tracker. It won't break it, but it'll look broken and discourage anyone from using it."

He walked even further down the road so he could get an early look at oncoming drivers. They checked their radios again and settled in to wait. Only a few minutes had passed when Popoford's voice sparked Millie's nerves to sharp awareness.

"Bogie One approaching. It's Diomed. I have my gun trained on her. Millie, if the trunk is locked, forget it. Just get off the road and wait for me. But if you get in trouble, take the driver out."

Diomed's car came around the bend and she immediately slammed on her brakes. She stopped thirty feet further down the road than expected. Millie quickly sneaked downhill until she was a few feet behind the car. She radioed Popoford and watched as Diomed opened her door.

Millie scrambled to the back of Diomed's car and tried the hatch door. It was unlocked and she rolled into the trunk and closed it as Popoford reported Diomed's movements. "She's getting back in."

Millie heard the engine start and soon she was on her way.

When the car was gone, Popoford ran to the tree limb and pulled it back into position. Then, he went to Millie's previous position and waited. In another twenty minutes, another car was approaching. He picked out the heavy thump of a subwoofer drawing nearer. The sound was blasphemy to God, His wilderness, and Popoford's ears.

Tamisra, the dark one, pulled her car to a halt and got out to inspect the blockade.

She left her car running and her boombox thwumping. Popoford did his best to ignore the insulting pounding and huddled near the passenger door.

Tamisra returned to her car and slipped behind the wheel. The shock on her face as Popoford slid into the passenger seat while screwing a suppressor to his threaded barrel made him laugh.

"Not what you expected, is that it?" he said. "Too bad for you. Your day is going to be so short and so bad."

When Blagden arrived the tree limb would not delay him.

CHAPTER FORTY-NINE

Popoford checked in with Millie and received a two-click "all's well" signal back from her. He kept his eyes on Tamisra at all times.

"What's your real name?" he asked, but she didn't answer. "I just thought you might like me to contact your next of kin."

"Go to Hell," she said.

"Not before you show me the way."

They drove a half-mile up the road and Tamisra turned into a narrow drive where there was another Columbia Outfitter's Spike Camp sign posted.

"What are your orders?" Popoford said and pushed the barrel of his gun against her head, "Give it to me straight."

"I'm to go to the Pine Bark cabin."

"Then what?"

"There's a computer there. I'm to turn it on and wait until I'm contacted."

"Are you on time? Not too early or late?"

"I'm here when I was told to be here."

"Sig Heil!" Popoford mocked, and he noted the smirk on Tamisra's face. "You would die for the Fuehrer. Is that right?"

"I will die for my Master," she said.

"Don't worry. I'll see to it. There's the sign now."

He kept his gun locked to the base of Tamisra's head as he took a quick look up the road. The cabin with a "Pine Bark" sign was just ahead. He could see smoke rising above the trees and a soft breeze brought a whisp of its scent to his nose.

Tamisra pulled up to the cabin and parked the car. She shut off the engine and pulled out the keys. Popoford snapped them out of her hands and slipped them into his pocket. He took a second to inventory her appearance.

She was a handsome woman, a description almost all unattractive women receive; not plain, not ugly, not masculine, not feminine, just not attractive. Her fingers were adorned by a collection of rings as if she were beholden to a collective. Her clothes were top drawer; plenty of money was spent on her suit, yet all it did was enhance her handsomeness. Hidden in all he saw was the demon that she was, the fixer who groomed deviant judges for Contlerust's courts. She appeared to be quite pleasant until she spoke again.

"I can't wait to see your hide underfoot, a rug to be trampled for eternity."

Popoford didn't take the bait. "Stay seated until I open your door," he ordered and got out of the car.

He scanned the trees and listened for the slightest sound. Hearing nothing but birds and a light breeze overhead, he ordered her out with a flick of his pistol.

"Grab your stuff and get inside," he said, "And don't do something stupid."

She led the way into the cabin, Popoford's left hand on her shoulder keeping her from dipping or dodging, his pistol barrel cold against her neck to discourage flight.

"Snap on the light and keep the shades drawn," he said while casing the single room. There was a queen-sized bed, a small desk next to the front door, and an open wardrobe. The bathroom door was also open.

"Have a seat at the desk," he said giving her a shove to help her out. "Boot up your computer and log in."

Tamisra opened her case and removed the laptop. She switched it on and waited for the operating system to boot.

"What's next," Popoford said.

"I'm to wait to be received."

"Received? By whom?"

"I don't know. I'm assuming it's Lamia."

"Are you that much in the dark?"

"What do you mean?"

"Nothing. Get your gear out and set it up."

As she worked, Popoford returned to the door and opened it sneaking a look outside while he kept his gun aimed in her direction. Seeing nothing, he called Millie's radio.

"Alpha Check," he said. "All eyes on target's cabins. Bogie contact soon."

The double clicks were comforting but his gut warned him of impending trouble just as it happened.

There was a quick movement from Tamisra's position, a movement he mirrored in a fluid motion as he responded to the sudden appearance of a revolver he had failed to secure. He dropped flat on the floor. Two rounds snapped from his pistol with a suppressed pop before he landed with a thud. That was followed by the crash of Tamisra's gun and then by the muffled thump of her body hitting the edge of the bed and sliding to the floor. She was still alive but wouldn't last until sundown.

Popoford jumped up and checked outside again. He dropped his magazine and topped it off while he peeked out the door once more. When he was sure his path was clear, he stole out of the Pine Bark cabin and darted into the woods.

"One down here, what's your status?" he asked Millie. "Report," he said when there was no response. He didn't bother to say more when the response finally came.

"Said the spider to the fly, I see you, Steven. Count the minutes you have remaining here on Earth. Soon you'll precede me into Hell." It was Contlerust whispering his venomous words into his ears.

Popoford's immediate adrenaline dump countered his impulse to collapse and surrender. His survival was dependent on training and the resilient remnants of his Resurrection Runner infusions.

Training had taught him to seal probable results in discrete mental containers where they'd stay until he could confirm their validity. Millie might be in trouble, but she couldn't be dead. He might have failed, but he needed proof to say it was so.

The Resurrection Runner drugs had provided his body with a practiced feature that infused endorphins into his system whenever he was dealt a crappy hand. As possible as Contlerust's declaration was, Popoford's emotions would not deflate to depression but inflate to optimism. He was a single-minded creature when under attack.

Since Contlerust either had Millie's radio or he'd scanned their frequencies. Popoford turned his microphone down but kept his earbud in place. He moved uphill, deeper into the woods where he hoped to find temporary shelter from Contlerust's prying eyes. He stepped behind a large tree and then crawled through the brush to his next cover. Doing this several times, he stopped and peeked around an outcropping to confirm his location and try to locate the other cabins in the spike camp.

"Nice moves, Steven," he heard Contlerust say. "96.3 Fahrenheit. A little cool, but not cool enough. I still see you."

Thermal imaging, Popoford realized. What could he do to counter that?

Clouds were moving in from the north and the wind was picking up as he spotted another series of boulders twenty feet in front of him. He dashed to them and squeezed into a crevasse splitting the largest rock.

"That's a slick little trick, Steven," Contlerust said. "You can stay there as long as you like. As soon as you duck out again, I'll pick up your image. You can't get away. I've got some staff training to take care of. When I'm done, I'll come for you. Have a good rest. It will be your last. Where you're going, you will crave rest that will never come."

CHAPTER FIFTY

Diomed pulled her car alongside the log cabin called The Meadows that appropriately faced a vast, gently sloping pasture. A flock of sheep grazed along a wooden fence line and a border collie kept an eye out for mischief. A shepherd slept in the verdant field; his straw hat pulled over his eyes. The gathering clouds moved unhurriedly by, casting lazy shadows upon the meadow. It was an idyllic scene and settled Diomed's nerves. Yet there was bitter irony in it that was missed by the Director of Propaganda until she opened the cottage door. A man holding a gun on his lap was sitting on the bed. He had a glass of scotch in his other hand, the corked bottle at his feet. Diomed froze.

"Do come in and take a seat," Contlerust said, gesturing toward the desk chair with his gun. "I've grown impatient waiting to talk to you."

Diomed took the seat as directed. "Who arc you?"

"Your best friend," he said and paused. "...or your worst enemy. Maybe both."

"How cryptic. Are you going to kill me?"

"Do you believe in an afterlife?" he asked.

"No."

"Too bad for you. You and I will be spending eternity together."

"Eternity and an afterlife are mutually exclusive," she countered.

"Fool!" he shouted. "Your propaganda has damned countless sycophants. For that, alone, you deserve Hell. I will stand before the court of judgment and declare that you corrupted countless souls. Not even the Christ who you disparage will save you."

"You must be nuts! Put that gun down and tell me who you are."

"I'm your Master," he replied.

"No man is my master!" she cried, jumping to her feet.

Diomed barely had the words out of her mouth than Contlerust pulled the trigger. Her mouth dropped open in astonishment as blood freely flowed from her inner thigh. The bullet had destroyed the femoral artery of her right leg. She desperately grasped her wounded flesh pressing with all her might to stanch the blood flow. It was a demoralizing effort. No pressure, no protestations, no confounding lie could save her. Moment by moment she slipped away, her desperate thoughts turning hysterical, then plaintive, then, as her last thought bridged her synapses, it verged on repentance as her final words escaped her lips.

"Forgive me, Lord..."

Infuriated, Contlerust jumped to his feet and emptied his gun into her chest.

"You damned Bitch!" he cried. "You traitor!"

And he slumped onto the bed again, downed his scotch then poured another and downed it, too. His nerves settled, he left the cabin.

CHAPTER FIFTY-ONE

Millie overheard Popoford's request to report but caught herself when she heard Contlerust's reply. She had just managed to get out of Diomed's trunk. When she first tried to get out, she found that it had locked automatically. She couldn't find an emergency latch on the inside of the trunk, but she was able to force the backseat forward and wiggle out. She stood up and closed the car door quietly. She saw the same pastoral scene that Diomed saw and marveled at its serenity, then she heard the conversation between Popoford and Contlerust, but she kept quiet and waited for the talking to cease. It ended and she rapidly tapped her send button twice, expecting no response. With their prearranged signal, Popoford would know she was still in action.

What she heard next altered her plan.

"Millie! My way."

It was Popoford telling her to abandon her plan. She acted immediately by pulling her cellphone out, tapped in her password, and switched to the tracking app. Two blips popped onto a toposheet. The orange one in the middle was hers and the green one Popoford's. He was located on a line that ran directly up a gentle slope about fifty yards away. She moved without hesitation directly toward him but came up short when she spotted a cabin ahead of her.

Millie skirted wide of the cabin when she saw movement through a cabin window. She was pleased with herself when she looked back through the trees and saw Contlerust step onto the porch. She was even happier when she heard him call Popoford.

"I see you haven't left your hide, Steven. You're not doing any good there. Come out and play."

Millie could see that he wasn't looking at anything and had no idea where Popoford was. He was just faking it.

As she continued toward Popoford's location, she considered turning back. But she let the thought drop knowing that she was better off combining her skills with Popoford's.

The app indicated that she was right on Popoford's location and she called out to him in a low voice. "Steven, are you there?"

"I'm back here between these boulders."

Millie joined him and filled him in on what she had seen.

"He doesn't seem to have a heat-sensing device. He was just standing on a cabin porch and talking on a radio."

"Okay. It's time we finished this. I want you to go back the way you came and set up on this side of the cabin where he is. I'm going to swing around to the other side. I'll draw him out, and you come in from behind. This shouldn't take long but be especially careful. He's a demon and can't be trusted."

CHAPTER FIFTY-TWO

Millie crept from the woods to the side of the cabin and inched her way to its front corner. She waited there until she saw Popoford on the other side of the cabin coming closer to her and raised a hand to signal she was ready. He acknowledged her and slipped even closer to the cabin.

"Simon," he called. "Simon. It's over, come out of there. The state patrol is on its way. You can't escape. Come out now and be done with it."

At first, there was no response, then the headsets awoke to this news: "Millie is dead."

"You lie!" Popoford said, not wanting to let on that he was looking right at her.

"Don't be a fool, Steven. Come and see if you don't believe me."

Popoford remained silent.

"You have your doubts, don't you," Contlerust said. "Don't you see how little resolve you have? You're afraid to see her. Afraid to face me."

Popoford lost his temper and started to run toward the cabin even as Millie stepped out and frantically waved him off. He only took one step when he heard Millie shouting in his earpiece.

"Behind you! Look out!"

Millie raised her gun in his defense as Blagden clamped a strong arm vice-grip around his throat. Instinctively Popoford lunged into a forward somersault landing facing the sky and lying on top of Blagden's body. But Blagden wasn't out of action. His grip was steel and his continuous pressure nearly fractured Popoford 's spine. Soon the pain would defeat him, yet with a tremendous thrust, he managed to roll over taking Blagden with him. Blagden's weight crushed him even harder. He was passing out when Blagden suddenly relinquished his grip. With an anguished cry that turned quickly into gurgling nonsense, Blagden went limp. Popoford rolled his dead weight off and wiped the man's blood from his own throat. He stood up and saw Millie finish cleaning her knife on Blagden's stomach and was slipping it back in its sheath. She reached down and gave Popoford a hand up.

"Thank you," he said as she hugged him. "I was almost dead."

"You're still almost dead, Steven." It was Contlerust standing in front of the cabin, a rifle aimed at Popoford's head. "I do wish Millie hadn't killed my new TAP Number One. The good news is it makes it easier to kill her. I have so many things to be thankful for."

"Like what?" Popoford asked without moving.

"I'm thankful for my earthly domain and for all the foolish souls who inhabit it. My playthings. The countless millions who have passed this way and have given themselves to me instead of the Other One. The tears of God are shed each time another turns away from Him. And each time, I get closer to victory. Prepare to die, both of you. I'd suggest you say your prayers, but that's not what I do."

"You're sick!" Millie said. "Who is my real father?"

"None of your business."

"You don't know, do you?"

"Shut up and prepare to die!"

"I am preparing. You should have known that if you are who you say you are. Listen to these words while you gloat: "Hail, Mary, Full of grace, the Lord is with thee, Blessed art thou among women and Blessed is the fruit of thy womb, Jesus."

"Stop!" Contlerust shouted and took a step back. He raised his arms to protect himself even as Dracula had raised his arms in the movies to shield himself from the Crucifix. Now Popoford joined in. "Holy Mary, Mother of God, pray for us sinners now and at the hour of our death. Amen."

Their prayer completed, Contlerust recovered and a blinding rage enveloped him. Bringing his rifle to his eye, he once again aimed at Popoford's head pressing the trigger ever so slowly. Too slowly.

Before he fired a round, his left arm flung into the air as a bullet shattered the bones in his trigger hand. He spun around attempting to maintain control of the rifle and saw Tamisra lying on her cabin porch, her revolver in her limp hand, glaring at him as her eyesight failed, and silently cursing herself for her errant shot. Popoford gave him a shove and Contlerust staggered forward but didn't fall. Instead, he took off running at great speed.

Millie was raising her rifle and setting herself for the kill shot when Popoford turned to her and placed his hand on the gun.

"He's mine, Millie, not yours. I told you that earlier. I have to finish this for my friend, Sheriff Florter. I'll track him. He can't get far with his hand blown out."

Popoford quickly kissed Millie and made sure she was armed. Then he took off after Contlerust.

CHAPTER FIFTY-THREE

The sky was now rapidly becoming leaden. Popoford saw sun-blocking darkness thicken almost to black while lightning bolts rioted silently within them. Thunder was conspicuously absent. Indeed, the earth had gone silent: even the wind refused to howl.

He walked over the first rise and followed Contlerust's straight trail down the other side, through the pines, and up another hill. At its crest, he stopped, astonished at what he saw.

The meadow beyond sloped sharply before him to a stand of tall grass, untouched, as if no creature had passed that way before. He scanned the horizon and the ground near him for a sign of Contlerust's passing. He took his time, making sure that there was no mistake. And then, reluctantly, he gazed at length upon the scene in front of him. He crossed himself, and as he did a thunderclap so loud that it rocked the world vibrated in Popoford's head and guts. He reflexively scrunched his eyes at the shattering sound, slowly reopening them as the thunder rolled to the heavens and finally fell utterly still.

Ozone was heavy in the air. A headache made him nauseous.

Looking across the field once again to the tall grass, he saw a new cleft of trampled stalks. A chill rippled up his sides and down his back.

With deep trepidation, Popoford slowly advanced to the opening in the tall grass. As he did, he reached down the front of his shirt and retrieved his crucifix and the brown scapular he habitually wore. He kissed them one at a time and let them fall back behind his shirt. He recited the Our Father out loud and took a timorous first step into the thick growth.

It was a narrow path no wider than his shoulders and it meandered in snaking curves, never crossing over itself but continually undulating. There was a time he was certain he'd walked in a circle and must soon pass over the path he had already followed, but he hadn't found an intersection no matter how far he'd walked. And then he decided upon another course of action and turned around.

Much to his horror, there was only undisturbed tall grass behind him and no indication that he had ever passed that way. He turned back again and the path was still there, yet now it opened on a small, circular clearing and Contlerust was standing across from him, muttering a chant, his lips bubbling with saliva, his ruined hand visibly recovering and resting on his opposite hand, an insane look in his eyes.

Popoford's mouth had gone dry leaving a metallic taste. He started to sweat and his face flushed. He took a step forward and stopped at once when a wave of vertigo washed over him as the horizon tilted. By taking a long stride and stretching his arms out like a tightrope walker he managed to regain his equilibrium and squat on his haunches to recover.

"Feeling light-headed, Steven? Perhaps you should have left well enough alone."

Contlerust burst into a guttural laughing spasm that echoed through Popoford's head. His laugh finally petered out and his comments continued.

"The longer you stay with me, the closer to death you will be. Not the death of peace you hope for, but the death of perdition my master will provide. There is no hope, Steven. Not now. Not ever. Yours is a puny dream, a hoax provided by my Master for mankind; a devilishly cruel joke foreshadowing the suffering of disappointment you all will suffer in Hell. There, each desire, lust, and dream will forever go eternally unfulfilled. There is where you will soon be. Forever."

Popoford was nauseous. A headache pressed on his temples and got continually worse. He fell forward on all fours and vomited.

"Poor thing," Contlerust said as he took a few steps closer to Popoford. "It's a pity that we should part in this way. I'll tell you what. I have a bad hand and you feel like hell. Let's fight it out and see who's the real warrior."

Contlerust took a few more steps and reached down to pull Popoford to his feet. Popoford got up bending forward as if he would retch again.

Contlerust backhanded him and then grabbed him by the collar and pulled him erect.

"There. That's it. Stand up like a man. Take what's coming to you, you failure. You never were any good. Hendricks was right. It's one of the only times he told the truth."

That comment stirred rage in Popoford. He bent again, and as he did, he reached into his shirt and pulled out his Scapular. At the same time, he wrapped his other arm around Contlerust's neck and pulled him close, pressing the Scapular against Contlerust's forehead, and holding it there.

This would appear to be a foolish attack, let alone a defense, but it was a campaign made in Heaven. For reasons of faith alone, he believed in God's grace, and that the intercession of The Blessed Virgin Mary would save him. His hand was unharmed, but the demon's forehead was scorched and aflame.

Contlerust finally tore the Scapular from Popoford's hand and tossed it aside. Stepping back, he staggered and nearly fell. He caught himself and quickly realized that he was looking down the barrel of Millie's Rifle.

"Hold your ground!" she ordered. "Don't make me do it."

"Millie," Contlerust said, waving her off with his once-injured hand. "Don't waste your time. You can't hurt me. See, my hand has already healed. Only my Master can crush me."

Millie and Popoford were amazed and Contlerust erupted in a damnable, cackling laugh that rose to an ungodly volume. It was so loud that they both had to cover their ears in an attempt to stop the pain.

Contlerust finally went silent and backed up slowly and disappeared once again into the tall grass. The instant silence that embraced the scene was stunning. Popoford was shocked, but Millie overcame her astonishment and scrambled after him.

She broke through the edge of the tall grass and ran into the open, Contlerust was facing her, his arms stretched out and his head hanging to the side in mockery of the sacrifice of Christ.

Millie ignored his satanic smile, raised her rifle, and emptied her magazine. Her shots made a trail of bullet holes from his crotch to his forehead and nearly cut his body in two. His face split apart while ripped slices of brains, bone, and flesh, burst into the air, his lurid grin still in place.

She didn't bother to reload but fell to her knees as a massive earthquake jolted the earth. Her eyes remained fixed on him, and she saw his wounds heal.

The quake continued until his body was restored. Then, in eerie silence, the granite beneath his feet split wide open and he fell, a sardonic smile on his lips, into the chasm. He vanished and the ruptured rock healed itself.

CHAPTER FIFTY-FOUR

It took Popoford and Millie several minutes to gather their wits. He felt fear and she felt sorrow. They finally walked over the second hill, their arms around each other, and descended slowly. Without thinking she turned her head in the direction of the bucolic scene she had enjoyed earlier in the day.

The view was empirically similar to what she remembered but was substantively transformed.

She closed her eyes for a moment thinking she was delirious, but when she reopened them the transformation remained: the sheep had become horned goats, the Border Collie a snarling wolf, and the shepherd had vanished. Millie knew her father, not a shepherd had been the one lying with the flock.

Popoford climbed the porch steps of the first cabin they came to, his blanched skin and hollow eyes telling the story, and sat on the top step. Millie leaned against the cabin wall, her head hanging down.

"He's gone," Popoford said. "He escaped."

"Not really," Millie said. "He vanished would be more accurate."

"That's impossible," Popoford said.

"For us, yes. For him, no."

Millie and Popoford sat for many minutes without a word. The burden revealed to them, the unfathomable truth about the man they knew as Simon Contlerust sunk in.

He wasn't Millie's father at all. They agreed that they had no idea what he was, except that he wasn't Satan. He referred to his master many times, so there was one more evil than him. They each had several wild fantasies, but none of them could be verified. He'd been swallowed up and they came to believe they had battled the Devil's minion. Shudders rippled throughout their souls. This was not the war they had signed up for. Their war was against existential corruption and political domination. This was the war the fallen angels waged against their Creator and His creatures.

The realization weighed heavily on them and the sun was close to setting when Popoford finally rose and took Millie in his arms.

"Come on, girl," he said. "Let's get out of here."

He stood and walked down the stairs. Millie quietly leaned on him as they walked together.

"Where are we going?" she said.

"We're going home. To Whimsy."

Millie's smile reflected less than she felt.

"We need to figure this out together," he said. "We need to have a plan. Whatever happens next, you can be sure we'll be marked for destruction. We need to stick together."

Millie nodded. "Someday Sarah needs to know what's happened. Maybe we can see her after we decompress."

"Of course," Popoford said, and they collected all the evidence that could place them at the spike camp and took all the TAP ID they could find.

Next, they searched each cabin for the Resurrection Runner serum Contlerust had stolen. But they came up empty-handed. For all they knew, Contlerust had taken the serum with him.

As the moon came up, they were driving away, eventually heading west to what they hoped would be a respite before they were attacked again.

Two days later after an unhurried drive to the eastern Sierras, they pulled into the clearing in front of the little house in Whimsy, a place a little large for one person and perhaps too small for two. Popoford stopped the car before driving to the front door.

"What's going on?" Millie asked.

"Nothing. I just wanted to access our security before we go back inside."

Satisfied that all was well, he pressed the gas pedal again and rolled up to the front door. He shut the car off and was about to open his door when his phone rang.

"It's Sarah," he said and answered the phone. "Sarah. How are you doing?"

"I'm fine. Things are going great with Dean Wrenbutt. Are you all right?"

"Yeah," he said, casually. "We just got home."

"Great. Is Simon with you?"

"No. He decided to go out on his own."

"Wow, then you were successful in putting down TAP?"

"Not completely," he said. "but mostly."

"That's great! Do you know how to get a hold of Simon? He's not answering his phone."

"No, I don't. I don't know where he went."

"Oh. Well, can I talk to Millie for a minute? Girl talk, you know?"

"Sure. Here she is."

Popoford handed the phone to Millie. "Hey, Sarah. Is everything okay?"

"Sure," Sarah said. "I'm just anxious to reach Simon."

"Why? Hasn't he hurt you enough? Is something wrong?"

"Well, yes and no."

"What's going on?" Millie asked.

Sarah's answer came with a sigh. "I'm pregnant!"

The End

Please write a considered review of
Reluctant Runner on
Amazon,
Barns and Nobel,
and Goodreads

Keep up to date on Book Three,
The Rising Runner at
https://rwanderson-author.com

Here is the first chapter of
Book Three of
Popoford's Run series to be Released in 2022

THE REVENANT RUNNER

It was a black hole concealed in the depths of an abysmally dank architectural horror, an exemplary example of the modern, perniciously minimalist mistake. Grey slabs pierced with trapezoid holes mimicking gunner's ports served as windows yet let in precious little light. The floors from bottom to top were strewn with scrap paper most of which was labeled "Top Secret."

No one protected the halls of Section 33. No one cared. The agency had been brought to its knees three years ago and the secrets it had concealed were no longer of value. But the shriveled biped that sat in his unique chair five feet off the floor was oblivious to his accommodations. His synapses were focused on the chart he had drawn on his green chalkboard.

His white-on-green masterpiece was everything to him, so much so that he didn't hear the elevator door opening in the third sub-basement where he lived and work. Nor did he see the shadow that was cast on the wall behind his chalkboard, nor did he hear the steps slowly advancing, toe, heel, toe, heel, toe, heel.

When he sensed the intruder and froze in his chair, he was startled by the hand reaching around and pressing his head against the cushioned seatback. There was no time for terror. The straight razor swiped a clean slice from ear to ear destroying his carotid arteries and slicing his vocal cords.

He was peaceful in dying for the last thing he saw was the mistake in his formula. The mistake he had been searching for these three years. He was thrilled that he had solved the problem, and he was certain that he was the only one who could understand what he had just discovered.

As he bled out, he tried but failed to sing a tune he remembered from his childhood. It was the one that the nuns had taught him when he had first been given up to them:

Jesus Loves Me. This I know.
For the Bible tells me so.
Little lambs to him belong.
We are weak and he is strong.
Yes, Jesus Loves Me.
Yes, Jesus Loves Me.
Yes, Jesus Loves Me.
The Bible Tells me so.

The scent of frankincense and myrrh filled his nostrils and its pungent smoke wrapped around his distorted face, stinging his eyes as life passed to death, judgment, and eternity.

His assassin snapped a picture of the chalkboard and made a call.

A phone rang in a darkened office three-thousand miles away. An iridescent wrinkled hand shimmering with a weakening inner light reached for the receiver and tentatively raised it to withered lips. The wretched creature did not speak, but his gurgling breath and slow exhalation were enough for the caller to begin his report.

"The dwarf is dead. Photo proof on the way along with the formula. The location has been cleaned. There will be no evidence remaining, but the dwarf is expected to make a report tomorrow at noon to his handlers. Details of his report will also be sent to you and identification will be found in his apartment when you arrive. I have been paid in full. You know where you can reach me whenever you have further need of my services."

The killer ended the call and the black angel's malignant servant replaced the receiver and turned his chair to the window. There he saw the lights asparkle, sad shimmering dots so cherished by men yet so insignificant in comparison to Godhead's beams the creature most intimately feared. Still, none of his terrors mattered for he was a soul wholly-owned, a slave of the underworld returned to complete what he had left undone.

In the stupor of rebirth, he tried to close his eyelids but the city lights kept coming. His lids had not yet developed muscular connections and as yet could not be controlled.

From within the blackness of his overhanging hood, he felt his lips maturing from withered husks to supple tools exquisitely eggar to speak artful lies of craft, cunning, and deceit. His mind was racing ahead out of his desire to please his master.

He forced himself to relax and dissolved his desirous longing into a dew of patient faith. For he was the one sent. The one named to deliver the lingering faithful to the master of the pit of fire and eternal hopelessness. He was the chosen one sent to ensnare the world in his master's name. He had been known as

Simon Contlerust in a previous incarnation having taken on the body of the dead former Home Office operative. Now his new human form was slowly emerging one trait at a time.

He made s quarter-turn away from the window and caught slices of his image reflected in a large mirror. The city daubed an evolving light picture in reflection, and he marveled at the transformation of the black spirit he saw before him. It was not the image of mortal beauty. Rather, it was a cluster of amorphous cells devoid of grace and compounding by the second into a creature that only a dead mother could love. It was a hideous sight yet gloriously pitiful. For the miniature creature he saw in reflection began as a strapping young man but soon reduced into a compressed, short-legged, barrel-chested dwarf.

His head, elegant at first glance, evolved into a solid Balkan cube: ears protruding and large eyes emphasized by perpetually startled eyebrows. These static attributes were countered by his silvery-thin skin that appeared to be sliding off his face, hampered only by a solid attachment to the deflated bags under his eyes. His lips were puffy and pale, his throat a stack of pancakes. He was transformed. His phone flashed an incoming message tone, and he reached for it, missing it by a foot though his arm was fully outstretched. Bending closer to the desk, he managed to activate the phone. The first image was a full-face and sliced-throat shot suitable for the morgue. The second was its companion shot showing the dwarf genius full body.

The evil spirit returned his gaze to the mirror and contemplated his situation. It was perfect irony. Here he was, having been sent, and here he would do his master's bidding. Not with splendid beauty, but with infirmity. Not as a pampered fool but as a brilliant castaway.

Yet even as he began to play the unfortunate, his brain reached a cognitive threshold where he could distinguish between norms and actualities.

The murdered dwarf was an honored genius no matter what his appearance, no matter how closely he had been held secretly to the chest of America's espionage universe, his public existence denied, dismissed, and scorned. He knew that it is neither the nature of the man nor the rouge on his powdered face but the grit of his heart and the wit and wisdom of his mind that marked him a man and not a fool. The dwarf had been a man.

His master knew where he would have the greatest leverage: he was headed inside Section 33 to rebuild it. Then, from deep in the bowels of his corrupt renovation, he would wreak havoc upon the world. All for his prince.

His master demanded absolute loyalty without the expectation of reward. He was ineligible for false promises. Such false pledges were reserved for the yet-to-be damned.

His master had equipped him with the power to guide, seduce, and corrupt all that he laid his eyes upon. Earth was his playground and nothing but failure conjured fear in his black soul.

www.ingramcontent.com/pod-product-compliance
Ingram Content Group UK Ltd.
Pitfield, Milton Keynes, MK11 3LW, UK
UKHW041829290726
14061UKWH00004BA/154/J

9 781734 769869